THE (NOT SO) SECRET LIVES OF FOOD PACKAGING

T0322354

Food in Modern History: Traditions and Innovations

Series editors: Peter Scholliers and Amy Bentley

This monograph series pays serious attention to food as a focal point in historical events from the late eighteenth century to present day.

Employing the lens of technology broadly construed, the series highlights the nutritional, social, political, cultural and economic transformations of food around the globe. It features new scholarship that considers ever-intensifying and accelerating tensions between tradition and innovation that characterize the modern era.

The editors are particularly committed to publishing manuscripts featuring geographical areas currently underrepresented in English-language academic publications, including the Global South, particularly Africa and Asia, as well as monographs featuring indigenous and under-represented groups, and non-western societies.

REBELLIOUS COOKS AND RECIPE WRITING IN COMMUNIST BULGARIA
Albena Shkodrova

FOOD AND AVIATION IN THE TWENTIETH CENTURY: THE PAN AMERICAN IDEAL
Bryce Evans

CHAMPAGNE IN BRITAIN, 1800–1914: HOW THE BRITISH TRANSFORMED A FRENCH LUXURY
Graham Harding

FEEDING THE PEOPLE IN WARTIME BRITAIN
Bryce Evans

GLOBALIZATION IN A GLASS: THE RISE OF PILSNER BEER THROUGH TECHNOLOGY, TASTE AND EMPIRE
Malcolm F. Purinton

EATING IN EIGHTEENTH-CENTURY PROVENCE: THE EVOLUTION OF A TRADITION
Barbara Santich

A HISTORY OF BREAD: CONSUMERS, BAKERS AND PUBLIC AUTHORITIES SINCE THE 18TH CENTURY
Peter Scholliers

THE (NOT SO) SECRET LIVES OF FOOD PACKAGING

Anne Murcott

BLOOMSBURY ACADEMIC
LONDON • NEW YORK • OXFORD • NEW DELHI • SYDNEY

BLOOMSBURY ACADEMIC
Bloomsbury Publishing Plc
50 Bedford Square, London, WC1B 3DP, UK
1385 Broadway, New York, NY 10018, USA
29 Earlsfort Terrace, Dublin 2, Ireland

BLOOMSBURY, BLOOMSBURY ACADEMIC and the Diana logo are
trademarks of Bloomsbury Publishing Plc

First published in Great Britain 2024

A catalogue record for this book is available from the British Library.

Library of Congress Cataloging-in-Publication Data
Names: Murcott, Anne, author.
Title: The (not so) secret lives of food packaging / Anne Murcott.
Description: London ; New York : Bloomsbury Academic, 2024. |
Series: Food in modern history : traditions and innovations |
Includes bibliographical references and indexes.
Identifiers: LCCN 2023026057 (print) | LCCN 2023026058 (ebook) |
ISBN 9781350022119 (hardcover) | ISBN 9781350022102 (paperback) |
ISBN 9781350022126 (adobe pdf) | ISBN 9781350022140 (epub)
Subjects: LCSH: Food–Packaging–History.
Classification: LCC TP374 .M97 2024 (print) | LCC TP374 (ebook) |
DDC 664–dc23/eng/20230727
LC record available at https://lccn.loc.gov/2023026057
LC ebook record available at https://lccn.loc.gov/2023026058

ISBN: HB: 978-1-3500-2211-9
         PB: 978-1-3500-2210-2
         ePDF: 978-1-3500-2212-6
         eBook: 978-1-3500-2214-0

Series: Food in Modern History: Traditions and Innovations

Typeset by Integra Software Services Pvt. Ltd.
Printed and bound in Great Britain

To find out more about our authors and books visit www.bloomsbury.com
and sign up for our newsletters.

For my children, grandchildren and great-grandchildren
with love and thanks – and in very special memory of my elder son
Toby Murcott
(August 5, 1963–August 28, 2023)

CONTENTS

ILLUSTRATIONS

PREFACE AND ACKNOWLEDGEMENTS

'What is so important about food packaging?' asked a friend of a friend curiously. This is the book that gives him some answers. Producing it has led in, what for me, are experimental directions. None the less, the career-long allegiance to an ethnographic outlook, instilled by training in anthropology and sociology, has shaped my expeditions, initially into history and then Science & Technology Studies (STS). As a result of well-engrained ethnographic habits of work, I have amassed materials that could, one way or another, have some bearing on food packaging. There is now a cloud full of documents, cuttings, links to videos, screen-shots, advertisements and notes of incidental conversations. In the real world, my study is still 'very messy' – as pronounced many years ago by my youngest granddaughter with all the scorn a tidy-minded three-year old could summon. Overflowing with storage boxes crammed with assorted packs, pouches, boxes and bags, shelves bulging with company histories, grey literature in lever-arch files alongside sepia photographs of factories, a 1920s Nuttall's Mintoes tin and the Virol box (Figure 3) it gives a false impression of being indiscriminate.

Instead, it is all stimulated by the thinking of two mid-twentieth-century sociologists. Herbert Blumer talks of 'sensitizing concepts' which give a 'general sense of reference and guidance in approaching empirical instances' (1954: 7). The other is C. Wright Mills' 'intellectual craftsmanship' to which filing and re-filing materials are central (1959). Together their writings have inspired unexpected juxtapositions or altered angles in repeated inspections of those amassed materials to configure the discussions developed in this book.

Sources have ranged widely. In addition to yards of specialist trade journals and technical books shelved in the British Library, they include:

~ company archives
~ early editions of food packaging textbooks bought online whose post/packing cost more than the pennies charged for each book
~ asking at formal receptions (to which seniority brings invitations) of those in the food industry for introductions to colleagues in company packaging divisions and in trade associations
~ capitalizing on decades-long pre-existing contacts in the food policy community seeking additional introductions
~ discovering that entrance to trade packaging fairs at London or Birmingham exhibition centres is often free, easily allowing finding more friendly industry insiders willing to help. I repeatedly returned home buzzing with new information, a sheaf of business cards and armfuls of intriguing free samples

~ cautious online-searches aimed, largely, at seeking lines of enquiry to be followed up in libraries and archives rather than simply relied upon *per se,* although they also turned up valuable primary sources

~ thirty audio-recorded/transcribed interviews, each over an hour long, with packaging experts and technical specialists carried out between 2016 and 2022. Only one request was apologetically refused – on the grounds of commercial sensitivity.

Interviews built on one another – earlier ones informing those coming later, repeat interviews doubling back to enquire more deeply than the first time. Given pandemic restrictions, the whole project was saved by internet opportunities, video-calling, email, open-access journal articles and JSTOR. During pandemic closures, archivists undertook searches for material on researchers' behalf sending the results electronically – prompting the heartfelt if unprofessional response of 'magic'.

A word is needed about the arrangement of references. Paramount for a book on food packaging is broadly to distinguish between primary sources – of which there is a multitude – and secondary sources – of which there are very few. Reference to online primary sources is presented in the end notes, following the standard format of Harvard referencing where possible, and where not, simply by the provision of the URL. Access to most online sources was double-checked in the spring of 2023 with others carrying the original date of access. It is important too to recognize that some sources are treated as primary here even though in other contexts they are firmly secondary scientific/academic sources, e.g. packaging textbooks, biographies, articles in scientific journals.

There are many people I must thank for their help. Credit for first suggesting studying food packaging is due to Katarzyna Cwiertka. The initial plan was to collaborate, but incompatible schedules led us to proceed independently. Grown since then is a long list of people who helped – far too many to mention them all – to whom I am most grateful. The book would be much the poorer without the support of librarians and archivists, colleagues and contacts, as well as many packaging 'insiders' willing to be interviewed, happy to invite me for site visits, ready to provide documents and search for materials, offer comments and effect introductions, including Christine Anders, Liz Anders, Klarijn Anderson-Loven, Suzi Barber, Jon Bell, Venita Bryant, Richard Burt, Rachel Butler, Paul Carrington, Katherine Carter, David Clark, Eibhlin Colgan, Catherine Conway, Jon Davey, Robert de Villiers, Scarlett Dennett, Colin Dennis, Toni Desrosiers, Nigel Dickie, Ayleen Driver, Malcolm Finch, Sophie Finn, Paul Gardner, Rachel Gidlow, Jack Green, Vincent Greenwood, Liisa Hakola, Raija-Liisa Heiniö, Richard Hemming, Nicola Herbert, Julie Hunton, Merja Itavaara, Spencer Johnston, Raija Lantto, Ruth Loughrey, Adam Manley, Sharon Maxwell, India Mary Mauback, Paul Morris, Tina Pajula, Clare Panjwani, Kaisa Poutenen, Michelle Patel, Mark Rawson, Ben Richards, Dick Searle, Mrs Shah, John Sherlock, Fraser Southey, Heather Stodolny, Sally Stodolsky, Andrew Streeter, Louise Streeter, Chris Sturman, Dorothy Thompson, Tony Thorne, Claire Tunstall and her colleagues, Barry Turner,

Mika Vähä-Nissi, James Ullman, Parul Vickers, Roger E. Wright, Paola Zanetti – along with Sarah, Taylor, Tom and Isaac in the butchery section, New World supermarket, Gardens Branch, Dunedin.

The enthusiasm of the anonymous reviewer is particularly appreciated. So too is the support of editors at Bloomsbury: Jennifer Schmidt (who originally commissioned this along with a textbook published in 2019, pitched at the same time), Miriam Cantwell, Louise Butler, Lucy Carroll, Lily McMahon and in the final few weeks before submitting the complete manuscript, Lalle Pursglove and Emily Wootton. I am also grateful to Kumaraguru Elangovan and Dharanivel Baskar for overseeing the book through production.

I have greatly benefited from invitations to present early versions of this work at academic meetings including: a keynote, the IV International Convention on Food History and Food Studies, Tours, 2018; and in 2019, seminar, Instituto de Ciéncias Sociais, University of Lisbon; seminar, 'FRIED' (Food Researchers in Edinburgh) Group, University of Edinburgh; 'Waste Not Want Not' Cambridge Body & Food Histories Group Conference, University of Cambridge; keynote address, Agri-food XXVI, University of Canterbury, Christchurch, New Zealand.

Completing a book means there is always much checking and sorting to be done. Karinne Faddy very kindly volunteered, undertaking a vital couple of days' work in the final stages. Charlotte Davey, Trina Moseley, Elizabeth Nichols, Elvira Tamus and Tom Cryer all accepted ad hoc employment variously visiting archives when I could not, undertaking bibliographic work, collating and tabulating material, transcribing audio recordings and helping manage requests for permissions.

Numerous colleagues and good friends have listened, offered thoughtful suggestions and invited me to give talks, seminar papers, etc. They include Jonas Bååth, Eleanor Barnett, Rosie Blau, Zofia Boni, Alice de Jong, Nuno Domingos, Diana Ellis, Nora Faltmann, Katie Graf, Louise Hide, Francisco Henriques, Visa Heinonen, Claire Holleran, the late Ian Jack, Peter Jackson, Hilly Janes, Tom Licence, Luisa Lima, Johanna Mäkelä, Pete Mills, Mari Niva, Jill Norman, Eeva Pyörälä, Emma Roe, Hilary Rose, Steven Rose (who never fails to ask 'how's the book going?'), Chris Rosen, Amir Sayadabdi, José Sobral, Kelly Spring, Jack Stilgoe, Johan Pottier, Charlie Taverner, Monica Truninger, Stefan Wahlan, Patrick Wallis, Geoff Watts, Harry West, Chenjia Xu, Sami Zubaida.

Some must receive very special mention for particularly valuable help and encouragement including Sue Aldworth, Paula Chin, Marion Familton, Xaq Frolich, Gabriella Petrick, Polly Russell and Rick Wilk. Others who also read drafts are Lizzie Hull, Jakob Klein, James Staples, with eleventh-hour exceptionally helpful reading by Sarah Weir and Caroline Stacey. Life would be a lot duller without Hugh Campbell and David Evans who are perennially encouraging close friends and colleagues. They too made time to read and comment on drafts and find me examples. Lindy Sharpe is simply irreplaceable for her shrewd observations, keen-eyed checking of drafts and staunch friendship.

Preface and Acknowledgements

A very particular thank you is owed to all NHS staff at both the local General Practice and University College London Hospital, for the unfailing care and attention that has kept me well enough to finish my previous book and to see this one all the way through to the end.

Finally there are not enough words adequately to thank my family for their help, companionship and just being there. In addition my younger son, Dominic Murcott, not only specially took photos for inclusion in the book but then made time to put all the illustrations into the appropriate format. My elder son Toby Murcott companionably took to phoning weekly, patiently to listen to whatever packaging preoccupation I was absorbed by at the time. Both my daughters-in-law, Sian Murcott and Karen Murcott, provided practical and moral support and, right at the very end, Karen also gave up time on an otherwise quiet Sunday afternoon to check a final section for me. Even later, having completed her GCSE exams, one of my granddaughters, Fenna Murcott, kindly agreed to help check at the copy-editing stage – in the process tightening up instances of slack sentence construction and teaching me the name for too many lapses into 'comma splicing'. I am immensely grateful to them all.

Any remaining mistakes or omissions are my sole responsibility.

PART I
PUTTING FOOD PACKAGING CENTRE STAGE

CHAPTER 1
UBIQUITY AND (IN)VISIBILITY

Food packaging is everywhere and nowhere.[1] As you read these words, ask yourself 'how far away am I from some food packaging?' It is so familiar that, as you reflect on the question you realize you are very likely to know almost without thinking, that much of it carries nutritional information, lists of ingredients, shrewdly designed, brightly coloured advertising, familiar logos and other features of branding. The chances are that, no matter where in the world you are at this moment, some kind of food packaging is pretty close by and, equally, the chances are that not a day goes by without your holding some item or other of food packaging: a plastic bottle of mountain spring water on the go; an aluminium drinks can; a cornflakes carton; a steel tin can of beans; a plastic tray of frozen lasagne sealed under a plastic film enveloped in a cardboard sleeve; a glass bottle of tomato ketchup; all loaded into the tall brown paper sack or plastic carrier bag picked up from the supermarket or corner shop on the way home from work. Once the cornflakes had been eaten, the beans tipped into a saucepan and the post-workout can of sports drink emptied, what remained was rubbish, waste, garbage – or at least it was until about two to three decades ago. Then, the lot was consigned to waste paper baskets and bins to go out for the weekly collection, part of the office, factory and household cleaning routines. Nowadays it is not quite rubbish, but few hold onto it as a matter of course: the aluminium can goes into the recycling bin, the empty cornflakes carton is dropped into the sack for cardboard collection, while in some places the plastic tray has nowhere else to go except the waste bin with all the other discards due for landfill.[2] Having come wrapped around our produce, confectionery and drinks its containing task done, it is disposed of in one or other prescribed direction. As a discard it can be seen as useless, something that came between the person and the packed item they want. The very act of removing it along with the packaging itself is still part of an almost unnoticed element of daily life – like the cage of discarded supermarket packaging waiting for collection outside its door (Figure 1).

All these things, all the associated daily activities, are part of the usual food packaging landscape. Yet it is highly likely, that in the ordinary run of things, most people barely reflect on how close they are to any of it, given it has as mundane a place in daily life as a cup or biro, door-mat or spoon. And it is not as if food packaging is insignificant: around 80 per cent of all packaging across Western Europe is for food and drink (Trentmann 2017).

Despite its ubiquity it is common to find commentators pointing to its invisibility. One of the earliest is Thomas Hine, an American writer on history and design who observed that '... I saw packaging as a major cultural, economic and social activity seemingly hidden in plain sight' (1995: 269). Even older is an observation initially made in a 1985

Figure 1 Awaiting collection.

conference paper by Laura Bix *et al.* at the School of Packaging, University of Michigan: 'Packaging is ubiquitous, yet invisible to many who use it' (2009: 859).

Although food packaging may well be abundant and commonly not noticed, it is not always so. There are times when examples are no longer taken-for-granted on the periphery of attention, but, highly visible, they move centre stage. Typically, this is when something goes wrong. Accidents when opening packages is one instance: 'a UK government report estimated 67,000 people in the UK visit hospital casualty departments every year due to an accident involving food or drink packaging' (Crockett 1985: 1768,

Stroud and Walker 2013: 152). Other dangers render food packaging visible too. Canned Argentinian corned beef was found to be responsible for an outbreak of typhoid in Aberdeen during the 1960s, attributed to imperfect packing procedures. In addition, there are dangers in the very materials of which the packages are made. Although glass is chemically inert, some contains lead which can leach into its contents, albeit at levels below those accepted as safe. Then, even if the whole pack's material is safe, adhesives, printing inks, seals and stoppers may be less so. And recycled paperboard can carry dangers left over from any earlier incarnation in printing inks trapped in the material itself 'potentially exposing consumers to phthalates as well as to other suspected endocrine disruptors including benzophenones and mineral oils' (Claudio 2012: A234). Although phthalates are plasticizers, widely used in food packaging, which have been the subject of safety investigation and regulation for a couple of decades (e.g. Freire, Santana and Reyes 2006), safety assessments remain current. In November 2021 the European Food Safety Authority (EFSA) opened an eight week public consultation seeking opinions on the exposure protocol currently being drawn up[3] while the health risks involved regularly turn up in mass media news reports.[4]

Food packaging is also noticed if it is missing from its usual, if inconspicuous, place. Major upheavals, such as war or – as recently – epidemics, tend to disrupt usual supply chains whose existence is exposed when shortages become noticeable. A widely remarked series of examples derive from governments' public health responses to the outbreak of the SARS-CoV-2 (COVID-19) pandemic.[5] Facets of food packaging abruptly became visible thereby underlining its significance in a smoothly running – and thus unnoticed – food system. While government agencies made clear at the outset that there was no evidence that either food or its packaging was a mode of transmission of the virus, it turned out later that frozen food and its packaging were occasionally suspected of carrying it.[6]

At the same time, members of the public quickly became aware of disruption to supermarkets' food stocks. This was less a result of the shortage of food, more a sudden halt to certain supply chains as food service – from restaurants to sandwich bars – had to close. Correspondingly there was as sudden an increase in demand for groceries: with schools and offices closed more people were at home for many more hours a week than usual, including lunch time, hence the increase in sales, especially those ordered online for home delivery. Shortages of eggs in supermarkets whether in New Zealand (Morris 2022) or the UK were not that the eggs themselves were in short supply but that the proportion packed on moulded trays, thirty at a time, for food service businesses was, abruptly, not needed at exactly the same time as demand for those packed for retail – in half dozen or dozen boxes – increased. Shoppers learned to keep those smaller boxes, order a tray of thirty from erstwhile suppliers to the commercial sector who switched to online/doorstep retail delivery overnight, and transfer six, twelve or eighteen into saved, smaller boxes to share with neighbours. Similarly, the shortage of flour was acutely felt as home baking of sourdough loaves and banana bread became the subject of lockdown jokes in the UK mass media, so widely was it newly becoming a habit. But the scarcity was not because less was being milled, but because the immediate increase in domestic demand exceeded the usual volume of retail size paper flour bags in the packaging supply chain as compared with the 22 kg paper sacks previously needed for restaurants.

Those fewer members of the public who were out during lockdown noticed a further unexpected change when buying their morning coffee. One chain of coffee shops had, in 2018, offered double discount to patrons who brought re-usable cups in order to reduce the burden of single-use items on the environment. Customers suddenly found that this had been reversed with re-usable cups banned lest they contribute to the spread of the virus.[7] People employed in the food industry were also affected. Clearly food provision is indispensable through a pandemic, and those working in the industries all along the food chains were designated 'essential workers'. COVID-19 showed up the circumstances of work in some sectors – meat packing is a key instance where rates of COVID-19 were noticeably higher, given the close proximity of work stations inside packing houses. At overall industry level, the US consumer expenditure on groceries forecast in April 2020 was predicted to increase very considerably, whereas most categories (alcohol, footwear or even alcohol) were expected to suffer significant decrease.[8] Those running food banks also faced dislocation: a dramatic drop almost from one day to the next in the amount of supermarket 'waste' – which ordinarily provided a regular fresh supply – as customers stocked up, stripping shelves bare.

Despite its ubiquity, most people probably pay comparatively little attention to the actual packaging itself – as distinct from what is printed on it – at least that is possibly so, until recently and, as noted, in specific circumstances. As cited above, Thomas Hine, the US design critic and journalist, talks of packaging as 'hidden in plain sight'. His is a sentiment put as memorably by the sociologists Franck Cochoy and Catherine Grandclément-Chaffy when they declare that it is often the material 'we see but don't see' (Cochoy and Grandclément-Chaffy 2005: 646). It is partly in this way that food packaging has a secret life. Its existence is not the least hidden, but many people take it for granted, largely paying little or no heed. Its presence is so familiar and the 'landscape' of food packaging on shelves in shops and in kitchen cupboards, so routine, that it simply seems unnoticed, a commonplace part of ordinary surroundings.

The lives of food packaging are also hidden in other ways. How many know how a plastic milk bottle is made or the name of the man often called 'the father' of canning? How many have heard of the late nineteenth-century American woman who took out a patent for her paper bag-making machine? Do many know what MAP refers to? And how many have ever stopped to ponder on what is quite so handy about the shape of a barrel or have come across household items made of old flour sacks? Answers to these – and many more – about the lesser known lives of food packaging are revealed in this book.[9]

In attending specifically to food packaging, Frank Cochoy is one of a notable, but very small handful of sociologists, human geographers and historians to do so.[10] Two social sciences much more likely to attend to packaging foodstuffs are archaeology but also anthropology, both of which include human artefacts at the centre of their purview. The research fields of the history, geography and sociology of food in general are proliferating at an ever-increasing rate on an ever-widening range of topics (Murcott 2013), but packaging barely features, commonly even absent from a book's index. It is as if food packaging is as invisible to many of these academics in their work as it is in many people's daily lives. Yet a recurrent theme across those academics' research is the global movement of foodstuffs, of people and their cuisines, the massive volumes of imports/exports in ever-lengthening food chains around the world – in short, 'the globalization of the food system'.

Certainly, the world-wide movement of food is nothing new, but it has been shown to have speeded up and grown ever more extensive and complicated. The world has become far more mobile. Without food packaging – the bags and the barrels, the cardboard boxes, the glass bottles and jars and, perhaps above all nowadays, the plastic bottles, trays and films – that enlarging global food system would look completely different. It would probably be far smaller in geographic reach, with far less variety in any one locality and some items likely much more expensive. Indeed it could be said that the contemporary food system is held together by packaging – no pun is intended nor needed. Leaving foodstuffs unpackaged makes them extremely difficult to move over even short distances, let alone along the current, elongated supply chains. They would get contaminated, losses would be considerable and keeping track of origins and destinations near impossible.

Yet, conspicuously absent in so much of that academic globalization literature is any curiosity about what the foods are moved round the world *in*. Indeed, even discussions of the extensive movement of foodstuffs on a more local scale barely attend to how they are carried. One swift example must suffice – a miniature snapshot. In a possibly surprising report, Derek Oddy observes that great quantities of liquid egg (preserved with boracic acid) were imported to London from China in the 1890s, likely used in the growing commercial cake manufacturing sector (Oddy 2007: 99). This intriguing record presented briefly, merely in passing, raises a good many questions: what were the circumstances under which those eggs were shelled and packed? Was that liquid egg conveyed in containers like wooden milk churns, or perhaps barrels? What were the decisions about containers and packages? Who made them? Is so much liquid egg still traded and transported internationally? If so, how has the packaging been updated and when? Answers to such questions in suitable detail appear hard to come by – appropriate records have yet to be identified.[11] Another gap remains to be filled.

Just a single source has been located thus far which is curious about the same question. In her book *Moveable Feasts: The Incredible Journeys of the Things We Eat* (2007), the journalist Sarah Murray observes that food has been hauled over long distances for centuries, e.g.

The Romans moved food all over their empire – British archaeologists recently discovered a 2,000 year-old food jar with a label showing it once contained fish paste thought to have been shipped to Carlisle[12] from Cadiz, Spain, more than 1,400 miles away.

(2007: 3)

Granting that some might wonder how Roman officers in a distant corner of their empire acquired a taste for fish paste, she is far more interested in

> how exactly did the paste get to such a remote corner of the Roman world? What sorts of containers did it travel in and how, in the absence of refrigeration and vacuum-sealed packs, did the fishy concoction not go bad during its journey?
>
> (2007: 3)

Several years before discovering Murray's inquisitive questions, preliminary work on which this book is based had already coalesced round a key question: 'how did the current food packaging landscape come about?' That question spawns any number of supplementaries: 'what was it like in different parts of the world and in different eras?' 'what is one or other package made of?' 'how did a particular package – or wrapper[13] – come to be contrived?' 'what sorts of reception do novel food containers receive from shoppers?' 'is it possible to trace the history of the expression "food packaging"?' 'why did it take half a century after tinned food was being produced for anyone to invent a can opener?' Did it have anything to do with initial use of canned foods by armies and navies – with strong men around used to wielding a stout knife or even hammer and chisel – and the wealthy – also with strong servants below stairs? Did a need only receive inventors' attention when canned goods could be afforded by the petit bourgeoisie with fewer employees, hammers and chisels regularly available ...[14] More generally, as Susan Leigh Star puts it 'What is the trajectory of social innovations? Who uses them and for what purposes?' (1988: 197). Asking questions such as these, self-evidently lead to enquiring about food packaging's history as well as its presence today. Accordingly, the enquiry on which this book makes a start covers a long span of time, occasionally millennia, certainly centuries, coming as up to date as is feasible to include some recent types of packaging.

A growing current concern about food packaging is, of course, its baleful contribution to environmental pollution and the climate emergency where it becomes visible for being in the wrong place. Campaigns drawing attention to this particular problem are not new. Fifty years ago, for instance, Britain's Women's Institute (WI) was agitating about the effect of plastics in the environment. In 1971, their National Federation proposed a resolution calling for research 'into the production of disintegrating plastic packaging materials' due to the increasing danger to livestock, other animals, spoiling beaches and the countryside.[15] And in June 2006, *The Daily Mail* reported that the WI had 'challenged supermarkets to cut down on unnecessary food packaging – or face a boycott'.[16]

For many, however, it is an episode of the veteran English natural historian David Attenborough's BBC TV series *Blue Planet*, screened in the UK late in 2017 (and then world-wide) which brought the environment's despoiling by discarded plastic packaging into the limelight.[17] Industry insiders consider the 'Attenborough effect' to have caused 'a tidal wave of change in consumer's attitudes towards packaging'.[18] In particular, commentators in the industry attribute the initiation of a public 'anti-plastic' attitude to that BBC programme.[19] And a 2018–19 market research social survey (not confined to its customers) commissioned by Waitrose, a UK supermarket, recorded that 88 per cent of respondents reported that they had altered their behaviour as a result of watching the programme.[20]

This book does not, however, directly intervene in current discussions about food packaging's environmental damage, of crucial importance though they are. Instead, the main purpose here is to contribute to understanding *precursors* to the current packaging landscape by asking that central question – how has it come about? Learning about those precursors is vital. For anyone concerned about the climate emergency – which arguably ought to be everyone – understanding what went before is essential to understanding the present. And knowing about the current food packaging landscape is as essential if any changes are to be made to it, or at least any changes which are effective in limiting factors that are long lasting if not irreversible as well as those propelling other environmental damage and the drastic loss of biodiversity.

Elements that need attention for tackling the book's main question about the origins of the current food packaging landscape include: changes over time; the historical parade of dramatis personae; the purposes to which people put packaging; the organizations and institutions involved; the knowledge and technologies that are brought to bear. As important are questions about what – the very stuff – the packages are made of and to initiate thinking about whatever difference that makes. Keeping all these in view results in a book that is located where the disciplines of history, sociology and Science & Technology Studies (STS) meet (Jasanoff *et al.* 2001). Despite its light hearted title, this book has a scholarly intent.

Each discipline has its own prime focus, as the historian and social scientist Xaq Frolich neatly puts it of the first two:

> Where historians see a series of people and events, sociologists see institutions and processes. Making sense (and use) of the past requires some reconciliation of both. On the one hand, past events are partly a (mere) consequence of chance, where 'the right person at the right time' is the only difference between one outcome and another. This speaks as much to the importance of individual personalities, as to the role of contingency in understanding the past and its legacy for the present. On the other hand, over time people's individual mark on enduring policies like food labeling become less important than the multitude of individuals and more permanent structures like institutions.
>
> (Frolich 2011: 19–20)

To history and sociology is added STS – for some, a sub-field of sociology (Star 1988) – which includes various traditions and concerns. Central, however, is the injunction not to treat science/technology as separate from society, but to recognize that they are part of society. By the same token it requires recognizing that the social is integral to science and technology – i.e. created and used by members of societies – and not to be apprehended as two distinct realms independent of one another. Such thinking paves the way for recognizing that science/technology are not exclusively investigable by the natural/biological/engineering sciences any more than their relation to the social is exclusively investigable by the human and social sciences. Science/technology is to be demystified by "'opening up the black box'", in other words, 'to analyze the process of production as well as the product' (Star 1988: 198). Tackling this book's central question about the precursors of the current food packaging landscape would be partial without aiming to focus on all three.

In the following pages, history in the guise of chronologies serves as a backbone throughout. The book moves very broadly from preindustrial food packaging via the tin can and canning to the modern and after-modern of its penultimate three chapters. But history also appears in recognizing several additional aspects: that there are commonly multiple rather than single histories to be written; that inventions do not necessarily have a smooth linear history culminating step by step in whatever are their familiar incarnations today; that earlier versions are not automatically inferior to or less sophisticated than those of the period when later their histories are written (Bijker 1997).

Sociology appears in attending to the sociocultural realm, especially in recognizing the human capacity for attributing meaning to inanimate objects – not forgetting that the attribution of some meaning or other arises in the social context of use (Mintz 1985). Much of the work in the sociology of food and eating[21] centres on consumption in the symbolic realm and on the sociopolitical significance of the social organization of institutions such as the household, education, health care, welfare provision, etc. (Murcott 2019, Murcott 2023). In the process, however, the material realm has almost completely been ignored as if closely following the working definition of culture presented by Giddens and Sutton for whom it is limited to the symbolic realm (2014: 135). What – to anthropologists and others – is missing in such a definition are artefacts.

Yet dealing with food packaging demands attention to just that sphere, the world of things. It is not only the materiality of the package or even the food – the very articles that packages are to contain – that is at issue but also the materiality of human beings themselves. The package's contents are intended to be ingested which means they must be protected from anything which renders them risky to the human body. As important, the package that is intended to keep out dangers must not, in the process, itself pose a danger. Of course, as creative beings, it is people who invent food and design packaging, people who manufacture and use it. But they are *also* involved as things and, moreover as things which can be fatally damaged. People and food both consist of organic (as distinct from inorganic) materials and both can decay or suffer chemical/physical/biological assault. It is partly in this respect the book turns to modes of thought developed in STS to help expose *material* features integral to the relation between people and the business of packaging their food.

In sum, all these components need to be accommodated in tackling that central question about the precursors and earlier incarnations of food packaging. Doing so is the main purpose of this book. In the process, it pulls in other purposes, such as drawing attention to the multitude of places food packaging has inhabited and continues to inhabit in the doings of one or other social group/society, demonstrating the roles it plays and highlighting the relation between people and the materials from which food packaging has been and is fashioned. In so doing the affordances – opportunities and limitations – posed by the very character of the materials is exposed to view – as, for instance, Gay Hawkins has pointed out, plastic's durability is a virtue when used as a water bottle but a vice once discarded in the ocean (Hawkins 2013). Above all, the ultimate purpose of this book is to support expanded understanding of food packaging. If its calamitous environmental consequences are effectively to be tackled, then a broad understanding of food packaging's materiality, its history, its place socioculturally, politically and economically is essential.

It follows that this book is written for more than one group of readers. Academics and students concerned with the analysis of modern food systems are a main group as well as those interested in technology/society. Those in the food/packaging industries as well as activists/campaigners may also share an interest in reading more about the precursors to their expertise and focus. After all they are typically invested in the futures of food packaging and, thus, by implication the history that has led to the present. And a further group of readers includes anyone simply curious about what some of the secret lives of food packaging are like.

Given the scant attention some academic historians and social scientists have paid to food packaging so far, this book can only make a start on contributing to such endeavour. The whole enterprise is far too big for itself. Masses of intriguing illuminating material had to be removed to keep this book a manageable length, a great many relevant lines of thought have had to be truncated with important topics omitted altogether – stoppers, lids, tops, caps and corks: packages' defects, bursting, leaking, collapsing: never mind insufficient attention to advertising, marketing and branding as well as to advanced technological innovations such as smart, active and intelligent packaging (Risch 2009). The whole is anything but comprehensive, trading depth for breadth – each chapter could be a complete book on its own and, indeed, deserves such treatment. Notwithstanding these particular limitations, it was decided to persist with attempting to view food packaging in general, aiming to demonstrate the huge potential for more detailed work in future and to start setting out a conceptual perspective at that junction of history, sociology and STS. The result is very firmly a first word, not the last. The book needs to be superseded, probably by several.

There are further limitations, one in particular.[22] Any book has to be written from somewhere – this one in London, with a few forays to an Irish and several UK archives. It is not just that its viewpoint is Eurocentric and at times North American. It also results in a sore lack of comparative perspective. Not only is Japan with its specific traditions, innovations and advanced food packaging industry (Hendry 1995, Cwiertka 2020) almost completely omitted. It is also that the kinds of assumptions and impressions about food packaging as hidden in plain sight of the project's point of departure are 'trapped' inside its primarily Transatlantic outlook. It is probably no accident that archaeology and anthropology are not nearly as guilty of ignoring the study of food packaging as much as are history, human geography and sociology. The former pair are both dedicated to the study of different times and places from 'the West' of other older eras and other contrasting cultures.

It is very possible that being able to regard food packaging as invisible is, if not engendered, at least aggravated, by its being set against a busy background of a century and more of 'Western' capitalist mass consumption – of huge volumes of consumer goods of as huge variety, of the associated regularly repeated rhetoric of choice and rights to exercising it (commonly forgetting completely this is available only to those with the means) and the sheer scale and sophistication of marketeers' activities and ingenuity of marketing practice.

Comparison with the work of anthropologist Elizabeth Hull (2022)[23] in rural South Africa is instructive. Poverty and scarcity and a far shorter history of mass consumption is noticeably associated with the careful re-purposing of a range of food packages, suggesting it is anything but invisible but valued, its potential for a new use clearly remarked. Similarly, anthropologist Jakob Klein (2022a) talks of food packaging along with so much else in post-socialist China attracting attention. For it stands in vivid contrast to the standardized, plain, serviceability of goods of the Communist era. Its novelty, brightness and originality have a special appeal, easily noticed against so drab a recent background.[24]

The book is organized with those several readerships in mind, aimed at making it easier for anyone to locate what they find more interesting and skip sections less relevant to them. Chapter 2 is the companion in Part I to the present chapter. It enlarges on the study of food packaging as a technology. In the process, it addresses the variety of answers to the question 'what is food packaging', to illustrate the inclusive view adopted throughout later chapters. In the main it introduces concepts worth keeping in mind when reading later chapters on specific instances of packaging. Above all it expands on the intellectual approach of the discussion's overall location at the intersection of the three disciplines noted above – the most academically technical part of the book.

Part II consists of a chapter each on major items of food packaging and the materials from which they have been and are made: bags and sacks, barrels and chests, bottles and jars, tin canisters and cans. All those chapters comprise some combination of: chronologies; inventors and their inventions; ingenious technical novelties; accounts of packaging and the activities involved in the industry drawn from interviews with key actors in the field; notes on how a package such as glass bottle or a wooden barrel is made, albeit from a non-technical viewpoint. Most chapters also include specific examples or cases – on the invention of canning, on the work of a waste paper merchant, on the engineering trial and error in producing a metal beer barrel – which are presented as self-contained 'Interludes'.

Part III changes tack with a trio of chapters each on packaged foodstuffs currently readily available in shops and supermarkets from South Africa to Canada, Finland to New Zealand, Singapore to Mexico to focus on the emergence of each of three processed items. These chapters too include 'Interludes' highlighting selected technologies or the portrayal of selected associated histories – on the microwave oven; on developments in processing tomato ketchup; on the part played in the preservation of raw salads by plastic bags – and social issues such as the differing public receptions accorded 'convenience' foods. The final chapter on its own in Part IV draws the threads together, noting the range of topics that this book has had to omit that still require close scrutiny. It lists selected considerations about food packaging's developments, directions and trends, notably 'unpackaged' retail set against a history of shopping, as well as moves towards novel environmentally friendlier food packaging materials. One purpose of the final chapter is to signal how much new work of the kind this book represents still remains to be done in order adequately to answer the question as to how the contemporary food packaging landscape came about.

Notes

1. This book refers to food packaging to include that for foods and drinks, alcoholic and non-alcoholic.

2. In principle, the act of recycling renders packaging more visible.

3. EFSA (2021). 'Phthalates: draft opinion and exposure protocol open for public consultation'. 5 November. Available online: https://www.efsa.europa.eu/en/news/phthalates-draft-opinion-and-exposure-protocol-open-public-consultation (accessed 6 April 2023). Unless otherwise specified, access to all websites cited was checked on 6 April 2023.

4. Westervelt, A. 'Phthalates are everywhere, and the health risks are worrying. How bad are they really?' 10 February. Available online: https://www.theguardian.com/lifeandstyle/2015/feb/10/phthalates-plastics-chemicals-research-analysis (accessed 6 April 2023). Swan, S. & Colino, S. (2021). 'How to avoid the toxic kitchen chemicals that could damage your fertility' 5 March. Available online: https://www.washingtonpost.com/lifestyle/wellness/fertility-chemicals-damage-count-down/2021/03/04/b491e220-6cad-11eb-9f80-3d7646ce1bc0_story.html (accessed 6 April 2023).

5. The UK public health response was to impose 'lockdown' in March 2020 with people allowed to go out for essentials only (e.g. food, medicines), a maximum of an hour's exercise daily, required to work from home where feasible. This book's spelling/capitalization of COVID-19 follows the practice in scientific/medical journals.

6. Southey, F. (2020). 'China detects COVID-19 on German pork knuckles, suspends imports from 20 countries'. 20 November. Available online: (accessed 6 April 2023).

7. Luxmoore, S. and agency (2018). 'Pret a Manger doubles discount for bringing reusable coffee cups'. 2 January. Available online: https://www.theguardian.com/environment/2018/jan/02/pret-a-manger-doubles-discount-for-bringing-reusable-coffee-cups?CMP=share_btn_link (accessed 6 April 2023). A good journalistic account of food provision in the early days of the pandemic in the UK is Rayner, J. (2020). 'From panic buying to food banks: how Britain fed itself in the first phase of coronavirus'. 21 June. Available online: https://www.theguardian.com/food/2020/jun/21/from-panic-buying-to-food-banks-how-britain-fed-itself-in-the-first-phase-of-coronavirus (accessed 6 April 2023).

8. Feber, D., Lingqvist, O. & Nordigården, D. (2020). 'How the packaging industry can navigate the coronavirus pandemic'. 16 April. Available online: https://www.mckinsey.com/industries/paper-forest-products-and-packaging/our-insights/how-the-packaging-industry-can-navigate-the-coronavirus-pandemic (accessed 6 April 2023).

9. Although commonly the word 'secrets' conjures something that is deliberately concealed, secrets here involves a much less strict definition, referring simply to things which are 'out of sight out of mind', backstage rather than on show, typically in the domain of insiders. Such secrets are, however, available for the asking, from specialist sources and to be acquired via the various techniques of enquiry used by historians and social scientists. There are still some deliberately to be concealed i.e. intellectual property, specialist patentable techniques, etc.

10. Others include: Simone Cinotto (2013), Katarzyna Cwiertka (2020), Adel den Hartog (1998), Jack Goody (1982), Gay Hawkins (2013) Gabriella Petrick (2010), Richard Wilk (2009), Anna Zeide (2018).

11. One small hint is found in the autobiography by Nathan Goldenberg, who led M&S' scientific and technical food divisions for almost forty years from 1948. Discussing efforts to improve the quality of eggs used in their cakes, he records the work undertaken with two firms, importers of frozen egg – from Australia and China to the UK (Goldenberg 1989: 80).

12. A city in north west England near the border with Scotland.

13. This is the word used in an 1892 practical guide for food inspectors when discussing the legal requirement to label margarine in England: '(U)nder section 8 (of the Butter and Margarine Act 1907) wrappers enclosing "margarine" are not required to be marked "margarine" exclusively, as previously ordered, but may be marked with a fancy or other descriptive name (approved by the Board of Agriculture and Fisheries) and printed in type not larger than, and in the same colour as the "margarine"' (Vacher 1892: 268).

14. Or was it that working-class women who kept wealthy households' kitchens going, were easily strong enough to use these tools to open a can, their arms well exercised by carrying heavy iron cooking pots and pans or lifting sacks of potatoes. Victorian images of women's fragility applied only to the more prosperous; working class women were considered 'naturally' physically strong as if of a completely separate species.

15. WI (nd). 'History of WI Campaigns'. Available online: https://www.thewi.org.uk/campaigns/100-years-of-wi-campaigns (accessed 6 April 2023).

16. Poulter, S. (2006). 'WI at war with stores over food packaging'. 21 June. Available online: http://www.dailymail.co.uk/health/article-391608/WI-war-stores-food-packaging.html#ixzz3QiS77Fus (accessed 6 April 2023).

17. BBC News (2019). 'Plastic pollution & Sir David Attenborough (Global)'. 19th November. Available online: https://www.youtube.com/watch?v=KQFdTGO6zTM (accessed 6 April 2023).

18. Kertész, Z. (2021). 'Choosing the best packaging in a post-pandemic world' 29 June. Available online: https://www.campdenbri.co.uk/blogs/post-pandemic-packaging.php (accessed 6 April 2023).

19. An interview with a very senior packaging industry leader in the UK revealed a rather different view, namely that it began earlier, prompted by a programme on Sky (a separate television channel) noting in the process that the then chairman of Sky happened to be an anti-plastic campaigner.

20. Waitrose (2020). 'Food and Drink Report'. Available online: https://www.waitrose.com/content/dam/waitrose/Inspiration/Waitrose%20&%20Partners%20Food%20and%20Drink%20Report%202018.pdf (accessed 6 April 2023).

21. Unlike the sociology of agriculture and food production.

22. It is limited too primarily to English language literature and sources. Inspection of archive materials nationally and internationally originally planned was cancelled under general pandemic restrictions and individual 'vulnerability' to COVID-19. The result is an unavoidable Anglocentric viewpoint to a project that had to be worked up and written in London with travel only possible via email and the internet, fortunately augmented by the invaluable help of four younger people able to travel, Charlotte Davey, Katrina Moseley, Tom Cryer and Elvira Tamus.

23. Hull, E. (2022). personal communication.

24. Klein, J. (2022a). personal communication.

CHAPTER 2
FOOD PACKAGING – A TECHNOLOGY

Self-evidently, food packaging entails technologies of many kinds. In just the same way that historians and other social scientists have not squarely examined the topic and its social implications, STS specialists mostly have not either – with honourable exceptions such as Henry Petroski or Gabriella Petrick.

This chapter's main purpose is to expand on the intellectual approach afforded by locating the book at the intersection of history, sociology and STS. In so doing, it considers a wide variety of answers to the question 'what is food packaging' *inter alia* introducing the inclusive view adopted in later chapters. Such a view is of an outsider to the packaging world and contrasts with insiders' viewpoints.[1] Drawing the contrast helps the search for secret aspects of food packaging's lives and supports opening the black box of increasing industrializations' wooden crates, sacks for wheat, railroad cars, tin cans and mass produced glass bottles for ketchups.

The chapter also introduces a few concepts and analytic abstractions used by historians, sociologists and STS experts that are worth keeping in mind when reading the rest of the book. The chapter eases its way in to the contrast between insiders' and outsiders' versions by discussing definitions of food packaging. Note that even if in many circumstances it is possible to talk of food packaging's invisibility, those for whom it is visible, indeed ever present, are the insiders to the industry with working lives revolving round it. These are insider specialists in paper and card, recycling, canning and more, not forgetting researchers representing many disciplines, independent institutes and R&D departments of major companies – valued from at least 1901 by Heinz in the United States (Foster and Kennedy 2006: 37) as well actively promoted in the mid-twentieth century by Marks and Spencer (M&S) in the UK (Rees 1969).[2]

What is food packaging?

The packaging expert, Diana Twede, authoritatively and succinctly answers this section's question: 'packaging functions of protection, utility, and communication' (2002: 98). Food packaging is something that may not only carry information but also protect and is useful. This view, as will be seen, is of a piece with definitions in food packaging textbooks and promoted by others on the inside of the contemporary industry. The words 'food packaging' commonly conjure images of things such as a pillow-like plastic bag containing fresh lettuce leaves, a tin can of water-chestnuts or baked beans, or a tube of tomato paste – in other words, ordinary items of industrialized packaging available at corner shops and convenience stores from Singapore to Scotland, Stockholm to Seattle.

Indeed it is likely that the very expression 'food packaging' is itself a twentieth century, industrialized invention. According to an influential industrial designer's 1939 discussion, the word 'packaging' was not in widespread use any earlier (Gray 1939). Instead, he argues, modern packaging dates from the rise of branding towards the end of the nineteenth century. Adel Den Hartog – industry historian – puts it later, thereby emphasizing a slow-ish process: '(T)he development of food packaging is linked with the making of modern food processing and food retail systems. In Western Europe and North America until the 1920s, most foods were sold unpackaged' (1998: 249). Their view is broadly shared by Waverly Root: in the United States packaging is a word 'which was not in the vocabulary of the nineteenth century, though the phenomenon which it represented was taking on substance then' (Root and de Rochemont 1976: 239).

Unravelling 'what is food packaging' is pursued here in broadly three interrelated ways. The first follows the lead offered Twede. Here the intention is attentively to learn how she and other specialists in the industry define it, alert to any changes over time. It also means looking out for any disagreements. A notable instance is the challenges to the definition from food packaging's critics about the silence on its darker side – 'overpackaging', the potential for harm to wildlife, environmental damage and negative implications for the climate. Despite such criticisms, both industry experts and detractors focus on what is still an insider's definition, albeit effecting small shifts in definitions. There are detectable signs of greater acknowledgement of negative criticism with statements about food packaging's purpose refocused to attend to ameliorating negative consequences. Inspecting the content of thirteen packaging textbooks published between 1980 and 2018 reveals additions in more recent years in references to 'biodegradability' (10 mentions), 'sustainability' (8), 'environment' (8), 'packaging waste' (7), 'recyclability' (7), 'compostable' (6) and 'greenhouse gas' (GHG) (5).[3]

Adopted in this book is a second way of disentangling the question: taking an outsider's or observer's approach. Where an insider's approach represents the lens through which to scrutinise, never mind engage in, the work of actually manufacturing, selling and using food packaging, the outsider's view moves to a different vantage point which *includes* that insider approach – both the lens and all shown up when looking through it – as part of the now expanded terrain to be examined. This second approach to identifying food packaging is stretched as widely and as inclusively as possible in order, among other things, to allow for firmer attention to differences in aspects of food packaging geographically and historically as well as socially and technically.

To underscore the point, the main concern of insiders' definitions of food packaging is to circumscribe characterizations that support industrial practicalities, including training the next generation to follow them into the industry. The outsider's stance caters for attention to the boundaries between food packaging and other things – an inclusive approach – as well as to other historical periods and societal settings in addition to industrialized contexts. Insiders' terminology largely assumes 'food packaging' refers to that of industrialized economies where packaging is mass produced for eventual mass distribution of commodities to consumer mass markets. Indeed, insider history tends explicitly to trace a progression from '(t)he earliest primitive packages … made from leaves, skins and gourds' with little change between the Classical world's amphoras and barrels until 'consumer packaging' began to emerge with that major shift when 'wooden crates and shipping sacks rode in on the industrial revolution with its boxcars, sawmills and textile mills' (Twede 2016).

While insiders' practical viewpoints note, but then by-pass, packaging of non-industrial economies – except when purposely writing a history of them – this book does not. Whether they be contemporary non-industrial economic sectors or those of the past, their packaging is, in principle, to be included in the purview here. In other words, neither time nor place is to rule out considering food packaging as a technology of interest. In part this is to evade adopting 'whig' history, one where the historiography of all earlier periods is deemed to present an inferior precursor to the successes of the present, conceiving history as proceeding in a straight line, with no offshoot 'blind alleys' or reinventions along the way – a position explicitly rejected by STS specialists (Bijker 1997).

The adoption of so inclusive a view in what follows makes provision for comparisons between the purposes and efficacy of packaging from different eras, keeps open the possibility of investigating how shifts come about and offers the chance of pondering on what happens when a food package looks to be disappearing. Above all it initiates attempts to study technologies from different eras and forms of economy from the vantage point of that junction between history, sociology and STS, thus allowing attention to the historiography and sociology of who, how and why anyone might be interested in the practical matters which preoccupy insiders – *including* the obstacles and opportunities materials afford – aiming to uncover how those matters are discussed, differences settled, or who has the final say.

All the same, both insiders' and a great many outsiders' approaches, by default, in silence and by implication, regard food packaging as passive and regard the field as crammed with inert objects, things that are invented, manufactured, distributed, used and, in some fashion, dealt with thereafter. By contrast, food packaging in this book's approach is to be understood as consisting of an assortment of items whose qualities, character and behaviour can make a difference to the manner in which people may invent, manufacture, distribute and use them. In this respect, food packaging is active, not passive and as much so as people in their dealings with it are active. Before enlarging any further on this less usual position, however, the first two approaches deserve more detailed discussion.

Insiders' views

If most people, in the usual way of things, pay little attention to food packaging or do not find it especially interesting, those in the food packaging industry are quite the opposite; it fills their field of vision.[4] As one packaging insider remarked in an interview:

> People (I work with) love talking about packaging because it's one of those industries where once you get sucked into it you're sucked into it for life
>
> (packaging specialist, 2018)

Whatever their expertise, responsibilities or allotted tasks, for these 'insiders', packaging is at the centre of their ordinary working days. The range of occupations is remarkably wide:

~ a supermarket's packaging manager, responsible for minimising the company's GHG (greenhouse gas) emissions

~ a materials engineer collaborating with a cell biologist testing the safety of a biopolyester

~ those in protective gloves standing at a recycling plant's conveyor belt in a vast, smelly, windowless box of a building checking the parade of crushed plastic bottles, used cans and jars passing before them

~ computing specialists responsible for the smooth running of a large factory making ready-meals' PET (polyethylene terephthalate) trays, ensuring real time data are transmitted into the parent-company's head office on another continent

~ an environmental specialist employed by a 'green' NGO as a policy adviser

~ an art college graduate specialising in food package design

~ a young woman in fleece jacket and gloves driving a forklift truck piling pallets of tertiary packaged frozen foods in a warehouse that is effectively a gigantic deep freeze compartment

~ a man with 35 years industry experience serving as director of a plastic-packaging trade association

For them and many more specialists associated with it, packaging represents among other things, their livelihood. And these specialists need to be able to communicate effectively: as in most occupations, specialist terminology develops in the process. As to definitions of food packaging itself, consider the following:

> To be an economic success a package must conform to certain basic and obvious principles. Firstly, it must be suitably constructed to hold and protect its contents, must be easy to pack in bulk and it must have good display value. Secondly, the reading matter must be legible and general design aesthetically pleasing and appropriate to its contents. Thirdly, the cost must be kept with a certain established margin.
>
> (BMRB 1950: 30)

> In addition to offering protection from the elements and a convenient way of transporting goods from store to table, food packages are indeed weapons in an ongoing war to win consumer loyalty ... For every popular brand, armies of tacticians, including brand managers, marketing experts and product, graphic and advertising designers expend a huge amount of resources devising the perfect attack.
>
> (Heller 1999: 213)

And displaying a view of the practicalities, Nathan Goldenberg, M&S' first technical manager, goes so far as to regard packaging thus:

> For many years I have learnt to regard packaging materials, in which foods are wrapped or packed in close and intimate contact with the wrapping materials, as *a food raw material*. Badly made or unsuitable packaging material can ruin the quality of the food packed therein.
>
> (1989: 88 emphasis added)

Each source tends to define packaging slightly differently. Indeed, as Coles observes, there are 'many ways of defining packaging reflecting different emphases' (2003: 8). Terms need to be defined in any activity where communication between those involved is essential to the smooth running of operations. A further distinction is made.

Packaging is classified into three levels: 'primary, secondary and tertiary' (Robertson 2013: 2). The first is the packaging directly enclosing the items themselves, serving as the main protective barrier and is typically the packaging at a retailer's premises, the level with which customers come into direct contact. Secondary packaging is a type which may hold one or several identical primary packages – quite commonly nowadays visible to food shoppers since some, often cardboard, double as display cases (i.e. 'shelf ready' Robertson 2013: 2). These also hold say, a collection of tubes of tomato paste, or small tins of anchovies whose shapes either make stacking awkward/impossible or even if they stack are relatively light and liable to slither.[5] Although customers may come into contact with them, they rarely do any more than select chosen items from the carton which they leave behind. Tertiary packaging is simply that which holds a collection of secondary packages together – nowadays, commonly plastic film stretched completely around a pallet-load.

Industry insiders also include trade associations and organizations. One instance is the Industry Council for Packaging and the Environment (INCPEN)[6] based in the UK whose members include packaging manufacturers, brands and retailers, recyclers and re-processors. A regular task they undertake is addressing public criticisms about 'superfluous' packaging, one that is couched in terms of exploding the myths criticisms are held to represent.[7] In the process, a 2011 discussion '(W)hy products are packaged the way they are' provides an elaborated definition:

> Packaging is an integral and essential part of the industrial and commercial supply chain. It protects goods from damage, allows efficient transport distribution, offers convenience, prolongs shelf-life, enables easy use, informs the consumer and helps to promote goods in a competitive market place.[8]

Incpen's position is echoed by Robertson who recognizes that despite its significance, packaging 'is often regarded as, at best, somewhat superfluous, and, at worst, a serious waste of resources and an environmental menace' (Robertson 2014: 232). But, he continues: '(S)uch views arise because, by the time most consumers come into contact with a package, its job, in many cases, is almost over'. In other words, when criticizing the volume of packaging people are not, he argues, including the part packaging plays from field or abattoir to shop-shelf, keeping foods clean, safe and tamper-proof. More to the point, as industry spokespeople regularly point out, food packaging limits food waste by keeping it fresh and contributing both to its extended shelf- and residency-life (i.e. the time between purchase and use).

Food packaging insiders who have to be concerned with definitions are not only those directly employed in its manufacture, use or disposal. Others, notably regulators, have to pay definitions even closer attention. One example is a 2022 New Zealand regulation banning the sale/manufacture of some single-use, hard-to-recycle plastics identified by the purpose to which they are put, namely

> rigid trays that are manufactured separately to the food it packages. The ban is not intended to cover PVC form-fill-seal packaging where the plastic is formed, filled with food and mechanically sealed on the same line.[9]

The distinction revolves around recent feature in food packaging history whereby factory production brought the process of food preservation and manufacturing the package so closely together that they are integrated on a single assembly line.

A second instance, also requiring detailed discrimination, is exemplified in a European Commission directive on packaging and packaging waste, urging reduction, reuse and recycling. Unavoidably, any such regulation has to specify what is *and* is not deemed food packaging: cheese wax, sausage skins and tea bags do not count.[10] In post-Brexit UK, the government has, at the time of writing, newly introduced a Plastic Packaging Tax (PPT) and the implementation of Extended Producer Responsibility (EPR) is underway. But a *Packaging News* editorial points out two key government departments involved have different ideas on the definition of a pack (Chadwick 2022).[11]

Public attention to food packaging – probably mostly complaint – tends in practice to think of examples of packaging in the same way as industry insiders, i.e. types of wrapping or container which are highly industrialized and often comparatively elaborate – finely corrugated card around biscuits, avocados in moulded plastic, cellophane wrapping tomatoes. Reference to a plain paper bag as food packaging can evince surprise, as if the words do not apply to something so simple. Outsiders' viewpoints on food packaging, however, take the focus much wider and encompass the public's/industry insiders' shared images of what typically counts as food packaging.

Outsiders' definitions

Tertiary packages are not simply contemporary inventions, even if the nomenclature is. Andrew Bevan, an archaeologist, makes no distinction between pre- and post-industrial third-level packaging. Sweeping up all levels into one observation, he declares that:

> (T)he Mediterranean basin offers perhaps our oldest, and certainly our most detailed, long-term record of trade in bulk and standardized goods. Associated

with these exchanges from the outset have been some highly distinctive physical media for maritime shipping and terrestrial carriage: animal-skin bags, pottery jars, wooden barrels, glass bottles, woven sacks, wooden crates, and, more recently, cardboard boxes, tin cans, plastic packaging, wooden pallets, and steel shipping containers.

(2014: 387)

Incorporating all of those distinctive physical media for transporting goods en masse is the shipping container. Its rise is sketched by a business administration expert:

(U)ntil the 1960s, maritime cargo was loaded, transported, and unloaded crate by crate. Once on the docks, crates were moved onto pallets. Forklifts moved the pallets into trucks and warehouses. A standardized, sealed shipping container was invented in the 1950s. In the second half of the 20th century, new shipping systems designed around these large (20, 40 or 45 feet long by 8 feet wide 8.5 feet high), interchangeable containers drastically increased transport efficiency allowing the seamless movement of cargo between ships, trucks and trains. By 2000, approximately 90% of all maritime cargo was shipped in containers.

(McGinn 2007: 267)

Thus, to the initial three has been added a fourth, the 'quaternary package' which can transport large numbers of tertiary packages. Such containers are moved on/off ships by crane at ports specially designed to handle such large items of cargo – the 40 foot/12.2 metres container became an internationally standard length by the late 1960s (Levinson 2008). Sometimes those ports are out of sight and earshot of major centres – such as one on the river Thames downstream of London, working continuously by gigantic spotlights through the night.

Like Lisbon's (Figure 2) they are not inevitably invisible, unlike containers' contents. Those responsible for a company's packaging need to consider all four levels, self-evidently they must dovetail with one another along the packaging chain especially when foodstuffs are to be moved by air, sea or road over very long distances.

Outsiders' approaches are more expansive. They thereby allow the inclusion of features adjacent, yet also integral, to food packaging's place in society. Note how disparate the sixteen disparate images in this book are, yet each has something to do with food packaging. It is not just that that there are multiple histories to be written of the invention and adoption of a novel food package, their forms and the materials from which they are made – the glassine, the aluminium foil, the plastic-lined tin can, the PET (polyethylene terephthalate) bottle and HDPE (high density polyethylene) tray. It is that to these must be added histories of a long list of other things:

~ barrels, bags, bottles, pottles, amphorae, tubs, jars
~ iron, steel, cardboard, glass, paper, cellophane, polythene, polystyrene
~ paper-bag-making – or glass-bottle-making machines

Figure 2 Lisbon's container port, easily visible to the public.

~ modes of food preservation, drying, salting, freezing, pickling, 'Apeel'
~ refrigeration, the 'cold chain'
~ logistics, 'just-in-time' supply, standardisation
~ can openers
~ containerisation, pallets and forklift trucks
~ transport, rubber tyres, road surfacing
~ food labelling, the creation of brands
~ excise duty, smuggling
~ food safety regulations
~ food-safe adhesives and inks
~ world fairs, great exhibitions' displays of model dairies
~ 'convenience foods' and the very idea of convenience
~ the invention of self-service grocery stores and the shopping trolley (cart)
~ the invention of the microwave oven

among others. As the STS scholar and historian Xaq Frolich observes of his own study of food labelling:

one could tell the history of food labeling as a proxy for the history of food packaging, which in turn is a proxy for the history of advances in transport and processing technologies which have extended the distances between production and consumption and played a part in creating the abstract relationships between manufacturers and consumers.

(2011: 439)

In sum, then, this inclusive, outsider, viewpoint represents the foundation on which this book's historic/sociologic study of food packaging rests – and which also provides the springboard for the third approach inspired by thinking developed in STS. It is an approach which affords a potentially far wider geographic, historic and sociologic view of food packaging. And instead of ruling in/out selected items, it allows the dissolution of everyday distinctions between what insiders regard as food packaging and other items that are closely related. Thus, when needed, a history of those very distinctions can be pursued exposing the social processes involved in the manner in which they arise to analytic view.

The kinds of distinctions being dissolved may well be mundane and familiar – a pizza's cardboard box is converted by the very way people use it, from container to plate. Other examples of highly industrialized food packaging are deliberately designed to be more than a container, self consciously blurring distinctions – the US company Emmerson Packaging's 'boil in the bag' food package highlights both 'safety and convenience for consumer and institutional uses' as both food package and cooking pot.[12] Other industrialized materials have been developed that are 'ovenable' in either a microwave or conventional oven: one is a cardboard derived from 'renewable farmed forests which can also be frozen down to −40°C'.[13] Popcorn was sold in another, available in the United States in the 1960s: 'a formed aluminium foil tray containing the raw kernels is used with an expandable foil cover. As the tray is heated, the corn pops, the foil cover expands and no cooking vessel is needed' (Sacharow and Griffin 1980: 407). More recent is a type used by supermarkets, a plastic bag completely enclosing a whole chicken which can be placed, still wrapped, straight into an oven to roast (Evans *et al.* 2020), thus protecting the shopper/cook from direct contact with the raw poultry thereby reducing the risk of campylobacter poisoning.[14] Further instances date from the nineteenth century of packaging that intentionally has a life beyond being bought/taken home so goods may be stored in the kitchen in their original pack: airtight cardboard drums containing cocoa or glass bottles of tomato ketchup designed to make continued use easily possible, while Huntley & Palmer's biscuit tins were intended for reuse in the home.[15]

Anthropologists record the widespread use of naturally occurring materials – leaves, stems, tree bark – all of which have been used for a long time to package, count, transport and store foods (Betzig and Turke 1986, Nelson, Ploetz and Kepler 2006, Densmore 2012, Ducos 2014, Ángel-Bravo 2021). Amongst the Tallensi, for instance, beef or donkey meat was dried, kept for many months. 'Such meat is carefully preserved in a pot or calabash among a woman's more valued possessions; but dried guinea-fowl is kept with her soup ingredients in the kitchen' (Fortes and Fortes 1936: 268). Banana leaves are widely used and there is the possibly unexpected instance of the use of a 'pitcher plant (*Nepenthes ampullaria*) to contain sticky rice' (Laistrooglai, Mosikarat and Wigran 2000: 18).[16] Archaeologists' work reveals pre-historic food storage technologies. Neolithic granaries found in the Jordan valley are an ingenious example. Their sophisticated design created suspended floors allowing air to circulate, limiting excessive moisture and helping protect against vermin (Kuijt and Finlayson 2009).

Anthropologists along with historians can readily list many more named items of wood, pottery, leather or textiles. Further nuances are found in work by Richard Bean, an economist, who created an extensive catalogue compiled from Naval Officer lists of 1688 and 1728–9 for Barbados and Jamaica as a basis for assessing colonial era imports to the West Indies. His list of containers includes: 'tuns, puncheons, butts, pipes, hogsheads, tierces, casks, barrels, aumes, rundlets, kegs, kilderkins, firkins, tubs, jars, cases, bags, serons, sacks, boxes, hampers, chests, quintals, flitches, pots, bottles and bushels' along with units such as pounds and gallons with 'tuns, pipes, hogsheads and barrels' as the relatively few standardized wooden containers (1977: 581). Here seventeenth-century usage also blurs boundaries: the names of containers slide into use as a unit of measurement. Recollect, after all, that crude oil is in the twenty-first century still measured in barrels.

A more inclusive observers' approach absolves the analyst of any obligation to decide whether or not, for example, a coating sprayed on to an avocado is or is not a food package. Such a novel 'skin' is reported in an industry newsletter; Apeel Sciences' development of an edible coating 'made from leftover plant skins and stems, could save suppliers, retailers, and consumers big bucks by promoting sustainable growing practices and reducing waste from farm to retailer to home. It could also be beneficial to the environment if less water, fertilizer or land is needed to grow produce to replace those items that are wasted'.[17] And, noted in 2019 issue of *Food Technology Magazine* is a different edible coating applied to frozen foods in order to reduce 'freezer burn'.[18] The purposes on which insider definitions rely are illustrated by items that may not, strictly speaking, count as a package from their point of view, yet share an industry viewpoint in devotion to lengthening shelf-life as well as to sustainability and waste reduction.

Most importantly, adopting an inclusive definition of food packaging caters for close attention to its many 'after lives'[19] (Hawkins 2013: 67) notably waste and its attendant problems. Criticisms aimed at altering insider activities have familiarly become louder in the recent decades well illustrated by growing attention to this post-use phase among insiders, manufacturers, regulators and so on, gradually replacing older attitude where what happens after use was an infrequently considered afterthought. Even a casual eye on the trade press suggests a considerable increase in attention to recycling, reuse and a circular economy whereby discards and used materials after suitable cleaning, etc. return to re-enter the circle as feedstock for new packages.

In any case, examples of mundane re-use by members of the public are very common and long standing. It is not hard to find a shelf or drawer in many households containing used and washed primary packs, yoghurt pots, ice-cream tubs ready for storing leftovers or freezing portions of batch-cooked soup. Cardboard boxes – i.e. secondary packaging for tins of baked beans or cartons of biscuits – are widely retained by supermarkets then made available, gratis, to shoppers to hold purchases carried out to the boot (trunk) of

Figure 3 Secondary packaging before the term was invented.

their cars. Another instance of secondary packaging, but far older, is the wooden box in Figure 3 which held a dozen jars of Virol.[20]

It was spotted, somewhen in the mid-1970s, pressed into service as a tray for deposit slips, perched on the window ledge behind the tellers in a small local branch of a bank. None of the staff could remember where it came from, none wanted any money for it as, bemused by anyone's even noticing let alone treasuring it, they readily handed it over the counter, replacing it with a standard office wire-basket.

Barrels are another package which continue to have several re-uses, familiar as garden planters, as tables on the pavement outside pubs and, of course for aging whisky, wine, port or vinegar. While used food packaging turns up in unlikely places to take on a new life as a museum curio. Clearing up after the earthquake in Christchurch, New Zealand, religious relics were found stored in an instant coffee glass jar.[21] Litter – an empty snack packet and fizzy drink (soda) can, presumably the remains of a building worker's lunch during the construction of London's Barbican complex in 1981 – got trapped somewhere in the building's fabric. Found during further works thirty-eight years later, they were removed for storage in the Barbican archive. Much nineteenth- and twentieth-century food packaging can be found in 'vintage' shops or second-hand on market stalls: Figure 4 shows a ceramic jar that once held cream.

Figure 4 Bought in a second-hand shop.

Online, items might be described as '1950s era' advertised as ideal as a film or TV prop – a large tin that held Nuttall's Mintos or some early Bakelite adding authenticity to a theatre set – now valued for their own sake as a collectible by historians of plastics.[22]

Food packaging could be said to have burst its boundaries of the insider, practical, working definitions essential for the provision of useful containers for the retail food market from which everyone benefits. Outsider, more extensive definitions help render more evident the places where many of those containers find a spot beyond that on which those working in the packaging industry primarily focus.

At this point, the discussion turns to present a handful of concepts worth bearing in mind when reading the remaining chapters.

Transitions and conversions – movement over time and space

Packaging, then, is prominent in the globalization of the food system. Though globalization is often loosely specified, it is generally understood to involve the accelerated movement of things, people and ideas around the world. Movement over both time and space is self-evidently implicated in a multitude of aspects of food packaging.

Several key features lie in the background. These include two types of time. Biological time is key when thinking about food since both people and their food are organic (not inorganic) – a fundamental feature of their materiality, with identifiable life cycles of birth, maturation, death and decay. Clock- or calendar-time is intertwined with packaging, especially in some accounts of its historical development – notably in respect of industrialization/urbanization and population movements from country to city, along with the associated separation of home and workplace and the novel significance of clock time (Thompson 1967). Feeding whole cities' populations was newly required – cities are built on land that, before their growth, could be used for food or fuel. Foodstuffs thereafter have to be moved from rural areas in something – eventually more technologically developed than a sack slung over the back of a packhorse or baskets of potatoes in a farm cart – thus highlighting twenty-first-century *mobilities* (Sheller and Urry 2006).

Two concepts are adopted in this book by way of summarizing aspects of packaging's movement. *Transitions* refer to instances when one item supplants another – barrels displacing amphorae containing olive oil – and *conversions* when the same item is subsequently used for a purpose other than that originally intended – the biscuit tin becomes a store for reusable string. Each, metaphorically, represents a form of mobilities. Both transitions and conversions may be large as well as small.

The significance of scale was described by a senior manager in the packaging department of a large UK supermarket in the decision to replace tin cans with laminated cardboard cartons for packaging chopped tomatoes.

> You can make a small incremental change to the product or the packaging or something to do with increasing efficiency in the supply chain ... (When it) is the biggest selling line in the business, your gain on that is going to be so much more because of the volume that it sells (rather) than focusing on a big win on a product that only sells a million SKUs[23] a year. The 'budget' tomatoes was one of the biggest examples of that ... (with) carbon reduction efficiencies in terms of transport, more products to a lorry, more products on each pallet, less lorries on the road, more space-efficient because you're not transporting air with those cans.

This transition was significant, not only for the improved sustainability of the operations involved but also because it contributed positively to the company's bottom line. Aspects of the decision are made visible.

An older example is a transition from wood to carton. By the 1960s, the British store M&S had established detailed investigations upstream to its primary producers' operations. Concerned with quality and standards including those affecting food safety, checks on the supplies of dried fruit (such as sultanas as ingredients for their cakes) were undertaken in Turkey, Greece and Iran. There the M&S contingent examined field-drying of the fruits, held meetings with government ministers and 'made a number of recommendations'. One in particular was that

> (C)artons should be used rather than wooden boxes, as the latter can contaminate the fruit by the bits of wood, nails, and piece of iron which fly around when the wooden boxes are opened.
>
> (Goldenberg 1989: 71)

Novel and perhaps more important are the movements of people *and* things at whose core lies food packaging – illustrating the intertwining of the social and the technological. Expert dock hands in Shanghai manoeuvred tea chests onto nineteenth-century clippers so the load did not upset the trim of the sailing boats plying their trade thence to Greenwich on London's River Thames. Romans – probably slaves – rolling barrels of Spanish olive oil trudged down gangplanks as they unloaded at the ports. Bagged salads packed in 'a protective atmosphere' (Chapter 9) are moved by forklift truck into the bays beneath the passenger cabins of airliners to transport them from Kenya to go on sale in Paris, London or Helsinki supermarkets only hours later. Shipping containers holding thousands of pallets of boxed cans of water chestnuts from South Korea to American supermarkets travel thousands of miles on huge ships with just one engineer on board, part of a crew of only a handful of seafarers (Levinson 2006). The packaged foodstuffs move, the ships, lorries and trucks move, customers' cars move them on roads nowadays smoothly paved, fuelled by petrol (gas) extracted yet more thousands of miles away and transported in oil tankers on their way to the pumps alongside supermarkets. Such movement of things and people is evident right down to the way 'travel patterns and distance to store' are implicated in explanations for local 'mode(s) of transport for grocery shopping' (Hagberg and Holmberg 2017: 991). Shoppers drive their purchases home to a kitchen-full of white goods – the refrigerator at the domestic end of the cold chain from which the frozen lasagne is carried across to be heated in the microwave oven, both appliances delivered by road to that house. Appliances made of steel are possibly smelted in another country, then manufactured in a third before being transported by container to the warehouse and thence the retailer's showroom. The relatively new specialism of logistics orchestrates the physical movement of packaged foods, the transport required, the information exchanged. Things, people, technologies and associated devices and know-how, all move.

This book's approach

Locating this book at the junction of history, sociology and STS this book is to help address this book's key question about how the food packaging landscape ended up as it has today. The question requires attention to chronologies, including consideration of inventors and factory owners, organizations and institutions associated with food packaging, the industry itself, regulators, NGOs and shoppers. The history and sociology deployed in the thinking can readily be understood as encompassing the social. But the book's key question also requires thinking about the packaging itself, its very materiality – what it is made of, the different types of matter used, why those and not others, and above all what difference does the actual stuff of which packing is fabricated make in its production and use. So doing is readily regarded as dealing with the technological – and any associated sciences, materials and methods, know-how, etc.

In order informatively to tackle the key question, however, STS as the third element cannot stand on its own any more than can the first two. The material/technological is relevant in relation not just to the passage of time – people and events – and the societal – organizations and institutions. All those elements in the creation of the modern food packaging landscape are also integral in its materiality and technologies. None can be sufficiently well understood without the others.

The aim of bringing the three together is to get away from thinking separately about society and technology, instead recognizing them as so intimately interrelated that they must be considered as a single entity. Certainly, some social scientists and historians, as well as several other contemporary commentators, separate them, notably when viewing advances in science and technology as independent factors affecting society, the polity or the economy, unhelpfully assuming technological developments are engines of social changes originating outside the social realm.

An STS attitude guards against such determinism, but not all expert technologists or scientists take this view:

[I]t turns out that, when we look at what technologists actually do, we find that they pay scant regard to distinctions between technology on the one hand and society, economy, politics, and the rest on the other. The disciplinary distinctions so dear to social scientists seem to be irrelevant to engineers. Thus, when they work, they are typically involved in designing and building projects that have both technical and social content and implications …. Engineers are not just people who sit in drawing offices and design machines; they are also, willy nilly, social activists who design societies or social institutions to fit those machines. Technical manuals or designs for nuclear power stations imply conclusions about the proper structure of society, the nature of social roles, and how these roles should be distributed.

(Law and Callon 1988: 284)

With these engineers in mind, return for a moment to the examples provided above of insiders' definitions of food packaging. Experts presenting those definitions can assume the materiality of food packaging – no need for a definition to state that it includes a collection of *things*. What they specify is societal. Twede's three-fold summary of the purposes of packaging as 'protection, utility, and communication' can rely on everyone's knowing that she is talking about primarily inanimate things that contain something people value such as food. Those things, their existence as a technology as well as the foodstuffs they wrap, are by their nature, indifferent to any of her three purposes. It is *people* who are to be kept safe from food poisoning; it is from an *economic* point of view (among others) that foods are to be protected from damage, spoiling or condemnation as waste. Utility is a massively condensed way of saying that food packaging has to be made for *people's* use, expediency and convenience by *people* charged with adhering to the regulations, organizations and institutions that have been developed according to *human* inventions of the organizations which govern the gamut of usages. Equally there is no need to spell out that communication refers to labelling, advertising and branding organized by *people,* regulated by *legislation and guidance* administered by certain *public and political* institutions staffed by *people* (ostensibly) for *people's* benefit. Anyone working through other definitions quoted above can readily identify the same silent assumption of the involvement of things whose technology exists to serve societal purposes.

If food packaging insiders do not separate technology and society then, following fundamental sociological principles of procedure, sociologically inspired studies of food packaging and the industry's denizens must follow their lead in not separating them either. In the process, it is essential to remember the eminent sociologist Everett Hughes' observation that "'it could have been otherwise'" (Star 1988: 198). So saying paves the way for studies to adopt further relevant sociological principles. Callon spells out three (1986). The first is not to take sides, but stand back from any controversy recognizing that not merely does one or other side have their own rationale, but that there can be no intrinsically sociological/social scientific basis for adopting either. Rather the sociological injunction is to take both equally seriously and learn using the same techniques and the same procedures to do so about both, seeking in the process to understand from multiple relevant angles the circumstances and origins of any fray from which investigators need to remain apart. This idea extends to include not just human protagonists but all phenomena involved, including the non-human. To these two principles is added a third, which is a reminder both of refraining from taking sides but also to follow human actors 'in order to identify the manner in which these define and associate the different elements by which they build and explain their world' (Callon 1986: 4).

The final element of STS thinking to be adopted is inspired by Actor Network Theory (ANT) initiated by Bruno Latour (1996). It is represented here by the term 'assemblage', a collection of phenomena with empirically specifiable relationships to one another in a given context. It is an expression that serves at least two valuable analytic purposes. One is that it allows summary/comparison across different empirical instances. In particular it strips away often dramatic differences between examples that can obscure what they may have in common thus making characteristics that are shared easier to see. The other is that it can – indeed must – include anything relevant to the discussion in hand. This discussion has already stated that the book's approach is to include both people and things, the social and the technological and, in effect, that neither is to be privileged over the other analytically. Relevant to answering the key question about how the food packaging 'landscape' came to be as it is now, are both the dramatis personae involved (along with the events, emergence of social institutions, etc.) and the things involved – *both* the social and the material.

It follows that the relationships to be encompassed are between people, social institutions, technologies as well as the things themselves, the manner in which they have been fashioned and the stuff from which they are made. STS thinking requires that they are all treated the same, setting aside everyday familiar assumptions about, e.g. any superiority of the human over non-human things. All are regarded as having agency in what goes on, they are lively, not inert. They all, in some fashion, act in relation to each other. To adopt Latour's terminology they are all actants – a term that replaces 'actor' and thus evades attributing motivation, intention or other supposedly peculiar human capacity to the non-human as well as evading privileging such capacities for the people involved. It highlights the character, the very nature, of the non-human which it is useful to think of as part and parcel of its agency.

So saying returns to the position adopted in this book, namely that food packaging – the various things themselves, including technologies, knowledges, relevant sciences that food packaging embodies – is not, here, treated as inactive or passive but regarded as active. That, however, is not to invite relapsing into some version of regarding technology as a 'driver' from outside the social realm. Doing so risks adopting technological determinism which can be shown to be flawed – e.g. the microwave oven illustrates that what its inventors thought of as a replacement for an oven for home-cooking complete dishes has been widely used as no more than a device for heating commercially pre-prepared meals.

Treating things as active not passive leads to focusing attention on the qualities or distinctive characteristics of one or other material, or on one or other thing's shape, size, varying behaviour in different temperature, levels of humidity, etc. This allows seeing the difference made by the distinctive characteristics of the material in question in relation to the activities of the people involved. It helps reveal the role a material takes in opening up opportunities for manufacture or purposes or alternatively limiting possibilities and novel uses. It is in this sense that materials have agency – but shorn of any sense of human motivation, intent or purpose – deriving from their biological/physical/chemical properties that represent affordances in relation to human aims and purposes.

Assemblages of people and packaging repeatedly take their place in the pages that follow, repeatedly helping reveal secrets in the lives of food packaging, repeatedly seeking to unpick how its landscape came to look as it does now.

Notes

1. Drawing this contrast between insider and outsider views does not imply that one or other approach is superior/inferior. It is to highlight their dissimilar purposes and differences in the direction in which subsequent thinking can proceed. This book too infrequently discusses such examples, for want of space not because they are less important.

2. By mid-twentieth century, training in packaging was sufficiently institutionalized for the earliest BSc to be awarded in 1955 – its inaugural curriculum composed of seven different courses – at the Michigan State University (MSU) Department of Forestry Products, now The School of Packaging.

3. Inspection undertaken by Tom Cryer.

4. In a three way discussion at a display stand at a trade exhibition with two representatives of a company manufacturing compostable egg boxes, one suddenly interrupted the flow of an animated conversation, to declare she had just realized how unusual it was to find someone outside the industry as passionate about it as they were. Answering 'what do you do?' at a party, she ruefully added, is an inevitable conversation stopper.

5. Shrink wrap, such as placed around say twelve bottles of water or four cans of tomatoes, is a form of secondary packaging not to be confused with plastic stretch wrap to hold palleted goods in place during transport i.e. tertiary packaging.

6. INCPEN (nd). 'About us'. Available online: https://incpen.org/about-us/ (accessed 6 April 2023).

7. The then Director, Jane Bickerstaffe, observed that '(C)onsumers and politicians see only two links in the chain – retailers and waste collectors'. Bickerstaffe, J. (2013). 'Packaging Myths'. 13 June. Available online: https://incpen.org/packaging-myths/ (accessed 6 April 2023).

8. INCPEN (nd). 'Why products are packaged the way they are'. Available online: https://incpen.org/why-products-are-packaged-the-way-they-are/ (accessed 6 April 2023).

9. New Zealand Ministry of the Environment (2022). 'Plastic and Related Products Regulations 2022'. Available online: https://environment.govt.nz/acts-and-regulations/regulations/plastic-and-related-products-regulations-2022/#:~:text=Banned%20items%20as%20of%201%20October%202022&text=The%20following%20products%20are%20no,subset%20of%20plastic%20type%207 (accessed 6 April 2023).

10. European Parliament and Council (1994). Directive 94/62/EC of 20 December 1994 on packaging and packaging waste. Available online: https://eur-lex.europa.eu/legal-content/EN/TXT/?uri=CELEX:31994L0062&qid=1684154260516 (accessed 6 April 2023).

11. A UK-based packaging trade magazine.

12. Emmerson Packaging (nd). 'BOIL-IN-BAG – BPA-FREE AND FDA-APPROVED'. Available online: https://www.emmersonpackaging.com/products-and-films/boil-in-bag/ (accessed 6 April 2023).

13. Starlight (nd). '124 x 155 x 43 oven-able BLACK trays'. Available online: https://starlightpackaging.co.uk/products/case-x-800-124-x-155-x-43-oven-able-black-trays.html (accessed 6 April 2023).

14. Poulter, S. (2014). 'How M&S plans to beat toxic bacteria bug that kills 100 people a year by selling roast in the bag chicken'. 21 November. Available online: https://www.dailymail.co.uk/news/article-2843379/Roast-bag-chicken-M-S-way-beat-food-bug-Supermarket-bid-beat-deadly-toxic-bacteria-kills-100-people-year.html (accessed 6 April 2023).

15. Huntley & Palmer (nd). Biscuit tins. Available online: http://www.huntleyandpalmers.org.uk/ixbin/hixclient.exe?a=query&p=huntley&f=generic_theme.htm&_IXFIRST_=1&_IXMAXHITS_=1&%3dtheme_record_id=rm-rm-tins_content1 (accessed 6 April 2023).

16. Note these authors classify packaging by process: folding; receiving plate (like a dish); containing; clipping and skewering; tying into a bundle.

17. Thacker, K. (2018). 'Why Costco's avocados will last twice as long'. 19 June. Available online: https://www.grocerydive.com/news/grocery–why-costcos-avocados-will-last-twice-as-long/533925/#:~:text=The%20company%20chose%20these%20retailers,healthier%20

country%2C%E2%80%9D%20Masek%20said (accessed 6 April 2023). See technical report of work to use discarded banana peel to create wrapping paper (Agustina and Susanti 2018).

18. Sand C.K. (2019). 'Frozen Food Packaging Heats Up' Food Technology Magazine. 1 November. Available online: https://www.ift.org/news-and-publications/food-technology-magazine/issues/2019/november/columns/frozen-food-packaging (accessed 6 April 2023).

19. Hereafter 'later-lives' to evade the implication that use is preeminent.

20. First manufactured at the end of the nineteenth century Virol was a malt extract used as a tonic for decades thereafter.

21. McClure, T. (2021). '"Only in New Zealand!"' 16 April. Available online: https://www.theguardian.com/world/2021/apr/16/only-in-new-zealand-relics-found-in-coffee-jars-in-rubble-of-christchurch-cathedral (accessed 6 April 2023).

22. Many now included in the Design in Plastics Museum: https://plastiquarian.com/ (accessed 6 April 2023).

23. Stock keeping unit.

PART II
HOW DID IT GET LIKE THIS? EARLY PRECURSORS

Part II: introduction

Each of the chapters in this part begins with something used to contain food. Each considers the material(s) from which the container in question may be made together with the something of the history of its design and use. Thus each illuminates something of the associated histories, whether they be of glass-making, of food preservation or the invention of techniques involved. Several Interludes enlarge on histories of adjacent things such as twentieth-century trading in waste paper; hardworking later-lives of sacks; how to load tea chests in the hold of a nineteenth-century clipper; or canning's English patent of a French invention. Some chapters illustrate a container's very early appearance in the archaeological and historical record. Their variety notwithstanding, these chapters revolve around the same question: how did today's package come to look as it does?

CHAPTER 3
BAGS, SACKS AND A LOT OF PAPER

Bags are everywhere, and have been so for a very long time in many different societies. Does that make them peculiarly unnoticed and ordinary? Very likely it does nowadays, if the bag is made of plain, slightly flimsy, brown paper in which the plums bought in the street were handed across by the market stall-holder (Figure 5).

But what about the small, stout plastic bag one supermarket calls a sharing pouch, filled with chocolate covered raisins or slices of liquorice?[1] Or maybe the bag is a leather sporran[2] which once would be filled with oats in which a nineteenth-century Scots student might have taken back his next few weeks' supply on Meal Monday.[3] Or perhaps it is a shopping bag with long handles, made by ten-year-old Daisy for her aunt out of an old cotton dress – secondary packaging for carrying groceries. Maybe it is a knee-high, double-walled paper sack holding 3 kg of puffed quinoa, its top securely closed with machine-stitched cotton thread.

Certainly a bag is comparatively simple, defined in one food packaging textbook as 'a tube with one sealed-end … made from a flexible material' (Sacharow and Griffin 1980: 55). Bags are 'mobile container(s)' allowing safe transport (Suddendorf *et al.* 2020). That they are flexible – as distinct, in the industry's classification, from semi-flexible and rigid – is a key defining characteristic. In other words, a bag is able to fit more or less closely round the contents rather than their being squeezed into a fixed shaped container.

Insider histories consider bags to be an exceptionally early form of food packaging: '(C)loth or paper may be the oldest forms of flexible packaging' (Berger 2002: 1 also Sacharow and Griffin 1980: 1). Various genres of insider commentary include the following materials from which bags have been made since then: textiles, skins/leather, paper, leaves, plant fibres such as those from flax or bark, kelp, oil cloth, glassine, cellophane and, of course, plastics. The use of flexible packaging has been dated to the first or second century BCE with the Chinese use of 'sheets of treated mulberry bark to wrap foods' (Berger 2002: 2). And there is 'good evidence' that the 'original inventor' … made paper by a series of operations much as we know them today (Gilmour 1955: 2). In principle, those operations are fairly simple, little different from the processes built-in to paper making machines, themselves differing little from the first 1804 machine. It is named after brothers who financed it – Henry and Sealy Fourdrinier 'two prosperous London stationers who purchased the patent interests of the Frenchman Didot Frères' (Robertson 2013: 175).

Paper making on any commercial basis depends on a suitable supply of feedstock. Richard Hills, an industrial historian, observes that the period of political stability following the Wars of the Roses was favourable to setting up England's first paper mill. The necessary steady supply of rags meant they had first to be collected, then sorted

Figure 5 Victoria plums sold on a market stall in a brown paper bag.

before arriving at the mill – journeys that would result in unduly great losses if the country continued to be war-torn. At that time the rags consisted primarily of 'hemp ropes and linen cloth' (1988: 5). Without the availability of bleaches, white paper needed white fibres – ships' old sails and worn-out clothes, the latter found most amply and easier to collect in towns near which mills would be established.

Any war typically creates changed circumstances, since all kinds of things have to be altered along with shifts in various activities to gear them to the 'war effort'. In the process, wars may make the thinking behind a transition more visible because it has to be deliberate, planned and accomplished quickly. Some packages announce their own provenance, such as the powdered egg the United States sent the UK during the Second World War to help relieve severe shortages (Figure 6).

With luck from a historian's point of view, records are created in the process and preserved – far likelier in more recent centuries. Bearing this out is a 1944 edition of *Science News Letter*[4] carrying a short piece by Caroline Parkinson (a freelance journalist?) which reflects some of the probable background to novel packaging adopted by the US forces for a good many necessaries. She notes that such packaging had to protect supplies for the troops (foods included) in conditions as varied as 'a steaming South Pacific jungle … the baking heat of North Africa or in the sub-zero

Figure 6 Dried egg canister announcing its origins.

cold of Arctic regions' (Parkinson 1944: 267). Metals were needed for the war effort, so replacements were required:

> (W)hen the supply of boxes and crates runs out, fruit and vegetable shippers use an open-mesh bag, made from strips of tough paper spun into yarn and woven into open-mesh cloth ... Because of their low cost, space and weight saving, and ease in filling and closing, they are likely to persist after the war as improvements instead of substitutes.
>
> (Parkinson 1944: 267)

She was right. This type of bag has indeed survived; net bags made of plastic yarn continue to be used for fruits, vegetables and nuts in twenty-first-century supermarkets. And, she adds, there is

> the good old brown paper bag. Impregnation with a synthetic resin to give it wet-strength properties has allowed the paper bag to save valuable cargo space and

weight. It carries vegetables, meats and chemicals, formerly packed in heavier metal containers.

(Parkinson 1944: 266)

The plain brown paper bag is a candidate as something so familiar that its presence is unnoticed – until that is, it is missing from its usual place. Not all are so unassuming. A Californian company, claiming to be the largest of its kind online, publishes a website blog describing nine very different types of paper bag and 'when to use them'.[5] The types range from 'S.O.S. bags' ('stand on its own') to 'pinch bottom bags' which also remain open making filling more efficient, while Bakery Bags are specifically made for food: '(W)ith glassine and wax paper linings, these bags preserve the taste and freshness of perishable items, making them perfect for bread, cookies, and even coffee'.[6] By contrast, Paine and Paine's textbook classifies the main types of paper bag in more technical terms, based on the design of the bottom of the bag: flat, gusseted, self-opening satchel and rose bottom (1992: 131).

More broadly, another textbook's listing of the materials from which bags are made (apart from plastic film) runs: 'kraft paper sacks, double-walled paper bags, window bags, fiber net bags, plastic net bags, paper mesh and plastic mesh bags'. They observe that 'field-bagging' grapes in HDPE (high density polyethylene) net bags is an 'excellent application', for losses are reduced and the fruits are 'easily visible and can be washed or stored right in the bag' (Sacharow and Griffin 1980: 252). Later, the same textbook weighs up the pros and cons of transparent versus opaque potato chip (crisp) bags.

Technically, opaque packages are superior to transparent packages. When exposed to light, potato chips are unsaleable in 6 days. The same chips shielded from light remain fresh much longer ... Other advantages ... are the nonvisibility of brown and broken chips. If the potato used in chip making contains too high a content of reducing sugars, brown chips result. Poor handling, cooking and consumer misuse cause broken chips. Opaque packages mask these problems and add to the overall saleability of the product.

(1980: 445)

That final, matter of fact note of the work opaque packaging does for the seller represents just the concealment that customers are said to remain suspicious of when the package obscures the foodstuff they are buying. The same tone continues: '(T)ransparent packages offer product visibility which may enhance merchandising appeal. Transparent packages also are "sparkly" or "glossy"' (1980: 445). Transparency or otherwise is, as will be seen, a recurrent topic in packaging decision-making. Other developments include lamination, a property widely valued. A 'greaseproof moisture barrier liner in multi-wall paper bags for biscuits' dates from the 1990s (Twede and Goddard 1998: 98). Bio-based packaging materials are another.

Bags well illustrate the persistence of one packaging material over several decades co-existing with the development of novel materials: the simultaneous use of paper and the development of plastic bags date from the 1930s. One example is the Cryovac process, shrink wrapping and freezing a whole turkey in a plastic bag. In his Cryovac company history, John Ross reports a 1939 *Life Magazine* article illustrating the 'innovative packaging concept' in four photographs. These demonstrate the cling effect of the process by enveloping Dorothy Andrews, 'a secretary' with the company, shown smiling throughout, dressed in no more than the corselette underwear of the period inside a pre-expanded latex 'lamb bag'. The first photograph shows two men in white lab coats, helping her step into the bag; the second, once it is pulled up over her shoulders, pinions her arms; third, one of the men uses a hair dryer to apply hot air to shrink it to 'form fit'. The final image shows her completely, tightly (and to twenty-first-century eyes unnervingly) enclosed up to her neck in the bag (Ross 1997: 4).

The bags, sacks and the occasional cardboard box of this chapter appear in different narratives in the sections to follow. First a historically and geographically specific bag is presented. Thereafter the narrative returns to the simple brown paper bag, to move along a chain from making the paper, to its recycling as feedstock to make more paper. Stages are illustrated in a two part Interlude, about two London based family firms, each originally founded in the nineteenth century. The chapter remains in industrialized settings to close even further along a chain, but double-backed to details of the use and re-use of sacks over a century ago, ending with instances of the later-lives of flour and chicken feed sacks. The first section records a more unusual example of a conversion, one that is caught up in the sensitive politics of post-colonialism. Varying assemblages appear: mutton birds (the foodstuff) bull kelp (the package) and two categories of people (Māori and Pākehā).

****

Interlude: Māori preserving young birds in kelp: pre-industrial

International visitors to Aotearoa/New Zealand today are likely to notice the ubiquity of Māori cultural symbols, not least in shops aimed at tourists. Visitors may hear of the 1840 Treaty of Waitangi between Māori and colonizing Pākehā (white incomers). They may be told of Māori customs, or learn that there is a distinctive Māori cuisine, few Māori restaurants but four Māori cookery books (Morris 2006: 395, Morris 2013). One or two may be lucky and eat at a (non-Māori) restaurant serving mutton bird – a fish-eating sooty shearwater found in Australasia. On the plate *titi* – the Māori name – looks like the dark meat of chicken, unsurprisingly tasting fishy. Many visitors, however, may never hear about 'the *paku* method' (Anderson 1981: 148) the South Island Māori means of preserving *titi* in the capacious pockets in bull kelp that keeps them edible and safe to eat (Whyte *et al.* 2001) for two or three years. The success of such procedures is recorded in 1827 by a ship's captain: 'and I have eaten of them after they had been 8 months in these bags, and found the meat as fresh as when put in' (Boultbee in Anderson 1997: 36).

The verb 'muttonbirding' apparently inclusively refers to a collection of linked activities associated with hunting the whole order of seabirds that includes the sooty shearwater, right up to the 'the body of techniques whereby the chicks and fledglings … were processed as preserved food' (Anderson 1997: 5) Those techniques, the *paku* method, rely on *rimurapa*, Māori for the long, ribbon-like bull kelp abundant in the waters around New Zealand. The kelp is split to make a bag, *pōhā*, which is inflated, filled with cooked birds then sealed with their own fat and/or the fish oil of their diet. As online photographs show, the bags stand waist high.[7] For transport and safe handling, *pōhā* are slid into woven flax baskets, secured with strips of bark – shown in a *c*.1920 photograph of a woman adding strips around the baskets for manageable transportation.[8]

The earliest historical record of New Zealand muttonbirding appears in the log of a cutter *Mermaid,* by Captain John Kent on a visit to Ruapuke Island[9] in 1823 (Anderson 1997). He noticed 'stacks of preserved mutton birds' leaning against a Māori hut, noting too that some of the muttonbirders had travelled from as far away as Kaikoura, almost 800km by sea. Another report dates from four years later at Bluff, where John Boultbee counted eleven canoes and some 200 Māori who had travelled from the east coast of South Island for the mutton bird season. Three local Māori travelling with him prepared the birds. After skinning them and removing the main bones they roasted them before putting them 'into large bags, made by splitting the immense sheets of kelp which abounds here – these bags being fastened up and kept airtight, prevent the birds from being tainted' finding it fresh 8 months later (in Stevens 2006: 279).

Those early reports are one-sided, created by incomers exploring what to them was still novel territory. Māori voices of the period are silent. This is partly because Māori had no written language, but it is also a product of the type of record available. Undergraduate students in anthropology nowadays learn that among the nineteenth-century precursors to their discipline are missionaries' reports and travellers' tales, in which accounts of novel ways of life are apprehended and evaluated via those authors' own cultural viewpoints. Modern ethnographic approaches to fieldwork would record far more detail of the succession of activities, capturing as far as possible the Māori viewpoint in their own words. Ethnographers would listen closely to Māori accounts of trekking to *titi* nesting sites, to conversations about all subsequent tasks and especially seek to establish what counts as skill in carrying them out. How does someone recognize a suitable piece of kelp, what is the best way of splitting it without damage, what is the best method for filling the *pōhā*, what has to be watched out for when sealing it, etc. Such approaches would illuminate the assemblage comprising the relation between the distinct material features of the kelp that constrain/enable what Māori regard as the proper way to accomplish the task.

Nowadays, this instance of pre-industrial food packaging is converted. No longer has it to provide a couple of years' safely preserved food for trade between *iwi* (tribes) or stored for lean times. Instead it persists in other modes. Certainly the 'customary harvest' is claimed to continue as a 'large-scale commercial enterprise for Māori', rights to which are enacted annually on the Titi Islands off the south of South Island. Procedures are much the same, except that splitting and salting the birds replaces packing under fat/oil and 20-litre plastic buckets have supplanted the kelp[10] – a transition among technical/technological components of the assemblage.

This packaging also persists intangibly, as an idea, in texts and photographs, preserved in libraries/online – e.g. where historians have attempted to date muttonbirding's longevity. Anderson reviews the historical and archaeological evidence to conclude that it is impossible to decide whether it began 'deep in prehistory' or in the early nineteenth century 'around the advent of Europeans' (Anderson 1997: 48). By contrast, Stevens, Māori historian of Māori – himself a veteran of a couple of decades' muttonbirding[11] – declares that for Kāi Tahu, a South Island *iwi*, muttonbirding dates from two to three centuries before their first, late eighteenth century, encounter with Pākehā (Stevens 2006) while an unreferenced *New Zealand Geographic* webpage, however, notes that radiocarbon dating indicates it is 600–800 years old.[12] Moller and colleagues, however, sidestep that question, instead discussing modern proposals for the simultaneous preservation of cultural inheritance/customs and environmental protection (Moller, Kitson and Downs 2009). The Otago Museum in Dunedin devotes a whole section to muttonbirding; the Otago University Research Heritage collection contains an account of 1940s childhood muttonbirding and there is a replica *pōhā* hand-made by a Māori expert.[13] These are variously caught up not just in preserving Māori traditions/artefacts and in teaching local school children but also in attracting tourists to Aotearoa/New Zealand heritage.

✳✳✳✳✳✳✳✳✳✳✳✳✳

The case of the Maōri *pōha* food package can readily be understood as an assemblage. The elements range from: people, Maōri and Pakeha; to the kelp and its naturally occurring pockets that can be enlarged by hand; the cooked and de-boned birds, along with the knowledge about how to catch the birds, cook and store them, sealing them with the fat and the craft of doing so effectively; the capability of carrying out all the necessary procedures. The result could not come about without all of these elements 'in play'. Attention to all those elements equally makes the secret life of this type of package available for inspection. In the process it can account for John Boultbee's astonished discovery that the meat was still fresh after many months as a matter of technique jointly harnessing biology and human ingenuity.

A pre-industrial food package possibly as long established in New Zealand as Māori themselves (they arrived from Polynesia in the 1300s) continues in several overlapping guises some seven centuries later. Answers to 'how did it get like this' have to settle for far more recent considerations: as a candidate for conservation as a museum exhibit and as an object of academic archaeological study, with the whole assemblage becoming a focus of the delicacy required of twenty-first-century New Zealand identity politics. Where *pōhā* can reasonably be described as anything but everyday packaging, that brown paper bag – also made from natural occurring material – returns this chapter to packaging as commonplace, 'hidden in plain sight'.

Towards the industrial era: plain brown paper bags

Addressing a 2005 conference on history in marketing, Diana Twede observes that '(W)ood fibers form the basis for the most widely used packaging materials in the world. Paper-based packaging is particularly significant in North America, with its abundant forests and well developed paper industry' (2005: 288). All the same, the use of wood fibres to make paper is recent. For, she adds, '(A) persistent theme throughout history is that packaging is made from the lowest cost materials. But most paper was, for a long time, too expensive to use for packaging. It was handmade from rags for 17 centuries after its invention. Paper use was hindered by the laborious process of papermaking and the limited supply of raw materials' (2005: 288).

How to make paper

Paper is made from plant fibres either from so-called virgin feedstock, such as freshly grown flax or wood, or from recycled paper and rags of cotton or linen. These materials have to be broken down, turned into a pulp, then mixed with water. A mesh on a frame is dipped vertically into the mixture, but removed horizontally so that the water drains through it leaving behind a layer of wet pulp produced by the overlapping fibres resting on the top. This layer is peeled off to go through pressing, drying and beating. These stages describe papermaking by hand, but the principles are the same when mechanized.[14] Diana Twede dates the earliest machine to make 'roll stock paper in a continuous process' to 1799, invented in Paris by Nicholas-Louis Robert (Twede 2005). Those were exactly the same stages Jonathan Jones[15] had to learn in the early 1950s at the beginning of his career in the waste paper trade. He was into his eighties when he talked of it, explaining that he was just sixteen when he began work in the family firm founded by his great-great-grandfather. When he started, a more senior member of the family would give him a lift to work each morning, using the time to teach young Jonathan some of the essentials of paper. An early lesson concerned the distinction between 'mechanical paper for newspapers' and 'wood-free paper for high-class paper'. Well, that's 'not correct. It's still made from wood, but wood-free has the lignin taken out. Therefore it stays white, stays bright', he explained.

Quite when (or who) decided to fold paper and close one end to make a simple bag is not known – not least because, being plant based, paper rots more easily than other packaging materials resulting in hardly any archaeological record. Wrapping goods for sale in paper dates, in England, from the seventeenth century co-existing alongside grocers' handing their unwrapped purchase over to customers' baskets, bags and jugs the goods doled out from the shops' supplies stored in chests, tubs, baskets, bottles, barrels and jars (Twede 2005). The frugality of eighteenth-century grocers' economising on expensive paper by re-using torn pages from unwanted books to wrap small items for sale is echoed in the frugality of those who in the 2010s sell snacks at bus stations throughout West Africa 'in slips of newspaper and recycled school exam papers' (Renne 2007: 620).

By the eighteenth century, explains the engineer and STS specialist, Henry Petroski, grocery bags in the United States were made on demand by storekeepers who 'cut, folded, and pasted sheets of paper, making versatile containers into which purchases could be loaded for carrying home' (2003: 99). The same arrangement prevailed in England where, right into the middle of the twentieth century, the work of a grocer included packaging.[16] Dividing large quantities of foodstuffs and packing them into papers and bags were 'central parts of the service that grocers provided to their customers' (Stobart 2013: 142). Sometimes this was done en bloc to build up a supply of ready-split and packaged items, mass production style. Yet it was common enough for goods to be weighed and packed to order while a customer waited, seated on a bentwood chair stationed alongside the counter – still widely prevalent in Scotland and England in the 1950s and 1960s. Items parcelled in paper tied up with string, a dab of sealing wax holding the knot from being undone too soon, continued into the 1930s (Milner Gray 1939). More goods were simply slid into a bag whose top was twisted round to close it: 'the grocer was most dextrous at conjuring up his own bags or twists' (Opie 1989: 15).

Stobart points out that by the early nineteenth century, grocers' 'packaging increasingly took the form of bags. The sale of one shop's goods in 1816 included various grades of paper (including blue paper, generally used for wrapping sugar), but also 109 lb of paper bags sold in seven separate lots' (2013: 141). Grocers were still selling two pounds' weight (approximately a kilogram) of sugar in distinctive blue paper bags in 1950s London. The simplest brown paper bag or sheets of white paper continue to be used in the UK today for bread, raw fish or meat as well as wrapping fish and chips hot from the fryer.

Predictably, hand-made paper bags were later supplanted by machine manufacture.

> It was in 1844 that the firm was founded of Elisha, Smith and Alfred Robinson of Bristol and played their part in the development of the paper bag. In 1860, the first bag-making machine was invented, and in 1873 Elisha Robinson brought back from America the first patents for the satchel type.
>
> (Gray 1939: 641)

Petroski regards the Bristol firm responsible for the first paper bags manufactured commercially. But, he goes on, '(I)n 1852, a "Machine for Making Bags of Paper" was patented in America by Francis Wolle, of Bethlehem, Pennsylvania'. Wolle claimed his machine produced '"complete and perfect bags"' prompting Petroski to remark wryly that though it produced them 'at the rate of eighteen hundred per hour' the bags 'were, of course, not perfect, nor was his machine' (Petroski 2003: 99).

Nineteenth-century mechanization of paper bag making came to be a competitive affair, Petroski explains, with inventors looking for ways of producing them faster, more efficiently never mind more reliably. In addition, there was the question of the shape of the bag; flat ones are fine for goods that are flat – a couple of chops, or a half a kilo of biscuits. But many grocery items are rounded or square-ish for which flat bags are singularly unsuited. Could a square bottomed paper bag be fashioned that would stand without being held upright to allow two handed packing – Petroski introduces the now famous story of Margaret E. Knight.

There are several sources recounting her achievements, including one for children (McCully 2006) illustrating the way women could be independent and successful in the nineteenth century, despite male obstruction. Born in Maine in 1838, then brought up in New Hampshire where her newly widowed mother moved, Knight is reported to have been an unusual child who preferred woodworking tools to dolls. Indeed, interviewed for *Woman's Journal*, 2 December 1872, she talked of following nature that she did so, adding her regret at not having had as good a chance as a boy with the same aptitudes. Later, employed in a cotton mill, the twelve-year-old Knight witnessed a serious accident when a fellow employee was badly injured: a shuttle shot from its housing in a mechanical loom. Knight devised a safety modification later adopted in other local mills – although records of the exact nature of her invention have yet to be located. Moving to Massachusetts in 1867, she worked for a paper bag company. A year later she invented an improvement to existing paper bag making techniques (which required flat-bottomed examples be hand-finished) by automating the process. Her machine cut, folded and glued brown paper to mass produce flat-bottomed bags. The male obstruction came in the form of a machinist who saw the iron model of her invention being made (needed in order to file a patent), reportedly stole her idea and patented it in is own name. On applying for her own patent, his theft came to light. Knight challenged him in court and won.

To serve their purpose well, brown paper bags full of groceries require a certain strength, lest they burst even when modestly loaded. As Petroski notes, to be as strong as required, these bags cannot be made from too much recycled material (unlike their successors, the 'T shirt' plastic carrier bag). His remark leads at this point to an earlier stage in the brown paper bag's production, providing a different view the life of a paper bag. The two part Interlude that follows runs from collection of feedstock for recycled components of paper (where the cardboard box makes a brief appearance) through to selling the bag itself. It begins with fourth generation Jonathan Jones learning about paper making from the day he started work in the London family firm.

****

Interlude: part 1 Abraham Jones & Co Ltd.

A little vignette of the firm's history was presented to those who attended the commemorative dinner to mark its centenary in 1975. Abraham Jones, it recorded, came from England's West Country where in the latter half of the eighteenth century a small Jewish congregation had been founded in ports along the coast. He went into partnership with a friend, then moved to London in 1875 where they set up as rag merchants. Jonathan was into his 80s when he added to this thumbnail history.[17] He reckons that knowledge of the trade was likely already to have 'been in the family' which had originally moved to England from The Netherlands. When the family was still in a coastal town in the West Country during Abraham's childhood, they collected rope – too worn for use on the high seas – from ships of the Royal Navy anchored just offshore, also gathering rags from local residents. That vignette continues: in the 1890s, the partnership broke up and Abraham set up on his own, forming the company Abraham Jones & Co Ltd., the name surviving until it was bought up in the 1960s although trading – plus the employment and 'know how' of family members – continued past the mid-1970s and its centenary under new ownership.

Around the early 1900s, Abraham had branched out to deal in waste paper and his eldest son successfully persuaded his father to let him visit France where soon he had created a market in waste paper, initiating sustained trading with mainland Europe which continued for another half-century and more. Indeed, a winter issue of the 1978 *Business America Journal of Industry & Trade* carried a small ad: 'Well established manufacturer and distributor of secondary fiber, pulp and paper substitutes is interested in producing any related products under license' directing interested parties to contact the Import/Export manager – providing some evidence of sustained interest in trading internationally.

Jonathan's lengthy, richly detailed account of his working life in the company gives a glimpse of what has to be considered when deciding which waste paper to buy and finding the right company to which to sell it. From his earliest days learning in the car on the way to work about the distinction between machine paper and wood-free paper, he was brought face to face with its materiality, its physical and chemical properties. As he noted:

> that sets you up immediately to know what you're dealing with. Because if you're dealing with mechanical paper, the paper is then your newspaper and your paperback book, and it will go brown because the lignin is still in there … it will go brown in sunlight. And if you test it with phloroglucinol, it will go red, if you test it with aniline sulphate, it will go yellow … they're the basic tests that the paper industry use.

He goes on to explain that knowing what type of waste paper was about to be bought determined to whom it could and could not be sold. But packaging, he observed, is a separate part of the industry 'which of course we have to take into account when we're processing waste paper, and when we're selling to the end user'. So the properties of the material are implicated in the selling stage bringing with it its own assemblage of the type/grade of paper and the associated collection of people, the clientele plus their specific manufacturing requirements.

The variety of waste Jonathan described is wide. Rag did not only consist of tattered cloth from old clothes or table-cloths, nor just ships' worn rope but also now and then damaged sails past repair. And, he added ruefully, it included mattresses: 'we took the springs out and we caught fleas'. As soon as I got home after work, 'I used to jump in the bath'. The aftermath of the Second World War continued: 'we were still moving camouflage netting from the war effort in about 1958 … Then when that ran out we got knapsacks, canvas knapsacks' from all three services. Around the same period 'we had a grade in our rag department called gunny … actually just waste (hessian) sacks'. They went for roofing, 'black roofing that you had on sheds … looks like a black tarmac, and that was made of rags'.

Between buying paper and selling it on, it had to be sorted and cleaned. The type of paper that was bought was separated into one of 175 grades in the 1950s, but by 2018 'we're down to approximately 12'. It might come in as old office records and spare stationery. In the early fifties, it was ledger, 'with leather covers, big ones … wood with leather on top. We had to take the covers off'. In the sixties it was punch cards for mechanical data handling, sorted on a Hollerith machine. Later still it was 'continuous stationery from computers, all in fan fold, (and) you have another grade'. A different grade consisted of Bibles 'because that's a very fine quality of paper'. Sorting was a central activity for the whole operation: 'everything you dealt with worked this way'. And whether rag or paper, it was the properties of the materials that shaped its fate – one or other grade required by one or other client and their manufacturing needs.

Sorting, however, only goes so far. In addition to the chemical tests to detect the presence/absence of lignin, Jonathan described other, simple practical tests that anyone can do, or rather anyone with the relevant knowledge. 'We lick and taste paper, there's a reason for that because we want to see how it breaks up, we smell it and see if it's got impurities in it, we tear it and you have to tear.' Whether it tears easily, how it breaks up, how readily it comes apart when wet all tell the experienced person about the quality and properties of what they are holding, and in turn, tell them to which range of uses the paper is best suited; 'see that loo roll core over there' if you tear it 'you can see the rubber bands'.

It was 'Marks and Sparks[18] who were bright enough to say on food packaging, we don't want your grey board, it's got too many impurities'. It must not have carbon paper[19] if 'it's got blue carbon paper, black carbon paper, rubber bands, plastics and other impurities, we don't want it'. The trouble is, Jonathan explained, 'you can't get it out, because the way we get impurities out is to put the paper into a hydropulper, we put a rope in which we call the ragger, as the hydropulper goes round, the ragger … collects all the other rubbish it can get hold of' but, cannot capture rubber bands or carbon paper.

Jonathan continues talking about food packaging when he turns to the cardboard box. After a merger between Abraham Jones & Co Ltd. with a paperboard making company, they were supplying a well-known manufacturer of breakfast cereal. Two different weights of board were produced: 'heavyweight thick chipboard, grey board with a white liner on it … also the outer cartons' – the former, primary and the latter, secondary packaging. Both met standards certified by the railways 'for packaging so the material travelled safely from A to B'. The outer cartons were very strong: if they survived being dropped from 60 feet, the certificate was given. These were 'solid boxes and the boxes themselves were very heavy … a pure brown kraft pack'.

Jonathan went on to Marks' and Spencer's next stage of negotiations. Instead of the impurities, they required 'a lot of our packaging pure pulp, a lot of the packaging we want a plastic liner to carry the cereals inside'. He sees mention of the liner as the start of a series of innovations in cereal boxes:

> then all sorts of plastic derivatives take place …. a cornflake packet in paper will pull apart. (And when) your wheat biscuits were once (wrapped in) wax coated (paper), it's now polyethene coated, so they can heat seal it round the biscuits. If you then transfer to puffed wheat or to cornflakes, you've got this heavy quality plastic which you have to really pull to open. It'll always pull this way … you can't tear it. That's a co-polymer, and you've got two types of plastic there fighting each other and they become extremely strong and extremely water repellent.

Once again he concludes with a knowledgeable comment on changes he has seen: 'so the developments on packaging for food have really taken off since the war'. Throughout his working life Jonathan has continuously had to grapple with the very stuff of the waste rag or paper itself, what different tests can detect, what can and cannot be done to sort and/ or remove unwanted materials like book covers, staples or rubber bands.

A key feature of Jonathan's life in the waste paper trade was not simply one or other assemblage, but a plethora of such assemblages and contrasts.

> So going out as a buyer, you were selling a service, buying the raw material. London was structured quite differently between the 50s and the 80s. You used to go to an office block and meet the housekeeper and the housekeeper kept everything he could sell … people didn't think about the waste they threw out.

At the time, buying from any of Britain's major companies – including one of the major supermarkets – you would need 'a bowler hat and a furled umbrella and a pin-striped suit … you had to go there properly dressed'. Jonathan goes on: 'on the other hand, if you were going out with one of your drivers and you were driving up to the Dorchester (one of London's top hotels) the driver would come (back) out … and say "would you like steak for lunch today" and you'd be invited into the kitchen with the driver'. On those days 'I wore dress-down clothing'.

Whatever facet of his job – and he talked of many more than have been recounted here – Jonathan was continuously having to take the chemical and physical properties of the rag and paper waste into account. It was not a case of trying to change those properties, but of testing, assessing and classifying accordingly, less to get round any obstacles thus presented, more to optimize the possibilities when developing relationships with those from whom he was buying and parallel relationships with those to whom he was selling. The materiality of the waste was and remains central to the various assemblages composed of Jonathan and clients, Jonathan and employees, Jonathan and the firms' Directors, older members of his family whom, when still very junior, he called 'sir'. Common to all the assemblages in which Jonathan was involved, however, were the physical and chemical properties of the materials. Altogether, they are at the centre of the relationships between the dramatis personae.

****

The first part of this Interlude concentrated on features of the business of scrap rag and paper merchants supplying the feedstock for and upstream of paper making. The next part also reveals assemblages of relationships between people as well as of materials in moving further downstream to the retail sale of paper bags, especially the ubiquitous plain brown one.

****

Interlude: part 2 *Gardners Market Sundriesmen*[20]

Like Jonathan Jones, Paul Gardner is a descendant of the founder of the business where he works.[21] It was his great-grandfather who started the shop in 1870 in Spitalfields, in East London, the last of its kind in the area, where, just before seven on a sunny June morning, he talked about his working life.[22] Spitalfields is a well-known, well-described area of London, not far from the Square Mile where in the late seventeenth century, a royal charter was granted to set up a market.[23] Fruit and vegetables were traded there until 1991 when for want of space and worsening traffic congestion, the whole market was moved further out to Leyton. Both Spitalfields and Gardners have a considerable online presence where much of the family history Paul recounted is reported.[24] Although younger than Jonathan, Paul also began work as a teenager: 'the very first day I left school. I didn't get a school holiday. My mum just got me up here straight away. But my mum had quite a tough time, so I can understand why she did want to get me up here': his mother had been widowed when she was only thirty-five needing to work hard to make ends meet.[25]

Paul's great-grandfather had started out repairing scales, the type which had a tray on which metal weights of various denominations were placed opposite the cradle holding the removable scoop into which the trader would slide the fruit or vegetables to be weighed. Such machines were essential: 'all the wholesalers had to have scales.' Paul hazarded that broadening the business to sell bags, sieves and other sundries 'was just people asking for stuff really. "Can you get bags?" Because they used to make paper bags' – just as did grocers of an earlier century. He added feelingly, 'It must have taken an eternity really.' He supposed they were made in the shop. He was certain they used to string them there 'because I used to have a piece of wood where they used to hammer into it to skewer the paper bags. In hundreds really'.

The stock expanded many years later into plastic bags, different shapes and sized bags, added to the Kraft and white Kraft bags, elaborately printed bags – a picture of tomatoes, bright red accompanied by their leaves, Christmas themed decoration. In addition there were the signs, eventually made of plastic, giving the price of produce, King Edward potatoes, apples or pears – comice, conference, ripe Williams, specifying their variety by name. He has plenty of carrier bags, kraft brown some with paper handles, others with string, piled up or hanging from string above head height.

Harking back, Paul remarked thoughtfully, 'it was much more basic in those days. I think it was just brown paper bags really'. And those same brown paper bags continue as the mainstay of his sales: 'I would say 90 per cent of people just buy the basic brown paper bags or striped bags' – both simple bags just folded over, the latter of brightly striped red and white or green and white paper, or simply the venerable brown. The old market building a little way down the road, like other long established London markets, newly houses expensive upmarket clothes shops, one or two specialising in vintage hats or jackets, and several fashionable 'food outlets' signalling its gentrification.

That process is reflected in some of Paul's sales: 'I sell a lot of (paper) carrier bags. The twisted handle carrier bags have got much more popular here because the shops are that one step up. Whereas if I supply people in the markets the likelihood is they would buy the cheapest plastic carrier bags really.' Consonant with the shop's old fashioned air, Pauls gets

a few film companies that come in and there is – I am just trying to think what was coming up. Oh, last week I had a girl in. There is a Disney film coming up. It was the prequel of Cruella de Ville before she got the 101 dalmatians. So I had to find quite a few old paper bags. Luckily, there were some odd ones which looked pretty old.

Since that conversation, Paul has moved from Spitalfields to Leyton, setting up his shop in what were once his mother's premises, now joined by his son to run the business. In 2022, they set up an online shop that Gardners' bags may be bought remotely. Scrolling down that page finds that below the various types of merchandise for sale – carrier bags, dayglo labels and tags, cotton tote bags – there is one brown bag very prominently featured. It is conveniently displayed on the home page, available in three different sizes and either 500 or 1,000 all ready for the customer to click on the 'add to cart' button without having to search. Here it is: 'Brown Pure Kraft Paper Bags.'

Certainly this is not an ordinary brown paper bag, but a superior version

made to a higher quality … more reliable and less likely to split or tear, giving you more peace of mind … a great option for food from bakeries, coffee shops, fruits, snacks and takeaways … brown paper bags have been a staple of the **green grocer** trade for decades.

(original emphasis)

At the same time as appealing to decades of tradition, Gardners is adroitly brought right into the twenty-first century: '(T)hese high quality brown kraft paper bags are fully recyclable, making them a good alternative to plastic as well as being environmentally friendly.'

****

Thus the ordinary brown paper bag of plums, potatoes or comice pears comes full circle – from the waste paper trade via retailing, then used predominantly for food, ending ready for recycling, thence re-sale as waste paper to be made into more brown paper bags. Exposed to view are the various assemblages. In Gardners' case the dramatis personae reflect the history of the market and its current gentrification whence the reduced volume of clients rendered retaining the premises financially impossible – a problem adroitly solved by going online. Central to all sets of assemblages is the paper and the paper bag, its distinctive appearance and material properties.

Sacks

Here the discussion shifts to bags on a different scale. Sacks are a form of bag, but distinctive in being longer, larger, probably more robust and not likely to be used for the retail sale of foodstuffs, more likely at the wholesale stage of a food chain – at least on the European side of the Atlantic. The word has, however, an additional meaning on the American side, to describe the tall, stout, brown paper version specific to grocery shopping. For a matter of centuries, sacks were typically made from hessian/burlap, a heavy duty fabric made from plants such as jute and sisal, but also cotton – stuff which can harbour fleas as Suffolk farm workers discovered (Barret 1967: 92–5).

Mention of textiles – typically defined as woven in some fashion despite the exception of felt – is extremely hard to find in textbooks on food packaging. But they do exist: 'bags' of mutton cloth – a type of soft cotton stockinette whose name derives from its use early twentieth-century wrapping frozen lamb imported to Europe from New Zealand to stop carcasses freezing together. Far more recent is novel packaging to replace domestic use of plastic cling film and storage bags. One instance is to replace the plastic bag with a wrapping made of a combination of beeswax and organic cotton cloth, mostly on the market as flat pieces of cloth not bags (see Chapter 10).

'A Sack's Journey'

The subheading quotes one used by William Cronon in his study of the growth of Chicago in the nineteenth century, in which he shows that the urban and rural are intimately interconnected. The coming of the railroad in mid-century was central to the history of this connection and key to that city's growth. Up to then, grain in particular, but also other farm products were transported by water and bad roads – often little more than dirt tracks in the rural areas – from farms west of the Great Lakes to distant cities, St Louis, New Orleans and Chicago itself. Sited as close as possible to the nearest waterway, pioneer farmers transported their crops on the first stage to market by wagon – as short a distance as possible – and then transferred them to a raft or flatboat often built by the farmers themselves. Thereafter, the crops were sold/bought perhaps to a wholesaler/merchant for sale further towards the city.

Cronon traces developments in grain marketing in Chicago during the 1840s and 1850s declaring that it all 'hinged on the seemingly unremarkable fact that shippers, whether farmers or merchants, loaded their grain into sacks before sending it on its journey to the mill that finally ground it into flour' (Cronon 1991: 107). Key is the simple fact that as the grain was moved from the farm, on the back of stevedores, pulled in wagons or floated by boat, the grain remained intact, in other words, not mixed with any grain from another farm. Not only did sacks make it possible for a man to manoeuvre them on and off wagons or in and out of boats single handed, '(n)othing adulterated the characteristic weight, bulk, cleanliness, purity and flavor that marked it as the product of a particular tract of land and a particular farmer's labor' (1991: 107). All that was needed was for a potential buyer – wholesaler or miller – to check a sample from just one sack in the knowledge it could safely be regarded as typical of the whole load from the same farm.

Such journeys could be perilous for the cargo – the grain might get rain-sodden, or in a warm spell start sprouting – and for the farmer should the bottom fall out of the ultimate market. At the time, it was the original shipper who retained ownership of the load, bearing any losses as well as hoping for a profit. Cronon signals the convenience of the sackful's service as a relevant unit for enumerating any particular load. Farms would likely only have modest quantities of grain to sell 'ideally suited to small groups of sacks' (108). Sacks also were convenient for flexibly loading what were often irregular holds in flatboats or steamships. Moreover, as Cronon observes:

(M)oving foods by water almost always meant transferring them several times along the way, from pier to flatboat, from flatboat to levee, from levee to steamboat, from steamboat to sailing craft. Such transfers worked best if shipments were small enough that their weight and bulk did not prevent an individual worker from handling them. Moving grain on and off a ship usually meant negotiating tortuous passageways – across gangways, down stairs, through corridors, into storage bins – and the more complicated the path, the more critical the need to keep down the size of the unit being moved.

(1991: 108–9)

Keeping one farm's modest group of sacks together meant not only that the whole output could be identified but it also preserved the link, as Cronon adds, between 'grain as physical object and grain as saleable commodity' (1991: 109).

This was the system railroads overturned: grain could be transported more quickly, more cheaply and undisrupted by bad winter weather. Not only was grain more speedily moved by rail, but it was transported in medium size, *standardized* carloads. Cronon remarks that once whole freight cars were carrying nothing but wheat, shippers, railroad managers and all concerned began to think not in terms of individual sacks but carloads. Instead of being a useful combination of food package, conveniently slightly flexibly shaped container that was readily counted and transported by a single stevedore, the sack became a hindrance to swifter movement allowed by the new invention of steam-powered grain elevators. Automated, they meant far faster (un)loading, smoothly shifting grain from train to train eclipsing the need for men having to heave sacks onto their backs.

The spread of the American railroads, design of freight cars and more, points to a transition of this particular package. Where once that package containing grain was the ancient-shaped bag, it was rapidly supplanted in the industrial era by chute-loads of unpacked freight, readily mixing grain from several farms, no longer keeping sacksful distinct and accountable farm by farm. This transition has persisted, shifting from sack to carload and subsequently to refrigerated shipping containers that control the temperature of the grains they carry and bulk lorries/trucks moving grains by road between farm and store then from store to mill.

That transition was not, however, the end of the use of sacks to carry food. As historian Heather Buechler (2016) argues, sacks 'became more prominently identifiable as a product *package* – designed and produced to *sell* its contents (and yes, still move them to some effect) – as opposed to a product *container* used *only* for *movement*' (2016: 41 original emphasis). In any case, sacks continue to be used for the resulting flour, with Italian pizza flour, for instance, transported to pizzerias in the UK arriving in 22kg double- or triple-walled paper versions. Cloth flour sacks at the end of their lives as packaging were given a further lease of life when the fabric was commandeered for domestic purposes in the decades before, during and after the Second World War. This was a practical conversion among the less well off.

'… sheets she'd sewn from ripped-out flour sacks.'

The sub-heading to this section is from the final line of 'In Memoriam M.K.H., 1911–1984', Seamus Heaney's poem to his mother.[26] Born in Northern Ireland in 1939, Heaney was probably tall enough to help fold the sheets when he was nine, ten or so before he went away to boarding school at the age of twelve. That would have been in the period of post-Second World War austerity where although the food supply was different from the rest of the UK, there was still rationing. Heaney was the eldest of nine children, suggesting, along with the repurposed sacks, there was little money to spare.

This kind of domestic re-use of flour sacks in early to mid-twentieth-century rural America and Canada is comparatively well documented. A note by Rita Adrosko, a Smithsonian curator, published in the *Textile Society of America Symposium Proceedings* of 1992 reports an exhibition mounted a short while before, which declares that it 'touched a popular nerve' (1992: 129). In amongst the handful of academic articles (e.g. Jones and Park 1993, Brandes 2009, Banning 2005, Powell 2012, as well as more popular coverage e.g. Nixon 2010) is online attention in the form of reminiscences and nostalgia now surrounding carefully preserved towels, tablecloths, dresses and more, which are deemed collectible and/or up for sale.

Between them these sources suggest that heyday of the re-use of feed-, flour- or potato-sacks in North America ran from the hardships of the Great Depression, via wartime shortages of fabric through to the 1960s. By that time sack manufacturers were anticipating their wares' re-use and pre-printing them with colourful, often floral designs. The domestication of flour sacks is also recorded in a possibly unexpected quarter. During the German Occupation of Belgium during the First World War, the United States exported grain to help relieve severe food shortages (Weinreb 2017). Local historical societies in Kansas – whence much of the grain originated – augmented the more formal academic histories concentrating on the fate of the sacks, emptied of their contents. It is reported that Belgian people recycled them into clothing and household items. But others returned them, first embroidering their thanks onto the sacks, sometimes embellishing them still further with silk ribbon and lace.[27]

For something that can so often be though of as 'merely' ordinary, the bag has a perhaps surprisingly varied past. Sacks' twentieth-century history has flashes of thrift in their conversion to sheets, dresses and thank-you notes. As for the paper bag, affordable and practicable on a mass scale only a couple of centuries ago, it has come to occupy a familiar, undramatic place in the food packaging landscape. And despite transitions to plastic, it has retained its place, more recently returning to the spotlight with moves to reduce single-use plastic packaging. Despite appearing plain and simply made, a brown paper bag's potentially circular life from old rags to feedstock for new bags can be detailed exhibiting a good number of overlapping assemblages along the way. One key impression to be derived from considering bags as food packaging is the variety of materials from which they have been and continue to be made. Concurrently, perhaps as a result of its relatively low price, manufacture from renewable sources, flexibility and recyclability, versions of the plain, brown paper bag continue in widespread use.

Notes

1. Sainsbury's (nd). 'Galaxy Minstrels Milk Chocolate Buttons Pouch Bag 125g'. Available online: https://www.sainsburys.co.uk/gol-ui/product/chocolate-pouches—bags/galaxy-minstrels-pouch-153g (accessed 6 April 2023).

2. Hung round the waist, it is the pouch worn at the front over a kilt, serving double duty as a pocket and small haversack.

3. That was the special day the old Scottish universities allowed students time to travel home and back to replenish their supplies for the porridge on which they subsisted for the remainder of the term.

4. Parkinson, C. (1944). 'Packaging for protection author(s): Caroline Parkinson'. *The Science News-Letter* 46(17): 266–7. Available online: https://www.societyforscience.org/ (accessed 6 April 2023).

5. https://www.papermart.com/ (accessed 6 April 2023).

6. https://blog.papermart.com/small-business/9-types-of-paper-bags/

7. https://teara.govt.nz/en/photograph/25761/poha-containers (accessed 3 August 2019).

8. https://teara.govt.nz/en/photograph/4602/preparing-poha-for-transportation (accessed 2 August 2019).

9. Lying between the southern tip of South Island and Stewart Island – information kindly provided by Hugh Campbell.

10. http://otago.ourheritage.ac.nz/items/show/8728; https://teara.govt.nz/en/titi-muttonbirding 'stored in plastic buckets' (accessed 11 April 2021).

11. https://www.nzgeo.com/stories/shearwater-confit/ (accessed 11 April 2021).

12. White, M. (2009). 'Sheerwater confit'. *New Zealand Geographic.* September/October issue 2009. Available online: https://www.nzgeo.com/stories/shearwater-confit/ (accessed 6 April 2023).

13. Murray, F. (nd). 'Sooty Shearwaters and Blue Penguins'. Available at: https://www.fergusmurraysculpture.com/new-zealand/stewart-island-bluff-foveaux-10-pages/vii-sooty-shearwaters-and-blue-penguins/; The Encyclopedia of New Zealand (nd) 'Pōhā (kelp)'. Available online: https://teara.govt.nz/en/photograph/11992/poha-kelp (accessed 6 April 2023).

14. Confederation of Paper Industries (nd). 'Papermaking Process'. Available online: https://paper.org.uk/CPI/Content/Information/Papermaking-Process; Global Equipment (nd). 'Fourdrinier paper machine'. Available online: https://www.youtube.com/watch?v=Vi4wBPWxxEs (accessed 6 April 2023).

15. A pseudonym.

16. The word 'grocer' in English previously referred not to retailers but to wholesalers who bought in bulk, thereafter dividing foodstuffs into smaller quantities for retail sale. 'Grocer' derives from the French word grosser, from Latin. Curiously the other main Romance languages do not use this derivation e.g. grocer is épicier in French, from the word for spice.

17. Interview, 2017.

18. A popular abbreviation for Marks and Spencer, a chain store with a significant food section, founded in 1884.

19. Carbon paper was essential before the introduction of Gestetner machines or, later, photocopiers, as the main way of producing typewritten copies.

20. 'the gentle author' (2011). 'At Gardners Market Sundriesmen' *Spitalfields Life.* 20 December. Available online: https://spitalfieldslife.com/2011/12/20/at-gardners-market-sundriesmen/ (accessed 6 April 2023).

21. 'the gentle author' (2020). Packing Up Gardners Market Sundriesmen'. 5 January. Available online: https://spitalfieldslife.com/2020/01/05/packing-up-gardners-market-sundriesmen/ (accessed 6 April 2023).

22. No pseudonym is used here, since included in the material discussed are segments publicly available online.

23. Londondwholesalemarkets.com (nd). 'New Spitalfields Market'. Available online: https://www.londonwholesalemarkets.com/spits.html (accessed 6 April 2023).

24. Rogers, K. (nd). 'Gardner's'. Available online: https://www.dailymotion.com/video/x866f3; 'the gentle author' (2021). 'Paul Gardner, Paper Bag Seller'. *Spitalfields Life.* 28 January. Available online: https://spitalfieldslife.com/2010/01/28/paul-gardner-paper-bag-seller-2/

(accessed 6 April 2023); 'the gentle author' (2021). 'At Gardners' Bags'. 20 October. Available online: https://spitalfieldslife.com/2021/10/20/at-gardners-bags/ (accessed 6 April 2023); https://gardnersbags.com/ (accessed 6 April 2023).

25. Interview, 2019.

26. Clothes in books (2013). 'Seamus Heaney'. Available online: http://clothesinbooks.blogspot.com/2013/08/seamus-heaney.html (Accessed 6 April 2023).

27. Anon (2014). 'Thank You, America: Flour Sacks from Belgium'. *Reflections* 8(2). Available online: https://www.kshs.org/publicat/reflections/pdfs/2014spring.pdf (accessed 6 April 2023).

CHAPTER 4
BARRELS, CASKS AND TEA CHESTS

What a barrel is made of is contained in an authoritative skilled cooper's definition: '(A) barrel is, in fact, a particular size of wooden cask, one holding 86 gallons, and other sizes of casks found under different names' (Kilby 1989: 17). Its material is also an issue for Alastair Simms, who was England's only remaining master cooper in 2009:

> I accept metal barrels are necessary for the long distance transportation of beer but it's a shame that has led to a decline in the coopering trade. In the past wooden barrels were the only way to store liquids and food. They used to be essential for trade but faded away with the emergence of cheap metal and plastics.[1]

Simms's comment about a point of transition has to be set against a historical background in which the use of wood to contain food and drink is very old and found worldwide. Barrels are historically especially prominent, from Asia – appearing, for instance, in Chinese drawings of 1000–1100 – to Europe (Twede 2005). But wood has long also been used for other food containers including boxes, buckets and chests, as well as for utensils, wooden bowls and spoons for instance, mortars and pestles in west Africa or food processing equipment such as butter churns in Europe (of similar construction to a barrel). In the late 1990s, an octogenarian in a rural area of Umbria in Italy cheerfully demonstrated how she made linguine for a neighbour's visitor from England. She began by scooping flour from a large, wooden chest in a corner of her kitchen where an open fire burned year round, over which she cooked the resulting pasta. Always, she said, that was how her family had made pasta, and she could not remember a time when the flour chest was not in its place.

Properties of the wood itself are commonly exploited. And it is not only the reuse of wine barrels for ageing spirits. Wood has been used for kneading troughs in bread making, capitalizing on residual yeasts from one batch to the next (Davidson 2006). Wood that is split into smaller, sometimes more pliable slivers, or slender whippy switches, reeds, or alternatively tough or fibrous plants such as yucca, New Zealand flax, as well as oak, hazel and particularly willow have all been widely used to make baskets for foods, boxes (e.g. 'Shaker boxes') and buckets. Twede observes that '(T)he earliest representations of wooden tubs have been found in Egyptian tombs. The tomb of Hesy (2690 BC) shows a wooden tub being used for measuring corn' (2005: 254). This would mean barrels or casks are some 5,000 years old. The material used for barrels for most of those millennia is wood, with vines or rope made of other plant sources in the earliest periods holding them together. For instance, soy sauce is said to have been transported in one of two sizes of wooden barrel made of cedar wood, with staves held together with braided bamboo hoops.[2]

As this chapter will discuss, a significant transition emerged with increasing speed during the twentieth century. Stainless steel, rubber, sometimes aluminium and latterly plastics (high density polyethylene, HDPE) supplanted wood for storing and transporting foodstuffs. Nevertheless the discussion to follow concentrates on barrels as a dominant, venerable, wooden food package. Twede claims that they are pre-eminently packaging for transporting foodstuffs – widely used for purposes that today would be considered primary functions, selling directly to customers. So much so that Cahn suggests that the cracker barrel itself symbolizes the American general store of the nineteenth century (1969).

The chapter begins with brief note of barrels' chronology, describing how one is made, noting the types of foodstuffs transported in them. The section that follows picks up on the relation between types of food container used across considerable distances and their co-evolution with modes of transport, illustrated with the special case of the wooden tea chest in the nineteenth-century tea clippers sailing between China and Europe. The penultimate section considers the manner in which the history of a food package is also the history of other phenomena with which it co-evolves. The final section continues the theme of technological development to focus on 'transitions'. It deals with the successive supplanting of amphorae by wooden barrels and thereafter to metals and more. That section includes an Interlude about one example of a transition of wooden barrels to metal – which serves as a reminder of Petroski's injunction that a good understanding of innovation requires attention to failures as well as successes (Petroski 1992).

Barrels: chronology, construction and contents

The earliest record of some sort of barrel dates, according to Twede, from 500 BCE by Herodotus. He detailed the way Armenians shipped wine from Assyria to Babylon down the Euphrates River "'stored in casks made of the wood of the palm tree'". She adds, '(P)alm wood has a hollow and soft centre that would lend itself to this form' and may thus be the first liquid-tight wooden barrel (2005: 254). Kenneth Kilby, however, goes far further back. He evades the undue speculation needed to imagine how prehistoric peoples may have used a hollow tree trunk to store food by paying detailed attention to the tools in the archaeological record. As an experienced cooper himself, apprenticed as a fourteen-year-old in 1941, Kilby well understands the types of tool needed to be able to make a wooden cask. So his history deals with flints, Copper Age adzes and Bronze Age chisels which survive long after any wooden vessels or casks they may have been used to make have rotted away.

The Romans used barrels which, lighter and not so breakable, started to supplant 'clay transport amphorae and storage dolias'[3] especially in areas of Northern Europe with a more plentiful supply of suitable trees than of clay. Several sources also point out that on its relief depicting the war it commemorates, Trajan's column of 133 CE in Rome shows an image of Roman ships well laden with casks which Elkington (1933) considers contained wine and vinegar for the army's use. The barrels are easily recognizable, made of staves of wood, a bulge in the middle and held together with hoops. Additional evidence of barrels in ordinary daily use comes from the same century. Several surviving marble reliefs from Ostia show food sellers presiding over their trestle table stalls in one of which a large wooden barrel is clearly displayed (Holleran 2016).

Towards the end of the first millennium, wooden barrels were probably well established for, at the least, making and storing wine in Europe. An outline drawing of a Carolingian monastery in Switzerland made around 830 shows fourteen barrels of different sizes in its storage room (Meussdoerffer 2009: 20). And the Bayeux Tapestry depicts a wine tun on a cart, hauled by one man holding a tall stick, his spine noticeably bent. By the Middle Ages, barrels were firmly established as containers for all kinds of goods as well as foodstuffs throughout Europe, transporting gallons of wine from France to England, never mind supplies for English armies fighting the French, of salted meat, fish, eels, peas and ship's biscuit (Curry 2005). For several centuries, well over twenty foods/drink were regularly transported in bulk in barrels and through the eighteenth and nineteenth centuries, dried New England cod was salted and packed in barrels for despatch to Europe (Work 2014). Joan Thirsk exemplifies a capital city's privileges: '(B)y 1724 London enjoyed fresh fish, which was carried regularly in waterbutts on wagons from as far away as the East Anglian fens ... The water was changed every evening on the journey' (2007: 159). Waterbutts were essential in a good many circumstances, especially for travellers. Those on mid-nineteenth-century sailing ships, early steam trains or horse-drawn coaches carried their own bottles or leather canteens which were filled from wooden water-storage barrels. This was, of course, especially significant on sea journeys which had to supply all on board with fresh water for an extended period.

Several sources declare that coopering developed alongside the development of ship-building. George Elkington who published a study of both the Coopers Company and the craft notes that '(I)t is put forward as a tenable and probable hypothesis that Coopering took its rise almost concurrently in time and place with ship building' (1933: 216). He goes on:

The use of thin slabs of wood, bent to curved shapes and bound together, was a necessity for the ship builder and similar materials and modes of construction would equally serve the cooper, whilst as soon as ships were capable of extended voyages, wooden receptacles for storage of water and some part of any cargo, were obviously convenient, being light, easy of transport and not subject to the risks of breakage of heavy earthenware.

(1933: 216)

He cites Herodotus' description of circular ships made in Armenia on the river to Babylon (c.900–800 BCE).

They cut frames of willow, then stretched hides over them making as it were a hold; the boats being round like a shield. They then fill them with reeds and send them down the river with a cargo; and it is for the most part palm wood casks of wine that they carry down.

(1933: 216)

He continues, reporting that the crew consisted of two men and a donkey and that 'the boats never returned up stream [sic] but were dismantled, the cargo and framework sold at Babylon and the hides carried back to Armenia for re-use' (1933: 21).

Here, incidentally, is a glimpse of one early version of a barrel's later-life. For some types of barrel, however, a conversion of that kind did not arise for many years. Depending on their construction and the purpose for which they were made, barrels can be reused for a good long time. For instance, casks whose staves were 1½ inches thick used by breweries could last thirty-five years – one brewery had some of more than fifty well repaired and in use (Kilby 1971: 29). Far older still, in her *Food in England* the historian Dorothy Hartley illustrates a different 'later-life'. She includes a line drawing of 'a simple "smoke house"' fashioned out of a wooden barrel, probably used for a couple of centuries in rural areas to preserve home-made sausages or fresh-caught fish for the winter. It was adapted 'by inverting a large hogshead' with tenterhooks driven through the bottom from which to suspend the hams and chaps, etc. (1954: 329). The bung hole served as a smoke vent. A neat trick was to use a red-hot horseshoe to get the sawdust and stick fire going inside – it could easily be hooked out for reheating if the fire died down. It was, it seems, advisable to keep a bucket of water handy to damp the hogshead in case the heat shrank the wood allowing the hoops to come loose.

There are several other examples of reusing barrels provided by an American cooper Henry H. Work. He notes that, historically, barrels were 'part of improperly disposed rubbish, with some simply thrown out, slowly to decompose, leaving bits of metal to damage the unwary'. Yet he also reports one source talking of throwing barrels overboard 'as target practice for the ship's cannons' (2014: 205). Otherwise he laments old barrels' use – halved as tubs for flowering plants – overpriced and thus unsuccessful conversion to furniture, although he describes as 'creative' the use of an old barrel under a mound of dirt and straw for storing apples. There is, however, a demand for second hand bourbon barrels. Made of sought after American oak, scotch and rum are aged in them:

After years of resting quietly on a rack or pallet within a bourbon warehouse, when finally emptied, the bourbon barrels are suddenly sent packing, often to the far ends of the world. Buyers from distilleries in Ireland, Scotland, India, Mexico, Canada, Taiwan, Thailand, China and the Caribbean circle like wolves trying to get the cheapest price for the best barrels – that is the ones with fewest leaks and defects.

(Work 2014: 191)

Each barrel's potential long life is just one of their attributes making them valuable.

Twede considers wooden barrel technology 'offered unique advantages'. The barrel shape is strong; it is easy to handle and ship. The materials were once plentiful and inexpensive. The form was versatile and could be used for wet or dry goods shipped in semi-bulk quantities. A barrel is a particularly tough structure, based on the engineering principle of the double arch. 'When a barrel is viewed from the head, each stave acts as a keystone in the arch construction, supported by the other staves as a base. When a barrel is viewed from the side, the stave is the keystone, supported by the two heads as a base' (Twede 2005: 255). And – recollect she is a packaging specialist – she explains that its 'handling characteristics' are unique. That it can roll, gives it a 'built-in wheel'. And even though one person can usually carry less than 100lb (approximately 45kg) they can readily roll a barrel that is far heavier. Given its shape – 'the bulging bilge construction' – just a small surface is in contact with the ground thus reducing friction to a minimum making it easy to roll and pivot round corners. It is equally quite easy to upend it for the chime – the lip at the top – provides a handhold allowing it to be to rocked backwards and forwards on the bilge (larger in the middle than at the top and bottom) to manoeuvre it upright. And, Twede continues, it can be transported quite simply on a wagon chassis, never mind being easy to load onto a ship needing little more than ropes and planks to for lifting and stowing.

The barrel's ease of handling is in complete contrast to the complexity of its construction. Twede also points out that although 'the craft required a great deal of skill, there was a successful training system for practitioners' (2005: 255). By the end of the Middle Ages, coopering has become well established in England with The Fraternity of Coopers granted its first charter from Henry VII in 1501. Sir William Foster's 1944 history of what became the Worshipful Company of Coopers of London documents the ensuing complicated politicking about bequests of property, the transformation of the company from its initial incarnation as a voluntary association into a legal entity and its eventual first Hall completed in 1547 (1944: 14). The Company's accounts which go back to 1440 are 'preserved with unusual care' (Elkington 1933: 5). They very likely reflect '(T)he increase of trade – especially seaborne commerce – that marked the early part of the sixteenth century did not fail to bring to the coopering industry a growing prosperity; while the development of a royal navy initiated by Henry VIII ended in the same direction' (Foster 1944: 13–14).

How to make a wooden barrel

A barrel has been made the same way

from its earliest known incarnation, a container constructed of staves of a straight grained wood (e.g., pine, larch, or oak) held together by hoops (made of more flexible wood species or metal). Such a vessel could be made watertight by a careful concave design and by lining with pitch. It could be rolled along ramps and other flat surfaces, hence avoiding unnecessary lifting, and it could be set in a stable position on one of its two flat ends or on its sides via the use of chocks. Its wooden, multipart structure allowed it to be disassembled for reselling or convenient relocation elsewhere.

(Bevan 2014: 395)

Kenneth Kilby describes in lucid detail how it is done. The task requires converting a collection of properly seasoned straight wooden staves, supplemented by a supply of straight strips of iron, into a rounded hooped container with a bilge. He introduces the distinctive tools of this intensely specialized trade as he goes – from flush borer to cooper's axe, topping plane to jointer plane. Intertwined with a description of the 'making of a cooper' from apprentice to indentures, he teaches his readers what he himself learned in those four or so years of progress from the most menial tasks at the start (sweeping up, keeping the fire in) and on to boring the tap and bung holes in which to fit the brass bushes.

He graduates to the job of sharpening the tools whose names he thereby learns. 'I soon knew the adze, the croze and the chive, the different types of knives, the jointer, the buzz and the downright, the various inside shaves and the swift, and I suppose I developed a pride in the efficiency of the tools by keeping them sharp and acquired a health respect for them' (1971: 20). In parallel he introduces the specialized vocabulary of the cooper's trade – listing, backing and hollowing out a stave, chiming a cask – as well as noting the very large variety of sizes and types of cask. A combination of autobiography and history, his book includes discussion of the trade itself, for example setting out the various branches of coopering associated with different qualities of cask used for varying types of contents. Wet coopering included the greater precision needed for casks to contain beer, wine and spirit, while those to contain oil, tar and pitch could be of poorer quality. Dry coopering, requiring less skill, made casks differing not only in the quality and associated cost of the staves, etc. but also as to the commodity for which they were made: herring coopers were in between known as 'dry-tight coopers' since they still had to make casks that were tight, i.e. capable of holding liquid without leaking.

The transformation from group of staves to barrel begins by bringing them together at one end to form a circle, held together at the base with an iron hoop from which they splay outwards, producing a 'raised up cask' (Kilby 1971: 24). Heat must then be applied to coax the wood to bend while first gently hammering then ramming the remaining hoops on to hold the curved staves in place as they cool. To top and tail the barrel i.e. fitting a head, would seem, from Kilby's account to entail even more skill than needed so far. By the end, a huge amount of very fine detailed work has been required so that not only is the barrel the desired thickness, will hold its contents securely but also is of a standard size so although hand-made, reliably holds the correct capacity.

The ubiquity of casks for close on two thousand years is striking. They were used for an impressively wide range of goods stored and transported across increasingly large distances. For several centuries they carried food and drink – butter, cheese, salted meats, fish, live eels, preserves of all kinds including jams and vinegars, soy sauces and olive oil, rice, grains and flour, milk and drinking water – as well as further necessaries, from nails and soap to gunpowder not forgetting other uses, such as laundry tubs (incorporated into early mechanical washing machines of the later nineteenth century). In certain circumstances they were essential: 'Until well into the nineteenth century casks were used for almost everything on board a ship food, drink, ammunition and much of the cargo as well; and in addition no ship put to sea without one or more coopers on board, to repair these barrels' (Foster 1944: 14).

Tea chests, loading a tea clipper – and smuggling

Those who are old enough to have moved house during the 1950s in England will remember tea chests used by removals firms in which to pack belongings as varied as books, china or clothes, ornaments or pots and pans. Some were lined with paper, that had become tattered with use, or tinfoil laminated paper. Now and then scatterings of black tea could be found caught in the corners at the bottom. Clearly this represented the useful later-life of a wooden food package of a distinctive type. Not quite waist high, the largest, Congou and Souchong being 23 x 17 x 21 inches (58 x 43 x 53 cm,) these wooden chests or crates featured centrally in the nineteenth century races among the tea clippers – triple masted, square rigged sailing ships – between China and England attempting to get their cargo onto the market as fast as possible (MacGregor 1952: 17).[4]

Loading the tea in Hong Kong or Shanghai was the exclusive preserve of Chinese stevedores. Certainly this particular cargo possibly presents fewer problems when transported than liquids whose behaviour when moved accelerates and exaggerates the movement, unbalancing the waggon, barge or ship in the process. None the less, stowage has to be done carefully not only to prevent the cargo from shifting during the voyage and to ensure the ship remains trimmed, but also to achieve the most efficient arrangement not to impede its speed – essential in a race.

In his detailed study of the 'China Tea Trade', David MacGregor describes how the tea chests were stacked for the journey. Ballast was laid first, then a flooring of 'chop' i.e. green or old tea, on which the chests were set. A very carefully judged series of procedures followed, including the addition of ballast, dunnage (loose wood chips or material packed between the cargo items to keep them steady) and chests were piled on top of each other. Work started at the sides ending in the middle. Once fully laden – and here MacGregor cites a Royal Navy Reserve Captain who had commanded a clipper in the mid-nineteenth century – the top tier was

> beaten even at the edges with a heavy wooden mallet about one foot square, and the chests are squeezed in so tight that the wing (or end) chests take the shape of the sides of the ship without injury to the packages when properly stowed.
>
> (1952: 16–17)

Illustrating his book himself, MacGregor includes a diagram showing a cross section through a fully tea-laden ship unsurprisingly bearing a strong resemblance to the diagram of a similar section Twede reproduces showing a 'bilge and cantline[5] stacking pattern' for amphorae (2002).

Reflecting on the transnational movement of foodstuffs provides a reminder of an additional purpose of packaging for which the neither packers nor shippers are directly responsible, even if they may be implicated in running orderly procedures. As soon as foodstuffs cross borders, specific dramatis personae come into view: guards and smugglers, those whose responsibility it is to enforcing collection of import/export tariffs, gangs dealing in forbidden goods, all well focus on what commodities are transported in. The anthropologist Richard Wilk points out that eighteenth-century British government policy included measures to reduce smuggling that prohibited exporting/importing wines and spirits in 'retail-sized' packages (2009: 92). And, he points out:

> (G)oods, packages and brands that became accepted and well known in the home market followed expatriate officials and military officers to the colonies where they became established in those markets as well: printed retail wrappers were used by British merchants throughout the eighteenth century for … tea and sago powder.
>
> (2009: 96)

A distinctive instance of a part food packaging once played is found in the records of the Old Bailey, London's Central Criminal Court.[6] Five men were indicted on 7 October 1747 for 'theft from a specified place'. What they allegedly stole was 30 hundred weight of tea unsuccessfully smuggled past the customs officers on the coast of Dorset in Southern England. This was a period when high rates of duty on tea made smuggling especially profitable. Testimony presented to the court contains the clue to the tea's being smuggled. Captain William Johnson – deputed by the Customs to 'seize prohibited goods' – described how he caught up with a cutter he had chased from the afternoon until around eleven that night. His testimony continued:

> After firing several shot at her, I brought her to, and took charge of her. I went myself on board, and found she was loaded with tea, brandy, and rum. The tea was in canvas and oil-skin, over that the usual package for tea intended to be run; there was a delivery of it, forty-one hundred three quarters gross weight, in eighty-two parcels; there were thirty-nine casks of rum and brandy, eight and four gallons casks, slung with ropes, in order to load upon horses, as smuggled brandy commonly is.

Johnson records how he knew the tea was smuggled – run – because of its packaging of 'canvas and oil-skin' rather than 'the usual package for tea'. Corroboration was provided by William Milner, the Collector of the Customs when questioned about the way the tea and brandy were packed:

> Q. Was the tea in such sort of package as the East-India Company have?
> Milner. No, Sir, it was pack'd as is usual for run tea, and the brandy was in small casks all slung.

These packages signalled nefarious doings. More generally – and legally – as the historian Jon Stobart notes, the use of containers later in the eighteenth century increased the recognisability of the foodstuffs inside afforded, for instance, by packaging tea in tin boxes (2013).

Transitions: amphora to wooden barrels, wooden barrels to metal

In 1795, The Swedish naturalist, Charles Peter Thunberg, is reported to have written that

> The traffic in *Soy* … is more considerable [than that of tea], and as the tea produced in this country is reckoned inferior to that of China, so the soy is much better than that which is brewed in China. For this reason, soy is not only exported to Batavia [Jakarta] in the wooden barrels in which it is made, but likewise sold from thence to Europe and to every part of the East Indies.[7]

A more recent comment about transitions is notably detailed:

> Ceramics which had been skilfully practised in Norway up to the age of the Vikings almost disappeared during the Viking Age. Pottery was mostly replaced by wooden vessels, soap-stone pots and iron cauldrons. The development of coopering would seem inevitable among a people living in a country having a plentiful supply of timber and needing large, strong containers for their provisions at sea. This is another instance where shipbuilding and coopering developed side by side.
>
> (Kilby 1971: 104)

But history is not chopped up into neat periods, one tidily following another. On the contrary: not only is it evident that overall, forms of packaging used for decades if not centuries co-exist with newer types. Even when a package made of one material continues in use for many years then supplanted by another, that transition is not necessarily immediate or complete at any one period.

This final section considers examples of such raggedy transitions. In the process it notes that it is important to pay as much attention to failures of innovations as to successes, remembering that what can seem to be a 'modern' type is not necessarily the culmination of a straightforward succession of incremental improvements on earlier versions. The 'evolution of a book or a design' involves 'the successive elimination of faults and error' (Petroski 1992: 79).

One such untidy transition – clay amphorae to wooden barrels – is illustrated in the work of classicists and archaeologists on the economics of the wine trade in ancient Italy. It is, at certain periods, sufficiently extensive to be describable as 'organized commerce', with the Romans transporting wine over considerable distances. Literary evidence on viticulture and archaeological work on amphorae combined supports the view that a 'complex economic symbiosis of landowner, trader, shipowner and terracotta manufacturer' lay behind the trade from around 140 BCE for the next century or so (Purcell 1985: 7W). Symbiosis may be thought of as a 'tighter' version of assemblage, involving a co-evolution of elements closely bound together.

Amphorae of clay date from far earlier. Their design, shape and size are remarkably varied. Illustrating their diversity Bevan presents a diagram of six centuries' outline shapes of about thirty-six types containing wine, twenty-seven holding fish products e.g. garum (a liquid salty seasoning made of slightly fermented fish, Wilson 1973) and a further seventeen for olives and/or olive oil. The contents are likely to have determined whether or not an amphora would be re-used. Olive oil penetrates unglazed clay where in time it goes rancid, thus risking tainting anything subsequently stored in it. This accounts for Monte Testaccio, a small hill on the River Tiber composed of the broken pieces of 53 million 'single-use' amphorae that had contained olive oil imported from Spain to Rome between the mid-second to the mid-third century CE (Beard 2016). Amphorae containing wine, however, were reused (Pecci *et al.* 2017).

These centuries' use of amphorae, Bevan notes, fit into a broader context of the study of the Mediterranean as a remarkable geographic feature that has been the site of sustained transporting of goods in bulk – especially oil and wine, but also grain and fish sauces – from Roman times onward. A component of that history has to include, he argues, studying forms of bulk packaging, including amphorae, used in Mediterranean shipping over millennia and with it, the remarkable longevity of the barrel as one major form of such packaging (2014). But that does not address the transition from amphorae to barrels, nor does it account for the brief period in which cistern boats were in use. Described as 'short-lived' (roughly two centuries) they were designed to hold *dolia*, large globular jars permanently installed in the hold for bulk transporting wine (Marlier and Sibella 2002) – the archaeological record cannot shed light on why these boats fell out of use. Another, transition, also with unknown reasons, along different sea routes, is noted by Twede: '(W)ine shipments from Bordeaux and Germany to the monks in England were packed in amphorae prior to 250 A.D. at which time they ceased abruptly, presumably superseded by wooden casks' (2005: 254).

Why was clay supplanted by wood? After all, as Estreicher observes, the former is 'found almost everywhere, and an amphora is easy to make ... It is easy to store and ship, and wine can be aged in amphorae for a long time'. But 'it disappeared' (2002: 992). For him, the reasons turn on the practical. Like Twede he notes different transport routes: an enlarging Roman Empire meant goods, including wine, to serve it had increasingly to be transported over land. Wryly he observes '(W)ith few or no roads, pulling a cart loaded with amphorae across bumpy terrain was a sure way to break the jars'. The local peoples, the Celts, had however solved the problem by developing the use of wooden barrels and, he implies, the Romans simply copied them, improving their manufacture in the process to make them tight. Although his chronology is not clear, Estreicher is firmly of the view that it has to do with the nature of the materials of which wine containers were made. Whatever spurred such transitions at the time, they remain inexplicable for want of suitable evidence. But evidence is exactly what is displayed in a report discussed next.

****

Interlude: from wood to metal

Beer (and wine) casks today are, worldwide, increasingly made of various materials' replacing the centuries' old wood. Metals (steel and aluminium), combinations such as a steel frame with stout rubber covering as well as plastics, are all extant. A manufacturer's online press release in 2018 strongly foregrounds their PET containers' recycling potential as one of the first to be so, together with promoting the keg's superiority to steel or glass packaging (by eliminating the costs to the craft beer sector – or the industry of cleaning or storage).[8] Another declares that, from the outset, their keg was designed 'with circularity in mind'.[9] The transition to plastic kegs is relatively recent – as is the transition to rubber covered steel. But an earlier transition from wood to metal emerged over half a century ago – raising, of course, the questions of how that came about, why, who were the dramatis personae and which organizations were involved. Some of the answers are found in an internal document of the 1970s for one major brewery, Arthur Guinness and Sons (now owned by the multinational, Diageo) whose archive is housed at its original headquarters at St James's Gate in Dublin. In turn the answers in this Interlude illustrate the manner in which assemblages' non-human actants routinely both thwarted and enabled human actants' aspirations and activities.

Little is known about how R. G. Audas, A. J. Cleave and F. C. C. Finch came to write 'Draught Guinness: 1929–1971'.[10] Nor is it (currently) known who the authors were, the qualifications they held, their responsibilities or their relationship to the type of experimental work their typewritten report covers.[11] All three are almost certainly men – along with all other people referred to in the report, they are known only by their second names, prefaced by the initials of their forenames and at times referred to thereafter solely by their initials, a convention of the period. None of this information nor anything about its own origins is, however, included in the report itself. Dated June 1971, it traces the development work undertaken from 1932 up to and beyond the launch in June 1959 of Draught Guinness – a launch which, in the process, celebrated the 200th anniversary since 'Arthur Guinness signed a 9,000 year lease on a disused brewery at St. James's Gate, Dublin for an annual rent of £45'.[12]

The report primarily deals with the experimental engineering work involved in the transition from the wooden to metal cask which resulted in the mixed gas Easy Serve Cask System. Its main thrust concerns the invention of a suitable cask (and associated arrangements for transporting, serving the stout, etc.). Along the way, however, the report notes associated company policies, key decision-makers, commercial interests and more.

In this respect it records and passes on secrets. It is an insiders' report written for fellow insiders (albeit in adjacent specialties and/or divisions of the same organization) possibly thereby obviating the need to include note of its own origins and, probably, the need to explain all the abbreviations used (i.e. suggesting their day-to-day currency in dealings among staff) and certainly obviating the need to explain the basic technicalities of brewing, cask manufacture, use, etc.[13] At the same time, those insiders appear to include those beyond (or new to) the department involved in devising and testing new casks, for it summarizes close to thirty years of repeated design, trial and redesign as if such efforts were previously unfamiliar to its readers. It is, in many ways, an archetypical insider history prepared for fellow insiders. Above all, the report records how, in the words of a 2018 blog, 'wood gives way to metal'.[14]

Tacitly the dual feature of the interrelation between things and the people involved is presented as the explanation as to why the transition from wood to steel barrels took so long. Arranged chronologically, the report gets to page 40 before eventually bringing its readers up to 1971 with the observation that:

> Later versions of the Alumasc lightweight have been modified mainly in respect of the chime construction and the aperture for the gas loading valve (G.L.V.). The aperture has been enlarged to accommodate a wider and stronger G.L.V. The present (Mark XIV) cask has both chimes consisting of one piece castings, which prove more resistant to bending and denting than the original extrusions.

That the version has reached Mark XIV references the extent of earlier work and the paragraph reminds its readers of significant modifications of at least two features. One is that changes had been made in the manner in which the metal was cast (one piece), the other that it represents an improvement in the strength on an earlier version.

The authors begin with the observation that up until the Second World War the casks from which Extra Stout was draughted were almost entirely wooden. In describing the process of draughting as simple, the implication is that the process was long established, widely and well understood, working perfectly well. But, '(A)s early as 1928, however, serious investigation of metal containers was undertaken, with a view to export trade and to supplying ships at sea where a long cask life was essential.' A transition is, then, under deliberate consideration, arising not (directly) from the casks' material or the tasks, tools or techniques involved in draughting, but from the company's commercial interests. Of course, indirectly, it was the material of which the cask is made that was inhibiting commercial expansion. Wood failed in that, presumably, it could not withstand the additional rigours of more distant transport or storage on board ship without either the barrels being damaged or the beer being spoiled (or spilled).

Thus is set a dominant theme of the report.[15] Repeatedly a thing's materiality gets in the way of the company's intentions as the following couple of instances illustrates. The requirement for packaging not adversely to affect its contents is perhaps especially significant in the case of beer. Associated with the very nature of beer's manufacture is that fermentation continues in the cask. Thus it may be distinctively prone to organoleptic difficulties (those involving the senses) particularly smell or taste but also sight and what the food industry describes as 'mouth feel'. The report notes that the earliest instance of such a problem, when aiming to move from wood to metal, dates from 1929 when 'a 30 gallon stainless steel cask produced by Krupps was tested at Dublin, but like other stainless steel and aluminium casks tried at the time, it was found to impart a metallic flavour to Extra-Stout'. Four or so decades later '(S)everal types of plastic container were all proved to impart unsatisfactory flavours to the Guinness.' Organoleptic aspects would also include the correct height of the head on a pint – visible, after all, to bar staff and customer alike. And head height – a feature of the way beer behaves – is affected not only by necessary processes of dispensing but also by temperature, both implicated in the cask, its manufacture and its use. Similarly associated with beer's organic (as distinct from inorganic) character, particular infections present problems, some attributable to direct exposure to the container or associated parts such as nickel lined tapping bushes.

More generally, the report summarizes developments and difficulties. Written in a condensed style, a typical example is the following account of the performance of the first design, MK. I Cask which led to improvements in MK. II.

The MK. I Cask for facilitating draughting of Guinness was developed jointly with E.C. Lewis of Alumasc, and the prototype arrived at Park Royal in September, 1957.[16] It was basically a standard Alumasc firkin with a central aperture into which a large Sparklets cylinder was inserted, containing mixed CO_2 and N_2 at 750 p.s.i. A reducing valve was also incorporated within the cask, and the gas passed through a flexible external connector back into the beer chamber. The reducing valve was of a spring type as used by Flowers in draughting their Keg Bitter. Major problems with the prototype were the pick-up of a metallic taste from the exterior of the gas cylinder, and the tendency of the cylinder to break loose when the cask was handled. The Mark II was produced soon after the prototype and three were made and tested at Park Royal in the Autumn of 1957. These were a type of enlarged Alumasc firkin of 11 gallon capacity, again with a top, central aperture into which was inserted a larger gas cylinder at a lower pressure (250 p.s.i.). The cylinder reached to the base of the cask and was loosely held there by the shaping of the surface, whilst at the top it was secured by a bayonet fitting and rubber O-ring. A single-stage spring type reducing valve was totally contained within the gas cylinder, the outside of which was epikoted to prevent contact between the beer and metal. Thus the gas cylinder came to be considered as an integral part of the cask, to be filled in situ at racking. Gas was returned to the beer chamber by a rigid, external connector. Whilst the casks performed generally satisfactorily, there was insufficient gas to dispense all of the 8 gallons of beer, and there was trouble with the rigid connector.

Disregarding details and technicalities, the point to notice here is that the text highlights the things – the cask itself, the gas, the chambers, the epikoting,[17] the connectors and their behaviour, etc. All these non-human actants and more are paraded as key to the move from MK. I to II pointing the way for continued development work.

The report, however, explicitly attributes some problems to people. Typical of handling beer is the need to ensure that wild yeasts, permanently present in the air, do not contaminate the beer whose yeasts necessary for fermentation are carefully selected. For a time, a 'two-cask method' was used for dispensing in the pub itself, an attempt 'to remove the possibility of aerial contamination'. But such contamination still occurred. The snag here is attributed not to the yeasts, the beer itself, the casks or associated equipment but to the 'publicans (who) rarely bothered to clean the second cask'. A second example is provided by the authors' explicit adoption of a version of 'great man' history, declaring that the late 1950s marked a period of the development of Draught Guinness 'whose course was greatly influenced by personalities'. But rather than detail how that played out, the section that follows continues in the same style as the rest of the report to refer to named people and continued work on the design of casks, equipment, etc. This is evident in the following paragraph which approvingly credits M.E.A. with important work:

M.E. Ash followed A.J.R. Purssell as Brewer i/c Sample Room in 1955 with a clear brief from C.J. Virden to develop the system of draughting Guinness. A.J.R.P had found that Extra Stout could not satisfactorily be draughted with a partial pressure of CO_2 above a certain low limit. M.E.A. resurrected the use of nitrogen, experimenting with separate cylinders of the gases until A.J.R.P suggested that they could be mixed in the correct proportion in a single cylinder. It seemed that the partial pressure of CO_2 controlled the size of the head whilst the partial pressure of N_2 primarily influenced the appearance of the head. Trial and error revealed the proportion in which the two gases should be mixed under given conditions of temperature and pressure. M.E.A.'s further major contribution was to appreciate that it was an interaction between the gassed beer and the tap which provided the fine bubbles that formed the head.

Approving of his 'major contribution', the authors go on to note that in 1958 more development was required for which M.E.A. 'felt that he needed some 6 to 9 months'. Pressure to speed up the work coming from the Trade Manager resulted in prototypes being ready earlier than that. Thereafter, however, the report's authors record that

it was decided that all the development of the cask should be done by Production Research without participation from the Engineering Department. This in effect meant that we left the engineering of this new type of die cast aluminium pressure vessel entirely in the hands of E.C. Lewis.

Written in the same, even tone of the whole report, these passages indicate the authors' discretion: how, why and above all, who made the decision, to exclude the Engineering Department is concealed by their laconic adoption of the passive voice's anonymity: 'it was decided'.

****

Broadly, the authors attribute responsibility for failure not only to people or their personalities, but also to the things in question while simultaneously crediting those same things with helping secure successive improvements. It is possible to continue working through the report illustrating the attribution of problems and reasons for failure or success in solving them to either characteristics of the things themselves or to the people involved. But doing so relies primarily on a literal interpretation of the text. Work through the account of the introduction first of MK.1 and then MK.2 again and, of course, people are implicated at every stage. Somebody made decisions – and had rationales for each – about the design, the selection of materials, the positioning of valves, the choice of coating to keep the beer from contact with metal and so on. Although the style in which much of the text is written accords responsibility for the difficulties to the non-human things involved, it is self-evident those difficulties are apprehended, evaluated, learned from and further manipulated by the human actants.

This Interlude, then, proposes answers to key questions about how at least one instance of the transition from wood to metal casks came about by turning to the manner in which assemblages' non-human actants both thwart and make human actants' aspirations and activities possible – and, technically speaking, vice versa. Moreover it illustrates the way that human actants well recognize the intimate *inter*relation between themselves and the non-human. And, much like Law and Callon's aircraft engineers they make no firm distinction between the social and the technical. At this point, the discussion moves from barrels as one very long established package for food and drink, to turn in the next chapter to examine another venerable example, glass bottles.

Notes

1. Anon (2009). 'England's only master cooper predicts demise of barrel making'. *The Telegraph*. 4 January. Available online: https://www.telegraph.co.uk/foodanddrink/foodanddrinknews/4108266/Englands-only-master-cooper-predicts-demise-of-barrel-making.html#:~:text=He%20said%3A%20%22Coopering%20is%20not,you%20can't%20learn%20it (accessed 16 September 2015).

2. Shurtleff, W. & Aoyagi, A. (2012). 'History of soy sauce'. *SoyInfo Center*. 31 May. Available online: http://www.soyinfocenter.com/books/153 (accessed 21 June 2019).

3. A dolium was a very large rounded fired clay container.

4. The interest in speed extended to unloading: 'the *Fiery Cross* docked in St Katherine's Dock (London) at 4 am on 20 September 1864, and by 10 am. next day had discharged her cargo of 14,000 chests' (MacGregor 1952: 13). Cutty Sark, a nineteenth-century race-winning tea clipper is moored in Greenwich, on the Thames in London. Now a museum, its website illustrates the re-use of tea chests in one of its holds as blackboards to provide information for visitors. A photograph is available at https://www.rmg.co.uk/stories/blog/curatorial/cutty-sark-china#:~:text=Cutty%20Sark%20usually%20loaded%20over,over%20%C2%A318.5%20million%20today (accessed 6 April 2023).

5. The space between the ends or the sides of stacked barrels.

6. *Old Bailey Proceedings Online* www.oldbaileyonline.org version 6.0, 14 August 2014. April 1749, trial of Thomas Kingsmill, alias Staymaker William Fairall, alias Shepherd Richard Perin, alias Pain, alias Carpenter Thomas Lillewhite Richard Glover (t17490405-36).

7. Shurtleff, W. & Aoyagi, A. (2012). 'History of soy sauce'. *SoyInfo Center*. 31 May. Available online: http://www.soyinfocenter.com/books/153 (accessed 21 June 2019).

8. Press Release (2018). 'Petainer Launches New Hybrid Kegs at Brau Beviale'. 13 November. Available online: https://wineindustryadvisor.com/2018/11/13/petainer-launches-new-hybrid-kegs (accessed 6 April 2023).

9. One Circle (nd). 'KeyKeg'. Available online: https://www.keykeg.com/documents/34/OneCircle_Brochure_ENG.pdf (accessed 6 April 2023).

10. Reference–GDB/CO04.05/0054, 'Guinness Archive, Diageo Archive' Dublin. Additional work in the Archive may yield details of the background to its compilation. The Archive catalogue entry notes that it was '(I)nstigated by A.J.R. Purssell'. The report refers to him as the Brewer in charge of the Sample Room. Describing the 'Guinness Hierarchy' until at least 1938, Byrne explains in his autobiography of a lifetime's employment at St James's Gate, that Brewers are one level down from The Board, to which in time many were recruited. 'It was top management who designed and executed the system whereby every department, brewing or otherwise, had a Brewer at its top. The fact that most of the time the Brewer in charge of any department other than brewing didn't have the faintest idea of the intricacies of the department's work didn't seem to have captured the attention of the Board' (1999: 15).

11. Their humour is wry: 'The use of the Barnes Bush and Patent Extractor was a major advance in cask tapping at this time. Barnes was an Australian who first saw his vocation on being drenched with ale whilst tapping a metal cask in Australia.' They are also entertained by a discovery. A covering known as a 'Nightshirt' concealing an unsightly cask on the pub counter 'provid(ed) excellent cover for the passing of betting slips' – an illicit activity only exposed when a new patent dispenser replaced the cask and abolished the Nightshirts.

12. Anon (nd). 'The Story of Guinness'. Available online: https://www.guinness-storehouse.com/en/discover/story-of-guinness (accessed 6 April 2023).

13. The report does, however, observe that 'The history of the "Easy Serve" cask should therefore begin in 1932. Should, because the design of this cask, and the lessons learnt with it, appear to have been entirely forgotten. The Easy Serve cask of 1959 incorporated a reduction valve exposed to the ravages of beer and weather, and in planning the cask little or no provision was made for the maintenance of the valve.' It may be that someone – one of the authors perhaps – was conscious of the loss of corporate memory and/or adequate notes preserved to guard against reinventions.

14. Boak & Bailey (2018). 'Draught Guinness 1958' *Beer History* 7 November. Available online: https://boakandbailey.com/2018/11/draught-guinness-1958-two-casks-one-tap/ (accessed 6 April 2023).

15. The authors are, however, conscious of types of factors involved in developments' origins, for they remark that 'In the course of the life of an industrial products [sic] there are frequent periods when its development is dictated within fairly well defined limits by past events.'

16. A Guinness Brewery in west London.

17. An epoxy resin sold under the trade name of Epikote™.

CHAPTER 5
BOTTLES, JARS AND GALLONS OF MILK

As a food package, a bottle or jar is mostly of hand held size. Containing liquids they may be crudely divided into three according to the rate at which the contents flow.[1] Water, milk, wine and fizzy drinks (soda) pour straight away when the opened bottle is tilted; many sauces just ooze while jams (jelly), mustards and similar preserves are far slower and fall at irregular intervals in varying sized amounts. But their properties of all are such that if not caught, they end up in pools and splodges on the ground. Bottles are typically distinguished from jars by their shape – the former having a tapering neck, opening with a mouth narrower than the circumference of the container, the latter typically being the same measurement bottom to top with a correspondingly wide mouth. Fast flowing liquids are conventionally contained in bottles, the slowest – jams and chutneys – are packaged in jars. Although probably most commonly cylindrical, neither needs to be. Indeed a square section of anything can in principle be packed for transport and storage more efficiently – although square shaped wine bottles gave way in the eighteenth century to cylindrical for better storage horizontally to ensure the cork remains wet (Meigh 1972: 20).[2]

How, then did these instances of food packaging end up as typical in the array used in the twenty-first century? This chapter tackles the chronological version of an answer by building on 'insider histories' of glassmaking and of the production of glass bottles and jars. Currently glass and plastic bottles co-exist as do cartons made of paper, laminated with plastic. Plastic may partly supplant glass. In a recent transition one UK supermarket replaced the dark green bottles for their own brand extra virgin olive oil with those of PET – except that in this particular the glass one was continued in tandem with its replacement for some time. Chick peas or black beans long packed in cans can now also be found in aseptic packs similar to Tetra Brik cartons. Milk and its containers are a special case, considered in detail in this chapter's three-part Interlude.

Bottles to contain liquid foods/drink have been and continue to be, made of other materials – from gourds to coconut shells, leather, ceramics, along with metal churns, wooden buckets and tubs. But, with the exception of ceramics, glass and plastic are today liable to be the most frequently used commercially for mass-market bottles and jars. Glass is possibly unique among food packaging materials in that it is both one of the oldest, most steadily used over centuries as well as continuing as such in global, mass-produced, commercial use today. Glass is also significant as a food package in that it can be permanently marked – branding on standard sized bottles could readily be instituted as soon as mass production moulding was introduced in the nineteenth century.

This distinctive material has a good many advantages as a food container, as one packaging textbook notes, for its 'chemical inertness, clarity, rigidity, resistance to internal pressures, heat resistance and low costs', set against just two main disadvantages of 'fragility and heavy weight' (Paine and Paine 1992: 78). All the same as just noted, significant transitions have been initiated, with glass, plastic and paper continuing to co-exist for packaging the same foodstuffs. This chapter also keeps an eye on the shifting multiplicity of assemblages that form, dissolve and reform over time. Glass is a good instance in which there are various sets of limits and possibilities of what people can do with it. Mainly these are associated with its thermal properties and its peculiar physical state between liquid and solid, whether as a hand-produced luxury bottle or machine-made, produced for mass markets. From early beginnings to contemporary mass production, glass is made in the same way.

How to make glass

Unexpectedly perhaps, a layer of glass coated a huge area of the Libyan Desert some 26 million years ago. Something unknown but extremely hot had happened. '(G)rains of silica melted and fused under an intense heat that must have been at least a thousand degrees (F)' (Johnson 2014: 13). Superheated, it liquefied. On cooling, however, it did not resume its original state. Unlike water which can change from steam, to water to ice and all the way back again, silicon dioxide can only change from liquid to solid. As it cools it remains in an irreversible state between solid and liquid. This does not, however, prevent its being re-melted – an essential property, it turns out, in glass-making.

Glass is so old that dating when it was first made can only be roughly estimated, several millennia ago in Asia Minor. 'The first glassmakers were motivated to create decorative objects' (Kurkjian and Prindle 1998: 797). Beads were found in Egypt dating from 2500 BCE (Carlisle 2004: 44) while Pfaender observes that 'Glass is possibly the oldest man-made material used without interruption since the beginning of recorded history' (1966: xiii). Most insider authorities note that the Phoenicians, followed by the Romans, made glass. Bottle making, they report, declined sharply from the end of the Roman Empire until the fourteenth century when following the sack of Constantinople in 1204, glass makers from Turkey travelled to Venice, heralding the city-state's ascendancy in luxury glass for the two succeeding centuries. Its widespread use for packaging, however, only goes back to the late 1700s (Twede and Goddard 1998: 49).

Glass is notable in that its constituents – primarily silica (sand) with some soda and lime – are plentiful and cheap, the least expensive of packaging materials compared to metals which are the most costly (Twede and Goddard 1998: 7). Ingredients can be added which change the colour, translucence and other properties; ingredients include lead, ash produced by burning kelp (Dungworth 2009) or boric trioxide (Pfaender 1966: 17). Modern additions include calcium, sodium oxide, traces of iron oxide, etc. for a typical bottle grade of glass (Twede and Goddard 1998: 49) and when colour is wanted, various metals are added – copper produces a light blue, cobalt an intense blue, manganese violet, etc. (Pfaender 1966: 30). A far greater cost than the main constituent materials is that of the energy needed to heat furnaces to sufficiently high temperatures.

In principle, the process is simple. The ingredients are crushed with, nowadays for commercial use at least, the addition of 20 per cent or more of cullet,[3] before firing at approximately 1,300°C. Cullet melts more easily so its addition reduces the heat needed and thereby the cost of energy. A key landmark in glass bottle making began with the unknown person responsible for devising a blow pipe (blowing iron), dated by Cable as around 50 CE (2021–2: 1), but as approximately 200 BCE by Khetarpaul and Punia (2008: 101). It remains in use today to make all types of glass whether machine-manufactured or to produce decorative objects by hand.

The steps involved in glass blowing are well described by the sociologist Paul Atkinson who attended a day-long practical class at a London studio (2013). Above all he records his awareness of the extreme heat and the potential dangers both of working so close to a furnace and handling molten glass. In principle, the procedures are simple: the 'irons' and 'pipes' are first heated in the furnace through a 'glory hole'. Then a 'glob' of molten glass may be 'gathered' onto the heated tip of the pipe by dipping it into a reservoir of molten glass held at about 1,100°C. As the 'gather' cools it can be shaped, either with spoon-shaped 'blocks' of slow-burning cherry wood stored in a bucket of water below the bench and used wet, or with a tweezer-like tool. The soft glass can be rolled into desired shapes on the 'marver' – once of marble, nowadays of steel – initially resulting in a 'parison' ready for further working, notably blowing. While making a piece, the glass can cool too far, reducing its malleability, so that it needs repeated re-heating. Once the desired shape is achieved, the third phase is 'annealing'. In glass-making this refers to the process of very slow cooling in a 'lehr', an oven whose temperature is lowered at a controlled rate. This reduces the internal stresses – caused by differential rates of cooling on the interior compared with exterior surfaces – that would otherwise weaken the final object.

'The story of the glass bottle'

This section's heading quotes the title of Edward Meigh the doyen of the glass-making industry's small book commemorating the first issue of C. E. Ramsden & Co. Ltd's *Monthly Bulletin for the Glass Industry* fifty years earlier (1972). Parochially, he writes from an English viewpoint primarily about the domestic glass bottle making industry. Meigh summarizes what looks to be an agreed periodicity across the insider histories consulted. From Venetian supremacy in glass-making, there were 'not any important accomplishment in bottle making' for the next two centuries when it was predominantly confined to making objets d'art (1972: 11). The seventeenth century, however, 'is a supremely important historical stage in the story of the glass bottle' as bottles began to be made for utility on a newly enlarged scale. Prompted by the 1612 publication (translated into English from Italian in 1662) of a 'scientific treatise on glass-making', the practice was spread by Italian glass makers travelling to France and thence England, marking the establishment of its hand-blown industry.

Harry Powell, an illustrious and energetic industry insider, a generation before Meigh, remarked in his 1919 lecture to the Royal Society of Arts in London that 'glass – making is one of the oldest of London's industries, and at one time was of considerable importance' with a continuous record for over 300 years 'of glass-making in London' (1919: 486). Other centres of bottle making in the eighteenth century include Bristol (Gregory *et al.* 2019), Alloa Glassworks serving whisky distilleries in the Scottish Lowlands, and Rotherham in Yorkshire specialising in bottles for medical, chemical and pharmaceutical use. For the nineteenth century, Meigh regards the Great Exhibition as a point from which the glass bottle trade really began to flourish extending more widely in regions where it was already established. This growth was, however, cut short as other nations imposed tariffs in order to protect their own domestic industries – the United States set theirs at 60 per cent.

Perhaps the importance of the industry may be measured by the way it 'spawned' a major contemporary literature on its manufacture, as well as a considerable technical literature on the development of furnace design and of bottle-making machines (Meigh 1972: 27). This literature makes it possible to trace the chronology of the mechanization and industrialization of glass-making; it can be followed in two ways. One is to note the shifts in the type and volume of fuel for the furnaces – and with it a reduction in the amount of fuel needed, thus lowering its cost to produce the very high temperatures required. Initially, furnaces burned wood but by mid-nineteenth century, it had mostly been replaced by coal (Shaw 1936: 296). Coal was succeeded by gas. The construction and control of furnaces fired by oil was respectively simpler and easier but by far the most expensive and presumably left unused. Shaw recounts the development of mechanization/mass production of glass bottles tracking the introduction of innovations he considers made automation possible, along with detail about successive amendments to the design of furnaces (1936).

A second measure of the industry's significance is to track the relationship between labour and development of bottle-making machines. This is a 'classic' economic feature of production during and since the industrial revolution whereby mechanization/automation displaces human labour – and needs little general elaboration here. Fine grained detail of this change is documented in Bernas (2011) who concludes by hoping that 'this research piece offered a window into the short and often *fuzzy period* bounded by the strictly hand and then nascent machine production of wide mouth bottles, jars and packers' ware' (2011: 23 emphasis added) thus underlining the manner in which this particular development was neither clearly chronological nor linear.

As Meigh summarized, the intricate history becomes even more intricate with the 'slow change from hand methods of bottle manufacture' to 'early attempts to introduce machines' and subsequently to 'complete automation in the glass container industry today' (1960: 1). He traces in considerable detail the incremental progress in the automation of glass bottle manufacture for the 'period of forty years, from 1880 to 1920, (which) saw the complete transformation of the glass bottle industry from a craft to a fully mechanised engineering activity' (1960: 1). He accords Owens' glass bottle-making machine pride of place in the automation of the whole process, from the initial selection of the molten glass to blowing it into its finished state. Owens' machine produced glass bottles at a rate of 240 per minute, and in some instances, reduced the costs of labour by 80 per cent. But Owens (1859–1923) himself is credited with much more than that.

Born in West Virginia, Michael Owens is described by his biographer as Irish-American who went out to work from the age of ten (his mother was widowed) and by twelve was employed in a flint glass factory (Skrabec 2007). Meigh observes that he 'passed through the various jobs for boys until the age of fifteen he learned to blow glass and soon became a proficient glass-blower' (1960: 5). These were his early beginnings in the industry later marked by the invention of a series of a dozen Owens machines, the first of 1903–4 and the last 1920–3 (Meigh 1959: 8). The intricacy of the machines is clearly displayed in illustrations accompanying Meigh's text (1960: 8–9).[4]

Skrabec (2007) enumerates Owens' contribution, declaring he 'was bigger than his forty-nine patents and automated glass-making machines', including:

(1) 'Owens brought automation to all the process industries, years ahead of Henry Ford's pioneering assembly line for manufacturing. His early glass plants were centers of automation.'

(2) It meant the production of 'standardized height of bottles (that) in turn allowed for the development of high-speed packing and filling lines'.

(3) Further, 'because of the uniformity of bottles produced by the Owens machine, the Pure Food and Drug Administration was able to enforce laws that assured proper amounts for the consumer'.

(4) More than that, '(T)o a large degree, Owens revolutionized the American diet as well as the glass industry by allowing for better storage and preservation of foods. Even pasteurization and bottle-feeding had to wait for Owens' commercialization of bottle (making)'.

(5) He 'even invented automated filling systems for the food and industry, making their processes continuous'.

(6) '(T)hanks to Mike Owens and his contemporaries, they made glass a commodity rather than a luxury and glass is now an important part of our environment.'

These features of his contribution are, self-evidently, closely allied to food packaging and its current place in the automated industrialized production of processed foods. The development of mass production of this container in turn made possible selling milk in glass bottles, an ideal material for packaging so difficult a foodstuff.

Milk – and its retail containers

To regard milk as a foodstuff has a history stretching back into the nineteenth century: '(M)ilk is not only drink but rich food' (Beecher 1873: 101). Yet, milk spoils so readily that for centuries it has been turned into cheese as a means of preserving it. Only those near enough next door to the cow, goat or sheep would drink it – or drink it moderately safely – scooped straight from the pail in which it had been collected. This also applied to those living in the rapidly growing cities of the nineteenth century, supplied by 'town dairies'. One way and another the scope for a retail trade in liquid milk was limited until the nineteenth century growth of cities providing a new market for those sufficiently close to rural farms for liquid milk to be delivered by cart. Cities were also supplied with milk from those town dairies where milch cows were kept in commonly squalid conditions to provide a typically dirty and often adulterated supply (Burnett 1999). Dr A. H. Hassall, the author of an enquiry that ran from 1851 to 1854, had declared:

> If the testimony of ordinary observers, and even of many scientific witnesses is to be credited, there are but few articles of food more liable to adulteration, and this of the grossest description, than milk.
>
> (Hassall 1855: 320)

Contemporary descriptions of its appearance are repellent. Watered down milk was 'washed' or 'bobbed', leaving it looking thin and blue-ish. As a remedy, dairymen added various substances, including flour as a thickener, the juice of boiled carrots for restoring both consistency and sweetness, chalk as a whitener, 'and even brains to froth the milk' (Atkins 1991: 320).

Urban food supplies in general were not that clean and adulteration – together with giving short weight – was common enough. But the creation in 1856 of the first Belgian public analysts' office in Brussels initiated the gradual reduction in fraud, adulteration, etc. in urban food supplies (Scholliers 2014). Milk was different. Widely recorded, the late nineteenth century difficulty with milk was its danger. Milk was not, however, the 'complete food' (despite Beecher's view) it was becoming by the mid-twentieth century. For centuries before then it was regarded primarily for infants and invalids. Until the late eighteenth century it was those in rural areas who had readiest access to liquid milk – a period, though, when cities were still smaller and market gardens and so forth penetrated well into the areas covered by buildings.

Drastically telescoping a detailed history, milk, notoriously, represented the last food item on sale to the public in the later part of the nineteenth century which continued to be adulterated in the rapidly growing cities of the United States, UK and Europe. Atkins (2010) is just one authority detailing the technical difficulties laboratory scientists and analysts faced in both detecting adulteration and devising improvements in preservation in the milk supply between Hassall's damning assessment and eventual moderate success by the 1920s by which time the milk supply was increasingly pasteurized.

The trade grew, supply and demand in lock-step. In the 1880s milk was transported considerable distances. The Gates family company (later Cow & Gate) built three creameries in England and another in Kildorrery in Ireland.

> Cream from Kildorrery was sent daily to England in 17-gallon churns … As a result of tests based on the work of the Lister Institute, cream was kept fresh for a week by adding 0.4 per cent boric acid.
>
> (Jenkins 1970: 57)

As most sources observe, it was the coming of the railways in mid-nineteenth-century Britain that made the frequent transport of milk from farms to cities far more practicable. Burnett notes that the railways carried milk 'almost from the start' (1999: 32). And, memorably,

> (O)n 1 December 1927 the first 3,000-gallon glass-lined rail tanks were filled at Wootton Bassett, Wiltshire and Calveley, in Cheshire, and made ceremonial journeys to London in a blaze of publicity.
>
> (Jenkins 1970: 60)

Milk as a food especially for children was heavily promoted in the inter-war years based in part on medical studies of primary schoolboys' growth (Burnett 1999, Smith-Howard 2014).[5] The idea of milk as special, a particularly good and complete food, was increasingly fostered. Indeed, building on this, a major advertising campaign for Cadbury's Dairy Milk Chocolate was launched in 1934, emphasizing its food value. Geared to defining the chocolate bar 'as a food rather than as a snack', it stressed 'the way in which the goodness of milk was complemented by the chocolate to provide a convenient source of essential nutrients' (Horrocks 1995: 12).

The pioneering nutrition scientist John Boyd Orr (1966), who also undertook studies of the nutritional value of milk in the 1930s, describes in his memoirs his view of the measures required to deal with Britain's oversupply of milk in that decade. He makes plain that he also took concern for farmers' livelihoods into account.[6] Success, he notes, came when, aligned with his own view, government funds were allocated to help solve the problem:

> £1,000,000 was to be devoted to propaganda to increase milk consumption to get rid of the unmarketable surplus … This enabled us to expand the Milk in Schools Scheme.
>
> (Boyd Orr 1966: 113)

By then the supply was certainly cleaner and less risky than it had been a century earlier.

Yet milk was still not regarded as safe. Indeed, in February 1938, the British Medical Association published an 'Announcement': 'Is All Milk Safe to Drink?' Answering its own question, it listed 'facts about unsafe milk', notably the extent to which milk was responsible for epidemic disease, not only bovine tuberculosis but also among others, scarlet fever, diphtheria and paratyphoid (Enock 1943: 68; for US see Smith-Howard 2014). Whether or not milk is pasteurized, it can still be contaminated during any further processing and eventual retail sale. After all, as Sir George Newman[7] observed 'Milk is a "tricky" article, extremely liable to contamination and *recontamination*, from the farm to the consumer' (1943: vi).

This is where milk's various retail containers enter the picture in the three part Interlude ending this chapter. The first part is about glass milk bottles, the second plastic milk bottles and the third paper cartons, or more accurately laminated paperboard as introduced and patented by Tetra Pak.[8]

****

Interlude part 1 – milk in glass bottles

It has been possible to buy milk in glass bottles since the 1880s in both the United States and the UK. By the mid-twentieth century, millions took it for granted that a milk bottle was made of glass and even if different dairies' varying shapes were unfamiliar, could recognize it as one. Familiarly too, millions have pressed it into a gamut of later-lives – from purposes as innocent as a flower vase to a Molotov cocktail, from a growing trade among collectors, to a pharmacist involved in developing ibuprofen in the 1960s recalling 'cultivating millions of doses of penicillin which he put in quart milk bottles for hospitals around Britain'.[9] Home deliveries were already established – reported in Vermont by 1785 when 'milkmen would come to the door with a metal barrel full of milk' from which customers' jugs, pails, jars would be filled.[10] In the UK, milk from town dairy cows (sometimes milked outside a customer's house) was hawked through the streets in wooden buckets hanging from a yolk round the seller's shoulders or carted from door to door to be doled out in the same manner as in Vermont.

The earliest patent for a glass milk bottle in the United States was filed on 22 September 1877 by George Henry Lester of Brooklyn.[11] In the UK George Barham's Express Dairy first bottled milk in 1884 as a convenience and safeguard to health. Barham is described in the company's centenary history as a 'typically Victorian capitalist-philanthropist' who may not have invented milk bottling, but 'pushed a system which benefited both his marketing convenience and his customers' well-being' (Morgan 1964: 31). Albeit initially slowly, how, then did glass bottles come to be *the* retail package for milk for a good half-century and more? What light can be shed on the decisions behind the transition to such a package?

The accelerating sanitary and public health movements of the nineteenth century represent the overall backdrop to concern with the quality of the food supply, milk in particular. But as Morgan indicates it was also good for business. The reasons for introducing a glass package are well described in the 1877 patent. Lester's invention, 'a new and useful improved Milk-Can', is designed to overcome the disadvantages of existing cans. In other words, here is explicit account of plans for what is hoped to be a successful transition.

The text of his patent begins by noting the existing arrangements for retail sale of milk in a major urban centres – New York City's population at the time is put at almost 2 million:

> Under the system of delivering milk established in the large cities of New York and Brooklyn, milk is delivered to the consumer in a nearly solid body, in a can, precisely as it came from the cow, without possibility of being tampered with, or of change from the shaking to which it is subjected while in transit.

He lists the existing cans' advantages in conserving the milk undisturbed in transit. The first difficulty[12] he seeks to remedy arises, for him, well after delivery, *after*, indeed, customers have used the milk and must prepare to return the cans to the dealer.

> The cans are cleaned by the consumer instead of the milk-man. Consumers are apt to neglect this most important duty. The milk corrodes the tin, exposing the metal, the corrosion of which injures the milk, and soon renders the metal can valueless.

Herein lies major and costly disadvantages. A corroded can is a useless can. It is the very materiality of the can which in contact with the materiality of its contents that lies at the heart of the problem. Noticeably, Lester does not seek to change consumers' behaviour but concentrates on finding a practical solution in terms of the materials used for a can.

> I overcome these difficulties by making my cans of glass, and by making them of a substantially plane surface inside and outside, without recesses in which unclean matter might collect. The can of this form is easily cleaned, and, being without the usual neck, of less diameter than the main body, it affords a large surface for the cream, which is all easily accessible; also, it is more easily emptied of its contents, and is more useful as a vessel to contain the milk while in the hands of the consumer. It is to be understood that the can, its contents having been used by the consumer, is to be returned to the milk-dealer for further like use in transporting milk, and the milk is used and the can returned by the consumer, as before.

Lester includes no technical details but presents his invention simply as a superior replacement for the existing metal can. It fits into existing arrangements – assemblages of the can, its contents, the milk-dealer and the customer – without disturbing them. In the process it continues to provide the delivery of clean, i.e. packaged, milk in a manner that retains the value of the can owned by the dairy. Those arrangements included the widespread assumption that customers return containers – an Australasian ceramic beer jar carried the return name and address (Figure 7).

Lester's glass can solves what he treats as purveyors' problems without involving customers, let alone attempting to 'educate' them into different habits. What he does not do, incidentally, is mention whether those customers would be content with a can of glass rather than metal – save for noting that dispensing milk from a glass bottle is far easier and claiming that it is more convenient for storage too.

****

This first part of the three part Interlude serves as a reminder of the manner in which the material can be said to thwart human use of a package, spurring attempts to circumvent the associated difficulties while retaining whatever advantages the package confers. In a small way, this patent illustrates one piece of the answer about what effected a transition from metal cans to glass milk bottles. The next parts of the Interlude identify

Figure 7 Beer flagon carrying details for its return to the brewers.

two more transitions, to plastic bottles or paperboard cartons. Both of these revolve around people's judgement of the earlier materials' limitations.

****

Interlude part 2 – milk in plastic bottles

Following directions towards an almost windowless, low-ish building strikingly painted in broad horizontal bands of sludge green, pink and fawn, first time visitors cannot see that it houses *two* factories. Each is owned by a separate company. One, A.R. is a dairy dedicated to milk processing and filling plastic bottles for the retail market. On the other side of the internal wall dividing them is a different company, A.L. dedicated to producing the bottles the dairy fills.[13] A.R. is this branch of A.L.'s sole customer. Coming in to the former is milk collected direct from farms, conveyed by road in bulk tankers numbering some 120 daily. Coming in to the latter are consignments of virgin HDPE pellets and rHDPE (recycled HDPE). Dispatched from A.R. are those familiar supermarket cages loaded with some 80/120 plastic bottles of milk each. The dairy is designed to produce 1,000 million litres/2 pints of fresh, bottled milk annually. The whole, symbiotic process runs continuously, 24 hours a day, 365 days per year.

A.L's factory, the bottle manufacturing side, is on two floors, all geared to meeting the dairy's needs, where bottles are made, stored and thence supplied. In order to accommodate fluctuations in demand from A.R. and ensure smooth continuous running, stocks are built up, warehoused in the store located on the upper floor. A.L's extrusion blow moulded bottles include 40 per cent of rHDPE. The process is simple, in principle. Echoing the manner in which a glass bottle may be made, first blown and then moulded to a desired shape, so the molten rHDPE is formed into a parison – the same word as used in glass blowing – which here is a hollow, commonly circular pipe around which a mould closes. Air is blown into the top so that the melted plastic expands to fit the mould's shape resulting in a bottle which as seen in Figure 8 still has ridged 'wings' of surplus attached at each shoulder and the base.

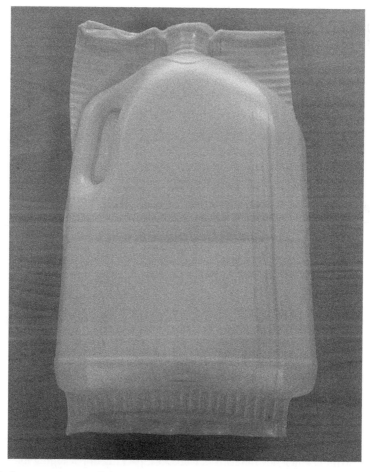

Figure 8 Stage in rHDPE milk bottle manufacture.

The surplus is automatically very precisely sliced off, re-ground and returned to an earlier stage as feedstock to form further parisons.

A line of continuously produced bottles snakes its way round the factory, to be warehoused or moved straight towards the dairy. Visitors are shown round the ground floor, past machines safely behind glass partitions manufacturing bottles at a speed so fast that the lasting impression is of no more than a blur of movement. They detour one floor up to the store to see packs of 160 watery greenish-grey semi-translucent bottles neatly packed upright alongside one another in perfectly fitting giant plastic bags, a pair piled one on another on a pallet – their stillness in marked contrast to the speed of their manufacture on the floor below.

Access to the dairy is controlled, but visitors may see its work through large picture windows along a broad corridor on an upper floor on A.L.'s side of the building. From here they can see down on A.R.'s eight filling lines supplied with pristine bottles that have moved continuously along that snaking line which runs right through the wall dividing the two companies. The visitors' guide explains that just a short distance after the line has arrived on A.R.'s side of the wall is the exact point at which ownership of the bottles is formally transferred from manufacturer to dairy – the precise point when the sale of bottles is effected.

Perhaps the most visually captivating part of a visit is to look down through those picture windows on to an area where the cages of filled bottles are housed. Here they are organized according to the orders A.R. receives from retailers and the correct consignments moved to the despatch bays. The whole space is chilled, essentially a fridge, whose dull yellow floor is marked by dark streaks where wheels have moved over them, tracing journeys round corners and in parallel lines where row upon row of cages are waiting to be moved along. Visitors looking down readily spot splashes of colour provided by the variously coloured capped bottles – blue for whole milk, red for skimmed, green for semi-skimmed.[14] The caps contrast with over 70 robots, painted the yellow of a hi-viz vest, which ceaselessly manoeuvre cages into position creating the wheel-streaks on the floor, obediently fulfilling orders to be loaded onto delivery lorries waiting outside.

****

How does the plastic milk bottle, that major feature of the current packaging landscape, come to be as it is now? A.L.'s processes illustrate one set of answers, converting a mix of rHDPE and some virgin HDPE pellets into bottles using a set of procedures whose principles glass blowers established many centuries ago. Certainly the machinery, computer controlled systems, the design of the factory, rest on decades of engineering, polymer science and technology and very much more. But what links glass bottle and plastic bottle making is blow moulding. A process developed in the glass-making industry in the nineteenth century, it recurs as 'extrusion blow moulding' in plastic bottle making.[15] Notable too is the simplicity of constructing two factories cheek by jowl effecting a striking efficiency in terms of transport, packing of packaging materials and, perhaps, land use too. It is an efficiency evident in accounts of packaging manufacture established in the United States whose huge distances prompted moving package-making and filling as close together as possible.[16]

****

Interlude part 3 – milk in laminated cartons

'Tetra Pak machines are available in the following sizes' – cut to images illustrating each of the six. This statement concludes a 1950s promotional film from the Tetra Pak archives.[17] Only on reaching the film's end is the viewer thus reminded that it must have been aimed at customers inside the industry to whom Tetra Pak sought to sell its tetrahedron shaped milk carton. The previous fifteen minutes or so began by listing the drawbacks even of glass milk bottles which were more hygienic than ladling milk from an open churn into a jug. None the less, the film goes on, as a 'return container' it still inconveniently needed rinsing and carrying back to the store. The film points out further disadvantages of glass bottles for the retailer which is to serve 'as a clearing-house for bottles, with concomitant inconvenience, deposit losses, and loss of valuable stock space'.

The first machine for producing Tetra Pak's 1 decilitre tetrahedron carton for cream began operations in 1952 in Sweden at the Lund Dairy Association and by 1957 the first 1 litre machine was installed in Linköping (Leander 1995). Yet the company's founder, Ruben Rausing (1895–1983) is recorded far earlier as having a question never far from his mind:

> (H)ow were 'loose'[18] milk and the glass bottles to be replaced? How could a sufficiently cheap and generally satisfactory package be created for such a vital daily food, with such small profit margins and special hygienic requirements?
>
> (Leander 1995: 20)

What happened between Rausing's quest for replacing glass bottles already in established use by the 1930s and the 1950s film promoting an innovative shaped pack with its own trade name? This third Interlude presents a sketch of how it came about.

Like the transition from wood to metal barrels for Guinness, the source for the relevant details is another 'insider history'. Unlike the Guinness document, however, this is a published book – one that is the size and weight of a substantial, amply illustrated, well-produced 'coffee table' book. Also unlike the Guinness document, it is very clear about why and for whom it is written. Beginning with its very subtitle – 'a company history with a difference' – a first Preface, above the signatures (dated 1995) of two of Rausing's sons, declares that 'this is neither a biography nor a conventional company history'. Instead of inviting a historian or other 'expert from the outside' they opted to have 'the narrative told from the inside, allowing the company to address the reader directly … through the medium of its own employees' (1995: 7). Those employees are also the intended readers: '(W)e hope that all staff in the Tetra Laval Group will find it absorbing and worthwhile: they are its main addressees'. Such points are taken up in his own, a second, preface by the author, Lars Leander, who, having spent decades as Tetra Pak's Marketing Manager, was, by then, Senior Vice President of Tetra Laval. Acknowledging the unusual entrepreneurial dynamism first of Ruben Rausing and then his descendants in running the company, Leander none the less points out that the book was 'never intended to be a family biography; rather it was conceived as an unconventional narrative chronicling the birth, and the unique evolution, of a company' (1995: 9). Along with the family were 'always pioneers and co-workers whose efforts were crucial to the success of the company'. They and their successors in 'the new Tetra Laval Group today' are the people intended to 'read these lines' – but, he concludes 'we would be glad if "outsider" readers were to find a certain measure of enjoyment in perusing the volume, too. One of our ambitions has been to tell the story of Tetra Pak in a different way: after all, Tetra Pak *is* a company with a difference' (1995: 11).

Leander, unsurprisingly, starts his book with the early years of Ruben Rausing himself. By the end of the First World War, and in receipt of a scholarship, the twenty-four-year-old Rausing went to the United States taking a course of 'advanced study' at Columbia University. One way and another, Rausing continued to look to the United States even after that first trip in 1919–20, not just at the economic theories newly evolving there, but also to study American 'big industry'. By 1933 he was sole owner of Åkerlund & Rausing (A&R) a company geared to building up a packaging industry 'where innovative forces prevailed from the outset', devoted to 'replacing unpacked and unwrapped goods by selling packaged foods designed for customer convenience – flour, sugar, salt, maybe even milk one day'. Rausing instructed one of his employees who was on the point of setting off for a trip to the United States to 'bring samples of milk cartons manufactured in that country' (1995: 18).

Even before the US first patent was granted in 1915 to John Van Wormer of Toledo, Ohio, the earliest record 'of paper being used to carry liquids on a commercial scale are found in reports, dated 1908, of a Dr Winslow of Seattle. He remarked on paper milk containers which were invented and sold in San Francisco and Los Angeles by a G. W. Maxwell as early as 1906' (Robertson 2002: 46). Coated inside and out in paraffin wax to render the paper moisture-proof, the pack was not always tight and even if effective, the adhesive risked tainting or contamination the contents. Van Wormer's patent was for 'a "paper bottle" (actually a folded blank box) for milk that he called *Pure-Pak*'. His patent includes diagrams showing that the bottle started life as a flat 'piece of paper or other suitable material and capable of being fabricated by hand or machinery … in such a manner that when its closure is opened a sanitary spout is formed from which the contents can be conveniently poured'.[19] As Robertson observes, '(T)he crucial and unique feature was that this box would be delivered flat to be folded, glued, filled, and sealed at the dairy. This offered significant savings in delivery and storage compared to preformed glass bottles' (2002: 46). He goes on to explain that the First World War shortage of tinplate for making cans spurred an increase in the use of paper for packaging foodstuffs, including soft cheeses and drinks, an increase that continued after 1918 with new companies starting up.

The advantages of paper over glass were readily listed. Not only was fabricating the bottle in the hands of the dairies, to whom the blanks were delivered flat, making storage and transport far easier and cheaper – using paper eliminated the need to collect empty bottles, return them to the dairy for inspection, washing and sterilizing. It also "'does away with bulk, weight, breakage, and waste, and effects a tremendous reduction in bottling costs'" (Robertson 2002: 47). Dairies were reluctant to make the change, partly because customers liked the glass bottles to which they had become accustomed. Robertson found the results of a survey published in a 1935 issue of *Fortune* magazine; 88 per cent of the 3,000 interviewees answered they would prefer their milk delivered in 'a glass bottle rather than paper container or tin can'. But dairies also preferred glass 'because they effectively created a monopoly where they established their collection system' (2002: 48). Yet cartons were far lighter than glass bottles, even after filling. It seemed to be a losing battle, for using paper cartons allowed supplying milk over a larger radius – up to 30 miles more (almost 50 km) from the dairy.

Switching over to cartons in the United States required updating health and weights/measures regulations governing milk containers since at all levels from federal to city and county these had been formulated before cartons were invented. In 1940, for instance, it required redefining 'milk bottle' to include:

A milk company's single serving container which is a prismatic box made of paper and paraffined on the outside and inside, is a 'milk bottle' within the meaning of an ordnance of the City of Chicago.[20]

The samples that were duly brought back from the United States to Å&R may have been attractive, but would not work for not only the paper but also the machinery needed to fabricate cartons was too expensive in Swedish conditions. Rausing's ambition remained. Employees continued to work on the problem, but during the Second World War, military service depleted their number. Leander records that Rausing visited the laboratory in February 1944 and was only half joking when he announced that 'I've just purchased a large number of cows; they're out there waiting to be milked' (Leander 1995: 27). A lab assistant, Erik Wallenberg to whom the milk package work had been delegated, had pondered on a selection of conventional shapes – square, rectangular, etc. – and then focused on a cylinder. 'What if the lid of a cylinder were to be replaced by a compressed, sealed top? And *what* if the round bottom, too, were scrapped in favour of a seal placed at right angles to the one at the top? The tetrahedron!' declared Leander. Having amended the shape slightly to make it equilateral, Wallenberg took his model upstairs to the office to present his idea to Rausing. Its reception was mixed; as Rausing was to remark later "'This is what you get for hiring people who have no idea how a package is made and what it ought to look like'" (Leander 1995: 27). All the same, the patent was filed in Sweden within a few weeks, on 27 March 1944.

What was then needed was to turn the prototype into a mass-produced effective container for a substance as 'perilous' a product as milk. While Å&R had sound expertise in packaging foodstuffs, its experience of packaging liquids had remained at experimental level. First the type of paper to be used had to be established, then what was to 'liquid-proof' it and how needed to be determined. Furthermore, there was the novel question of how a tetrahedron of a package was to be fabricated, filled, sealed in an automated continuous process. And, as Leander observes, 'nobody had any conception of what a suitable filling machine might look like' (1995: 28). Time and again over the next few years, the materiality of the various non-human items in the assemblage resisted human attempts to turn them to their advantage.

The work was divided up between teams in the company. Harry Järund had been recruited to the company in 1942 as a 'time and motion study man'. Although by then the company had grown with around 300 employees, he was the first member of staff with training in engineering. Duly attending to the tasks for which he was employed – he was 'technologically inquisitive by nature' – he studied the development work under way on a milk package. On his own initiative, he spent his evenings contemplating the associated engineering design problems, prompting his being asked to devise a transport box or crate for the tetrahedrons. He produced a hexagonal transport basket or crate into which eighteen packages were neatly nested in a specified pattern that minimized movement and thus damage. Yet, a means of mass-producing and filling those packages had still to be invented.

What is noticeable, however, is that for all his understandably triumphalist tone – or perhaps to underscore it – Leander records the struggle required to achieve it, the repeated trial and error. Over five pages, he uses the following expressions to convey the efforts involved:

> The great difficulty …
> … a compromise proposal … never realised
> … the fundamental principle … seemed reasonable, but the remainder of the proposal failed to win support, and it was rejected
> … a new working team was appointed … bringing fresh ideas to bear (on the problem)
> (following the illness and retirement of the key man of the entire project leaving it incomplete) nobody on the team was able to finish it. Uncertainty prevailed …
> … a few days of tension followed …
> one troublesome fact caused the machine designer much concern (there was no material suitable for a trial run)
> nobody was able to put forward an acceptable option
> a time of searching, hoping and suffering disappointment
> nobody had yet been able to attain a harmonious relationship between machine and paper.
>
> (Leander 1995: 40–5)

What some might argue deserves any triumphalism is the mode of filling the tetrahedron that was finally contrived. Backtrack for a moment, to the stage of working out how to mass-produce tetrahedron packs and fill them in a continuous, automated process. Not only must the (presumably pasteurized) milk not come into contact with any source of re-contamination but its tendency to foam when poured had to be counteracted in order to be sure that the identical volume of milk went into each pack. Rausing himself – or perhaps his wife – provided the ingenious solution – clearly demonstrated in the film. Leander reports his telling them:

> One day at home over lunch, I discussed the matter with my wife. Suddenly she said 'Why don't you add milk to the tube in a continuous process … sealing the packages right through the milk?' I replied that it would be a superb idea, if only it could be applied. It would result in completely filled packages, without oxygen which has a deleterious effect on milk. But it would seem impossible, as the hot clamps used for the heat-sealing would give the milk a burnt taste. All she said was, 'Have you tried it?' – That was a typical, logical reply from this remarkable woman. I returned to my office after lunch and had a cylinder made in the laboratory, filled it with milk, and separated a number of tetrahedrons with the aid of heat-sealing clamps. Some of us tasted the milk, and we were unable to detect even the faintest burnt taste.
>
> (Leander 1995: 40–1)

****

It is difficult to identify all the assemblages involved in moving from the initial inspiration of a package in the shape of a tetrahedron to the eventual appearance on the market of the first small, decilitre pack of cream. This is partly because unlike the Guinness document which remains close to the succession of attempts to perfect a metal barrel – also to the dramatis personae involved – Leander's book is written for a different purpose and far larger, more varied audience. So the detail is missing – clear listings of which group of employees were working on one or other aspect are not provided – and in any case the whole project is far more complex involving not just constructing the container but also the machinery for its continuous manufacture integral to the process of filling. So there are many more assemblages for the Tetra Pak case compared to Guinness, there are also many more human and non-human elements. What does come over clearly, however, is the interplay between people and things in that collection of assemblages, repeatedly requiring people's attention to circumvent materials' resistance.

Milk and its containers straddle pre-industrial and industrialized packaging. Glass, plastic and cartons continue to co-exist, despite the development of each as in part, a reaction to the limitations of its predecessor. As a food package still widely used, glass also co-exists with its supremely successful successor, the metal can – taken up in the next chapter.

Notes

1. Such a rough working definition is based on contemporary 'Western' packaging. Foods that are pickled and packed under vinegar or brine are obviously different, even if the liquid pours like wine the foods themselves are solid and behave accordingly.

2. But see Shaw, L. (2013). 'World's first square wine bottle released'. *The Drinks Business.* 17 October. Available online: https://www.thedrinksbusiness.com/2013/10/worlds-first-square-wine-bottle-released/ (accessed 6 April 2023).

3. Recycled glass with typical contaminants such as paper, plastic metal, etc. removed, then processed into smaller, different grades of near enough uniform pieces.

4. A ten-arm owens automatic bottle machine, *c.*1913, photo by Lewis Hine. Available online: https://en.wikipedia.org/wiki/Michael_Joseph_Owens (accessed 6 April 2023).

5. Modern reanalysis of some of the experiments has raised doubt about the scientific adequacy of the conclusion suggesting that the broader context of considerable milk surplus in which they were conducted may be relevant (Petty 1987a, 1987b).

6. Boyd Orr himself had a farm by Brechin, in north eastern Scotland, on which at least at some point in the 1940s he kept cattle. While he would likely have agreed that his own circumstances as farmer were a-typical, he would still have had some insight into farmers' viewpoints.

7. A public health physician who became England's first Chief Medical Officer of Health.

8. These by no means exhaust the variety used. In Finland, for instance a plastic pouch of milk was sold with the correct-sized jug into which to decant it. Image available online: http://suokatu14.blogspot.com/2010/08/maitopussi.html (accessed 6 April 2023).

9. Davison, P. (2019). 'Stewart Adams, British pharmacist who helped create ibuprofen, dies at 95'. 5 February. *The Washington Post.* Available online: https://www.washingtonpost.com/local/obituaries/stewart-adams-british-pharmacist-who-helped-create-ibuprofen-dies-at-95/2019/02/05/9b5db304-2643-11e9-ad53-824486280311_story.html (accessed 6 April 2023).

10. Anon (nd). 'A quick history of home milk delivery in America'. *Drink Milk in Glass Bottles.* Available online: https://www.drinkmilkinglassbottles.com/a-quick-history-home-milk-delivery/#:~:text=In%201878%2C%20the%20first%20glass,a%20year%20later%2C%20in%201879 (accessed 6 April 2023).

11. Lester, G.H. (1878). Improvement in milk jars and cans Patent: US199837A Patent. Available online: https://patents.google.com/patent/US199837A/en (accessed 6 April 2023).

12. His patent also deals with arrangements for secure and hygienic stoppering.

13. Both companies' initials are fictitious.

14. The codes are quite different in the United States, where red signals whole milk, for instance. In New Zealand the colours as well as colloquial classification are different again: Red: Cream; Dark Blue: Full Cream Milk; Light Blue: Semi-Trim; Light Green: Trim/skim milk; Yellow: Calcium enriched (Hugh Campbell kindly provided this information).

15. British Plastics Federation (nd). 'Extrusion Blow Moulding'. Available online: https://www.bpf.co.uk/plastipedia/processes/Extrusion_Blow_Moulding.aspx (accessed 6 April 2023).

16. The efficiencies of locating factories producing an ingredient or specific package close to a food product manufacturing plant is a recurrent theme in discussions about the industrialization of food production and packaging. Goldenberg refers to the realization that an egg-packing plant producing ingredients for M&S' cakes so near to the bakery, rendered preservation by freezing unnecessary, replaced by more efficient chilling and transfer by refrigerated tanker, insulated churn or pipeline (1989: 81).

17. Tetra Pak® (nd). 'From the Tetra Pak® archive: The first Tetra Pak film (1950s)'. Available online: https://www.youtube.com/watch?v=rQI9hZf6m6w. See also Tetra Pak® (nd) Full Plant Solutions from Tetra Pak®. Available online: https://www.youtube.com/watch?v=o0zWSBcZa7w (accessed 6 April 2023).

18. Milk dispensed with a ladle or cup directly from a churn.

19. Van Wormer, J. R. (1915). 'Folded-blank box' patent US1157462A. Available online: https://patents.google.com/patent/US1157462A/en (accessed 6 April 2023).

20. Anon (1940). 'Selling milk in paper boxes'. *The National Corporation Reporter*. 27 December. Available online: https://heinonline.org/HOL/LandingPage?handle=hein.journals/natcorpre p101&div=29&id=&page= (accessed 6 April 2023).

CHAPTER 6
CANISTERS, CANS AND CANNING

A lyrical account of a tin canister's later-life arrived in an email.[1] The tin's discovery was unexpected and its location even more so, fuelling an imaginative account of its journey. Its original contents are unknown, for its battered appearance has lost any description of its first use. This is how the account runs:

> The place I described to you was in the Tang Valley. Aesthetically it is spectacular, and the 'manor house' as they call it and the villages around it, are a brilliant example of (not quite) bygone feudal life in eastern Bhutan ... Various elements have come together for the production of this place. The manor itself is built around a Tibetan Buddhist temple which ties the area to the Nyingmapa Buddhism school. The house could have been constructed in the 15th century. It was refurbished, as many houses are in the earthquake prone Himalayas, in the late 19th century. These days it is marketed as Bhutan's only 'private museum'. It is only accessible along a dirt road and 4x4 cars are often required during the monsoons.
>
> It was my second visit to the museum and I spent it leisurely, walking up the three stories. The outside walls, painted lime white, were a stark contrast to the earth hues which clung to the dusty walls of the rooms. Typical of other Himalayan houses, there were very few openings in the outer walls, ensuring heat regulation throughout the year ... this made for semi-lit rooms ... As I walked through broken chain mail, brass drinking vessels and swords thrown in untidy heaps in ornate cabinets, I noticed a curious box. It was tucked between a lump of Tibetan salt and a hairbrush made of shell. While the writing on it was mostly gone, it was unmistakably one of those mass-produced European tin boxes which were ubiquitous in many industrial nations in the early years of the 20th century. Its contents could have been biscuits, marzipan or toffees, or even tobacco. Rust was slowly eating the sides, but one could make out the scene painted (printed?) on the lid: blue bunting, some ornately written yellow words, some Rubenesque children. I picked up the box, it was light, almost weightless. I ran my thumb over the hinges of the lid, grainy rust pushed back.
>
> The lands, I thought, that this box had seen, as it was jostled in the saddle bag of a Tibetan horse. A journey that may have begun on a conduit of the tea-horse road, in a ship, possibly on the shores of the Mediterranean. Then on the backs of Bactrian camels somewhere in the hinterlands of Persia, to be transferred to horse traders in the jagged Karakorum mountains. Then the traders would have walked the long arc across the roof of the world, passing through herds of yak, in

the trans-Himalayan dry-lands of Tibet. Finally in Lhasa, a trade would have been made with merchants going south. Another trip in a saddle, but this time crossing through breathless passes of the water towers of Asia, following the sacred rivers that feed half of humanity. Finally, as glaciers turned into the moist emerald forests of the lower hills, it would have passed through an ocean of lilac and white orchids, with lichen hanging ... from rhododendrons older than Christ. At the gates of the manor, the tired merchant would have dumped his load on the ground and been engulfed in the excitement that welcomes stories and artefacts from far-away lands. The box had travelled far ...

Unlike the one sitting quietly in the dim Bhutan museum, canisters tend to lead active, even productive later-lives compared to other forms of food packaging. A toffee tin, (Figure 9), bought around 1950 in Cape Town, was converted to a button store for decades after the contents had been eaten.

It returned with its owner to England later in the 1950s, remaining in continuous use until, on her death, her daughter inherited it, still using it for spare buttons. Tea canisters continue storing tea or are switched to hold biscuits, while little biscuit tins hold embroidery thread. Nowadays, canisters from the nineteenth century onwards are

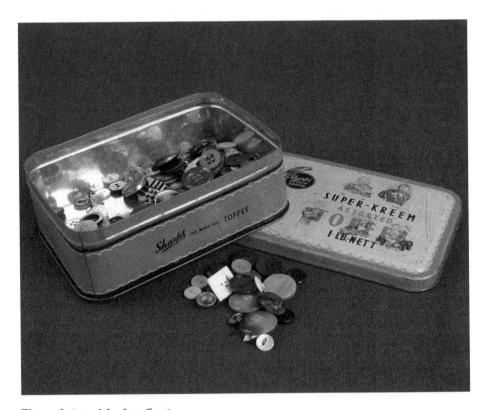

Figure 9 Later-life of a toffee tin.

collectors' items, commonly found for sale on stalls in 'vintage' street markets or on internet auction sites.

Huntley & Palmer, the English biscuit manufacturers, packed their wares in canisters for airtight storage transported to 'distant customers' staying 'oven-fresh and unbroken' in tins deliberately designed to be used for other domestic purposes once empty – no-one can have missed this would repeatedly publicize the company name. That well-travelled tin in the Bhutan museum turns out not to be as unexpected as all that. Not only did Huntley and Palmers serve the 1880s home market, the company 'lost no opportunity to expand into overseas markets. Their biscuits and tins appeared in the Royal courts of Europe, followed explorers like Stanley into Africa and were used for purposes as varied as keeping cremated ashes, valuables and as ballot boxes'.[2]

Canisters and cans mark the early industrialization of food packaging. While canisters became by the end of the nineteenth century more decorated than their initial incarnation, it is the tin can which contains far more varied foods, manufactured in far great quantities and, arguably associated with much more significant positive consequences for many more people's diets than ever has a canister. All the same, canisters and cans have an affinity in that both are (at first) made of tinplate – Huntley & Palmer are credited as the first to make dedicated use of tin for packaging.[3] What everyday name to give them was not, initially, stable. An 'insider history' notes, shortly after the first American patent on the tin container was granted to Thomas Kensett and Ezra Dagget in 1825, 'American bookkeepers began to abbreviate "canister" to "can"' (NCA 1963: 6) while the abbreviation which survived 'tin can' in the UK was 'tin' – and correspondingly the expressions 'canned' or 'tinned' meat, fruit or beans are now commonplace in the United States and UK, respectively.

What they also have in common is that despite cans being water-tight and canisters not, both are sufficiently stout to be air-tight and, even a canister is reasonably moisture proof. 'The great advantage of a tin is that it will keep air out and moisture either in or out, as may be desired for considerable periods' (Reader 1976: 6). But canisters differ from cans in that the latter are containers into which food is packed and then completely removed as needed, while whatever remains in the canister stays protected, unaffected by some contents being used. By contrast, canned food is processed – 'sterilized by heat in airtight containers' (NCA 1963: 13) and thereby preserved in the can itself, storable intact for years. Any food that is not removed once the can is opened will spoil fairly rapidly. In other words, the very procedures of canning have to be considered as part and parcel of the manufacture and use of a can in just the same way that preserving '*titi*' in *pōhā* is integral to the human exploitation of the kelp. On the face of it, making a canister is the simpler.

Canisters – and how to make them

The origins of canister making have faint echoes of grocers' wrapping their wares themselves, customer by customer. At first, the tin boxes were 'easily made with very little skill from easily worked material – tinplate – using hand tools or machinery of the simplest kind which need not necessarily be power-operated'. All that was required was somewhere to work, a suitable stock of 'tinplate, shears, solder and a soldering iron' (Reader 1976: 8). Companies with goods to be packed in canister turned to make their own as wanted – a practice which was widespread in the later Victorian period. It was not just comparatively easy, it brought with it the advantage of not paying for buying in completed – but empty – tins from a specialist maker, i.e. transporting air. It seemed to be a matter of no greater difficulty than deciding on the dimensions of the finished canister, folding and cutting the tinplate accordingly, soldering the seams and perhaps turning over any sharp edges for users' safety.

Huntley & Palmers, for instance, originated in a small shop opened in 1822 by Joseph Huntley who baked biscuits in a small shop on the London to Bath Road in Reading. His shop was not far from the Crown, a coaching inn where travellers between those two cities would stop and to whom Huntley sold his biscuits from a basket.[4] Those biscuits became sufficiently popular for Huntley to realize there was an untapped market further afield. But, as is well known, a biscuit left exposed to the air quickly goes soft and stale. Selling locally from a basket would no longer serve. Coincidentally or no, Joseph Junior, Huntley's younger son, ran an ironmongery in London Street over the road from his father's bakery. There he began making tin canisters – the origin of Huntley, Boorne and Stevens.

Simple as the manufacture of early canisters may have been, does not mean it could not be improved. Filed in 1891 by Samuel Beaven Stevens of that new company, a patent proposed a better 'method of closing tin boxes canister or receptacles which are used for packing biscuits cakes or other goods or articles which require to be preserved from access of air'.[5] He declares that his 'improvements will be found most useful' in regard to 'decorated tins or canisters of an irregular or ornamental shape', fancy canisters for which Huntley & Palmers were, by then, famous. The patent describes the technical detail, emphasizing that the amendment needed only thumb and finger (no 'tin opener or other instrument' required) to open it. And since the materials of which the improved lid is made are soft, never mind remaining attached to the box, they 'will not cut or injure the hand in removing the contents'. By only a few years later, Huntley & Palmers' was the largest biscuit factory in the world.

Simple canisters and their manufacture were not, apparently, that appealing to everyone in the early Victorian period.[6] What made the difference was the development of colour printing allowing attractive and, more to the point, distinctive designs which promoted the company making the biscuits, selling the cocoa or importing the tea. Part of the history of canisters, in particular, is the ingenuity involved in devising methods for giving them labels, by either printing onto a paper label, or coloured images printed directly onto the tin itself. Paper labels were technically easier to apply, but were more susceptible to damage or even complete removal. Large 7lb and then 10lb square tins with a glass lid were later made for retail display. Grocers would weigh out a customer's request from the tin then pack it into a paper bag that went straight into the shopper's basket.[7]

How to make tin cans

Not all metal cans are made of tin or tinplate (tin-coated steel). Indeed more are, apparently, now made of thin steel or aluminium, amounting in 2021 to 'around 12.5 billion cans are used every year in the UK alone.'[8] A decade earlier, the 'total world market for metal containers is estimated at 410 billion units per annum. Of this, drink cans account for 320 billion and processed food cans account for 75 billion' (Page Edwards and May 2011: 107). Mid-century, the canning industry was the US' third largest user of its total steel output (NCA 1963: 11).

Industry insiders are said to regard the first patent for manufacturing a tin can, as that taken out in England in 1810 and sold to John Hall and Bryan Donkin. Their factory produced cans 'made of iron coated with tin, which a good tinsmith could turn out at the rate of 10 cans a day' (NCA 1963: 6). Very early tin cans were particularly heavy: one calculation putting it at upwards of 8lbs (approximately 4 kg) (Howard 1949). An empty can at the time of writing can weigh 50g (less than 2 oz), successfully 'light-weighted' while retaining the necessary strength by beading, the concentric rings ridged round the middle of the can.

In principle a can's construction is simple. Shape a piece of tinplate into an oblong, measuring the shorter sides as the height wanted for the finished article. Curl it round a mould to form a cylinder. Then cut out a pair of circles whose circumference is the same length as the oblong's pair of longer sides. Fit one of the circles to the base of the cylinder, make a hole in the other to allow filling with the food, fit it to the top and close it ready for processing. Those discs could be made that much larger, allowing the creation of a flange all around so that the edges overlapped while the cylinder could similarly be cut larger to be soldered together forming a seam down the side (Howard 1949).

At this stage, a smaller hole is made in the top that steam may escape during heating. Solder is used to seam the cylinder, fix the discs top and bottom and eventually close the holes. One of Donkin's 1812 cans is held in The Science Museum, London – the website image clearly shows the soldered holes at the top and the vertical seam.[9] This one is topped by a loop which, presumably, makes manoeuvring it in and out of boiling water that much easier and safer. In addition to the introduction of steel, later aluminium, the design, etc. of cans has altered over the last two centuries (Geueke 2016). Their construction now includes two piece – typically aluminium drinks cans – as well as older three piece design. Any number of illustrations can be found online to see how details vary between them. Metal packaging has more recently departed from the long established 'can' shape to be formed into 'bottle cans' with a removable screw top lid and seamless body (Page, Edwards and May 2011: 109).

At this point, the chapter steps away from focus on the can to consider the process of canning foods. Preserving foodstuffs entails grappling with the biological certainty of their very materiality primarily in the tendency to relatively rapid decay beyond safe edibility. But the step away is only small, for the process of canning cannot happen without the can or its equivalent. The Interlude to follow concentrates on how that process came about and in particular the identities of the dramatic personae involved.

****

Interlude: the invention of canning

Time and again, histories of the ubiquitous tin can begin with the Frenchman, Nicolas Appert (1749–1841) and his inventions (Shepherd 2000). Long established too is the view that he is the 'founding father' of food canning, for instance: '(I)t was undoubtedly Nicholas Appert working quietly in his little house at Massy (Seine et Oise) during the troubled years at the end of the eighteenth century who laid the foundations of our modern canning industry' (Drummond and Lewis 1939: 9). Parallel histories of the process of preserving food in airtight containers may also begin with him. Jean-Paul Barbier cannot praise him highly enough – describing him as 'a merchant under Louis XVI, a revolutionary in 1789, a scientist under the Empire, but a researcher all his life', adding that he was a 'simple man, above all a disinterested man who chose to give his discovery away rather than patent it' (Barbier 1994). And his home town is proud of him: his biography appears on its website as if written by himself, translated more or less securely into a selection of languages.[10]

Not all agree that Appert should be regarded as founding father. Some argue it depends on the material of which the container is made (Jones 1949), or the method adopted. Others note that he stood on predecessors' shoulders, e.g. Spallanzani, an Italian naturalist (Howard 1949: 1). Apparently taking yet another tack by anticipating mass production, Garcia and Adrian still arrive at the same place. For they grant that 'Appert did not really invent the process' as it was thought 'homemakers could be doing this already'. His 'undeniable talent was to develop a precise, detailed and reliable method on a large scale' (Garcia and Adrian 2009: 118). None the less, these alternatives still opt for a 'founding father' approach to history.

Appert was a confectioner who had accumulated experience of varied responsibilities and occupations in what nowadays would be called the hospitality sector on top of running a wholesale grocery business (Barbier 1994, Summers 2015). His early excursions into methods for conserving foodstuffs were already under way by 1792. By the century's end he was, apparently, aiming to extend his capacity for producing preserved foods, resulting in his seeking to open and equip a factory. For the next decade he succeeded in preserving various foods, a success increasingly widely recognized by several influential authorities especially *La Societé d'Encouragement pour l'Industrie Nationale* (Summers 2015: 117).[11] Appert eventually convinced key authorities of the efficacy of his method of preserving a long list of foodstuffs in glass jars – heavy and breakable – stoppered with a judiciously carved cork to ensure an airtight seal.[12] The committee of *Le Bureau Consultatif des Art et Manufactures* set up by the Minister of the Interior to assess the innovation reported in July 1809.[13] It was very impressed, recommending Appert be awarded 6,000 francs.

Based on the committee's report, the Comte de Montalivet who set up the enquiry offered Appert two alternatives. He could either patent his invention and receive royalties, or he could publish his method at his own expense, provide 200 copies gratis to the *Bureau* and receive 12,000 francs – twice the recommended amount. The monies were in recognition of the social and economic implications of the invention and were to go towards defraying several years' expenses in developing the technique (Summers 2015). Appert elected to publish.

By chance the final sum he received was the same that Napoleon (as head of the army needing to feed troops on the move) had offered in 1795 as a prize for a way of preserving foodstuffs. The coincidence has led several commentators (e.g. Zeide 2018) incorrectly to assume that the prize was awarded to Appert. As Thorne laconically notes: '(T)his was not so. The *ex gratia* payment that Appert received in return for publication of his methods was the common practice of the French Government at the time' (1986: 33).

Publishing precluded his being able to patent his own invention or benefit financially. But Appert readily accepted the arrangement.[14] He noted later that he thought it 'nobler' and more likely 'to serve', proclaiming that he had 'sacrificed everything for humankind for his entire life' (Barbier 1994).[15] Nevertheless, he suffered the consequences, repeatedly very short of funds, eventually so impoverished he was buried in a pauper's grave. Apparently taking only two months to write, *Le Livre de Tous Les Ménages, ou L'art de conserver pendant plusieurs années toutes les substances animales et végétales* was published in Paris in 1810.[16] The initial print run was 6,000, selling rapidly from the outset; 4,500 copies were bought in four months (Barbier 1994: 128).

It is against this background that the discussion moves to consider another version of this book's question 'how did it get this way?' It concerns the manner in which Appert's invention, published in detail in France, came to be patented and successfully commercialized across the Channel, in England. The nub of the case emerges when realizing that Appert published his book – in French – in Paris in 1810 on or after 19 April,[17] while the patent[18] granted to Peter Durand – in English – in London is dated 30 August of the *same* year.

The speed is startling. After all, this was a period when the journey between Paris and London took at least two days, when translation would have taken its own time working in longhand, when type had to be set by hand, all undertaken during the turbulence of the Napoleonic wars when travel between the two countries could be perilous. Moreover, the wording of the patent is virtually identical to Appert's method. This led many, such as Bee Wilson in her popular history of cooking/eating if not explicitly to speculate (providing no source) about theft, at least to describe the rapidity as 'suspiciously' quick (2012: 291). Stuart Thorne is more forthcoming. He assumes that it is a case of plagiarism. He declares that the 'foreigner residing abroad' to whom Durand refers as the technology's source coupled with the fact of the near identical text 'must be assumed' to be 'Appert himself'. Although Thorne asks whether Appert authorized or even knew about Durand's patent, he relies only on the fact that Appert did not patent it himself instead opting to publicize his invention widely, stating that

> (I)t seems very unlikely that he would have condoned the grant of this patent and the inescapable conclusion is that Durand's patent was a straightforward act of plagiarism, taking advantage of the war between Britain and France.
>
> (1986: 37)

Once it had been granted, Durand then sold the patent to Bryan Donkin, an engineer who already owned the Dartford Iron Works near London. And it is Donkin who in 1813 opened a 'preservatory', a canning factory, in Blue Anchor Road, Bermondsey, in south London.[19]

Suspicion is one thing, but those of that opinion do not explain how any industrial espionage was accomplished, apparently neglecting to seek substantiation of their position. There is now, however, convincing evidence that Durand did not steal Appert's method. Based on archival work in London (especially in the Royal Society) for his 1994 PhD, Norman Cowell identified a third person, Phillippe de Girard. He reports circumstantial evidence that Appert and Girard were in contact. As Summers observes of Girard, this 'enterprising Frenchman … managed to cross the Channel to England, in spite of the naval blockade', taking news of Appert's increasingly well-known book with him (Summers 2015). Far from stealing the method, Cowell has established that when patenting it, Durand was acting as an agent on Girard's behalf, thereby serving as the latter's 'mouthpiece' in facilitating it.

Furthermore, it seems that Appert knew very well about Girard's trip. Barbier finds in the *Archives Nationales* a record of Appert's irritation. What displeased him had nothing to do with news of the invention's being spread – after all the work's publication was widely promoted in newspapers and word continued to spread among scientists for many months after first publication. What irked Appert was the theft of his status as inventor, writing that 'a Frenchman, M. Girard, a lamp manufacturer, having acquired my writings, went to England where he had the effrontery to call himself inventor of the process' (Barbier: 128). Some, however, suggest that, given Anglo/French hostility, it was wiser to take out a patent in an English rather than French name where its invention appears as if Durand's. Even so, Cowell's work in archives in London appears to corroborate that of Barbier's in archives in Paris.

The patent is not wholly identical to Appert's own account of the method which only used glass containers. It differs in one respect; the patent provides for alternatives: 'vessels of glass, pottery, tin, or other metals or fit materials' (Bitting 1937: 24). It is worth noting, though, that visiting England some years later, Appert was much struck by the superior quality of tin readily available in England but unobtainable back home. Perhaps this was one of the reasons for his persisting with the use of glass, despite its drawbacks. At this period, just two small areas, one in South Wales and the other in The Midlands in England, had achieved superiority over other nations' tinplate manufacture – an early stage in an almost century long world domination in its production (Pollard 1959).

Summarizing the upshot of his work, Cowell proposed that Durand could no longer 'be seen as a naked opportunist pirating Appert's invention: instead he appears as a London agent facilitating the exploitation by Girard (and probably Appert) of their inventions in the more technologically advanced world of British industry' (Cowell: 363).

First commercialized in England, canning spread rapidly and by the early twentieth century, the American industry was held to lead the world.[20] So said Arthur L. Judge ('of the canning trade') who edited the 'Souvenir of the 7th Annual Convention of the National Canners' and Allied Associations' held in 1914. It is a substantial booklet 'consisting of original articles and statistical data, illustrating the practical developments of the various branches of the canning industry and showing the present magnitude of the business' (Judge 1914:5). Judge's Preface observes that it was 'singularly appropriate' that the 1914 meeting should be held approximately a century after Appert's work was published in Baltimore, a city 'that has long been known as the "mother of the canning industry"'. The emergence of a domestic tinplate industry is likely to have played a major part in the spread of canning. For it was only in the 1890s that the United States was producing enough, suitable quality, tinplate to be able to stop importing it from Wales.[21]

Although modifications have been made to the technical specifications of the can since then,[22] the technology remains essentially the same as that described by Appert over 200 years ago. Those who are inclined to accord Appert the credit for that technology's invention should, however, look further afield to evade their ethnocentrism. The large-scale industrialized production of soy sauce satisfying a huge demand in late seventeenth-century Japanese cities also supported an export market – as documented in Dutch East India Company records held in The Hague. Among them is commentary by Carl Thunberg, one of the Company's ship's doctors who described the production method. They 'bottle soy sauce in ceramic containers after boiling in an iron-pot, stoppered then sealed with pitch' thus preventing spoilage and discoloration on the voyage. Fukushima laconically comments on Thunberg's records: '(T)his invention preceded the invention of canned foods by Nicholas Appert by 50–100 years' (Fukushima 2004: 10). In any case, anyone tempted to credit Appert with originating canned food needs to read even further, to realize that 'a canning industry of sorts had been established in Holland independently of, and prior to, Appert's work' (Robertson 2013: 188; see also Thorne 1986).

****

Towards universal distribution

Grandiose perhaps, but Appert's claim that his invention would be for the huge betterment of humankind was shrewd: 'My problem is, to preserve all nutritive substances with all their peculiar and constituent qualities ... (to which) I have devoted my fortune and twenty years of labour and meditation ... able to render service to my fellow-citizens and humanity' (Appert 1810). The use of canned foods made the most dramatic difference. In Europe, even the aristocracy let alone the populace at large ate meagrely in winter until, at least the sixteenth century, when trade over larger distances began to increase (Mennell 2022).[23] Being able to eat reasonably well all year round was a major contrast. If, however, there was mixed public reaction once tinned foods were more widely available – effectively, more affordable – it is probably no surprise. Bottles and jars, baskets and boxes, barrels and bags had all been in use for so many generations that they were ordinary and unremarkable. The tin can and canister, the first of the industrialized era, were wholly novel food packages (Petrick 2010). Appert's achievement was, however, no guarantee of the safe preservation of the contents.

Certainly the creation of a canning industry is undeniably associated with major nutritional and social developments – the historian Simone Cinotto compellingly details how this contributed to sustaining and cementing an Italian identity in the United States in which canned Californian tomatoes played a major part (2013). But there were setbacks, largely resulting from poisoning associated with tinned foods. Soon after the Great Exhibition was a scandal of 'putrid naval supplies' as Thorne has it. Whatever failures of cans there might have been in the half-century before then, these latest were widely covered in the British newspapers involving a 'public furore' that became sufficiently prominent to lead to a call to set up a Parliamentary Committee – acceded to in 1852 – to enquire into the matter (Thorne 1986).

In 1906, there were, once more, news reports of the dangers of canned food – illustrating *inter alia* that by then news travelled rapidly across the Atlantic. Suspicion in the UK of the safety of canned meat from America was already established, including claims of its being bulked out with cereals, contained pig bristle or skin, its 'nutritive value' deemed inferior to fresh with small quantities of tin held to leach into the food. Reports of a major canned meat 'scare' were apparently prompted by Theodore Roosevelt's declaring that 'his special investigators had revealed serious problems' (Lyon and Kinney 2013).[24] The safety of tinned foods remained a public concern, for good reason. Not quite a decade later the venerable medical journal, *Archives of Internal Medicine* carried a write-up of a fatality at Stanford University at which canned beans were served (Wilbur and Ophüls 1914: 589). In the event, it transpired that the source of the botulism was not the commercially- but the domestically- canned beans served at the same time. It is possible that the latter were not preserved in metal cans but in glass jars. Nowadays household canners in the UK (and New Zealand) who still do so know the process as bottling, using glass jars, commonly called Kilner jars after the company that manufactures them, with Mason jars in the United States, Agee jars the Australasian equivalent.[25]

Fatalities from microbiologically contaminated tinned foods hit the headlines now and then, despite steady improvements in what has been known (in industry, policy and consumer research circles) as 'consumer acceptance' since at least the 1970s. Nervousness recurred in 1964 during the Aberdeen typhoid outbreak which many in the UK will still recollect – traced to inadequately processed Argentinian corned beef (Smith 2005). Since then, adverse implications for health tend to derive from the cans – or rather their very materials and manufacture. For Anna Zeide the question of trust remains. She observes that one of the distinctive characteristics of food in cans is the opacity of the metal container – one of the factors (along with the unfamiliarity of canning processes) which made canned food a 'tough sell'. The product and 'the process by which it was created were opaque to the average consumer, both literally and metaphorically' (2018).

Extending her discussion of trust she details campaigns mounted in the United States to remove Bisphenol-A (BPS) – an endocrine disruptor – from can linings.[26] She regards '(O)ne of the great barriers' to achieving the transparency that 'consumers' call for 'has been the deep connection between industry and federal regulatory bodies' (2018: 165). Thereby she draws attention to one actor in a relevant assemblage that has barely been mentioned thus far, let alone inspected. The role in food packaging of regulatory bodies in principle and in practice deserves far more detailed scrutiny than has yet been devoted to it, and it can only be pointed to in this book. The next Interlude, however, provides a glimpse of two occasions when regulators succeeded in getting a change in food packaging that benefited everyone.

****

Interlude: removing lead from the manufacture of tin cans

This took place in the UK in the 1970s. At the time, Robert Smithson,[27] a scientist who had completed postdoctoral research before working in industry, had become a senior civil servant in the then Ministry of Agriculture, Fisheries and Food (MAFF). He served in the section of the Ministry with responsibility for monitoring foodstuffs for any dangers posed by heavy metals, which, of course, include lead. In the 1970s lead was contained in the solder used to seam tin cans and was also in the soft, tearable cover of wine bottle corks. A specific task was to establish the source(s) of measurably high blood lead levels in some sections of the population. Air polluted with lead deriving from the addition of lead tetra ethyl as an antiknock to petrol was the target of widespread campaigning (resulting, eventually in the production of lead-free fuel). Yet its inhalation was of insufficient scale to be responsible for the high blood lead levels being reported.

'(B)ut' Robert Smithson observed 'what about all the other sources of lead? Well, we in MAFF began to have a very hard look …. (One) unlikely source was lead from wine.' Preliminary investigations had showed, by chance, that a particular European wine contained '0.3 mg/kilogram of lead, nice soluble lead and very bioavailable'.[28] Further enquiries confirmed that European wineries had 'bronze fittings in them' some of which made from 'leaded bronze which contributed to the lead in wine'. The grape juice itself was ruled out. But '(W)e then started to wonder about the "caps" on the end of wine bottles covering the cork. You'll recall that the coverings had to be gently pulled off in a tearing fashion. You may have noticed from time to time a white deposit under the covering.' 'Well', Robert Smithson paused for effect, 'that was lead acetate'. Some wine can get through the cork 'the alcohol in the wine oxidised to acetic acid, and this dissolved the covering'.

Settling into his story of what looked like worrying news for the wine industry, Smithson described how he

> was invited to a meal at (a smart restaurant) to talk to representatives of the wine industry … The object of the exercise was to persuade me that no action needed to be taken, particularly because a lot of the more expensive wines had been in the bottle for a long time and certainly had lead caps. It could not have gone better. The experts ordered a pricey white wine to start with, the waiter removed the cap prior to removing the cork and I managed to arrest his progress just in time. The top of the bottle under the cap was totally encrusted with a white deposit, lead acetate. I was told not to worry this was just a one-off and most bottles were absolutely fine, there was no hazard to the consumer at all. Bottle number two was a fine red wine. Once again the waiter showed the wine to the experts, removed the lead cap, and … underneath the cap was a pile of white blue deposit, lead acetate.

That ended arguments from the wine trade, the upshot of which is that nowadays the packaging has been changed: 'nearly all bottles either have a screw cap or a plastic covering over the cork'.[29]

As the enlarged search for additional sources of lead in foodstuffs got under way, the focus turned to tin cans as one possibility. Robert Smithson crisply recounted a further instance in which he was involved.

> if you get it right … in a fruit can, provided the oxygen in the headspace is very low to start with, you don't get any lead dissolved. Virtually none. So, in a can of pineapple or grapefruit or oranges (it's alright). However, if you have something like fruit cocktails which has got glacé cherries in it, or anything highly coloured or pears (for various reasons) you do get lead dissolved.

And at the time, tins typically contained a certain amount of lead. For

> (T)he solder on the side seams of tin cans was made of, essentially, lead. As a consequence of this some canned foods had more lead in them than was desirable. We applied pressure, changed the lead limit for canned food and the like. Now cans are welded on the side seam.

'Success', he declared succinctly, 'no lead solder, no lead'.

****

At one point as he told the story, Robert Smithson triumphantly announced 'plus one for consumers'. In addition, his account illustrates some of the depth in the relationship between industry and regulator of which Zeide is suspicious. An expensive restaurant meal, presumably paid for by the company's entertainment budget, was intended to create a convivial occasion at which officials might be persuaded of the worthiness of the industry view. On this occasion the relationship between the two was neatly, if perhaps coincidentally, turned to wine-drinkers' advantage. The obligations that come with accepting a free lunch may result in events going in either party's favour – even if, as in Zeide's sceptical view, the continuing lack of transparency remains a barrier.

Also lingering are familiar aspects of tinned foods' public image as second-class (Bowen 2019). Published in 2020, Lola Milne's *Take One Tin* is designed to rehabilitate the image of tinned foods. She gives her cookery book the subtitle *80 delicious meals from the storecupboard* – each recipe including canned ingredients. She seems to be aiming to rescue tinned foods from humdrum, even negative overtones to something far more cheerily positive. Between them, her introduction and the blurb on the back cover, shrewdly mirror tinned food's public image, working hard to deflect any lingering ambivalence that it is for those with little culinary imagination or less skill, only used by the impecunious or stingy. Almost defiantly, she declares that the tin is indeed 'humble and always found in the storecupboard' but it is also 'cheap, nutritious and long lasting'. Her book 'showcases these versatile creatures and gives you all sorts of new ideas on how to use them'. The tin is also 'universal, affordable and accessible'; easily found, on sale everywhere, a sign not of destitution but thrifty provisioning. And while it 'shouldn't be bland or dull', it does not expose anyone to the anxieties of unknown or exotic foods, for it is safely found in 'the comfort of the tinned aisle'. It means that cooking can be 'achievable ... even joyous ... and doesn't always need to be about fresh or expensive ingredients' (Milne 2020: 6–7). It is hard not to read those last remarks as a rebuke to 'foodies' (Bauman and Bauman 2015) while the blurb on the book's back appeals to an even wider market; not only is it '(Q)uick, easy' it is also 'environmentally friendly'. It is noticeable that neither introduction nor blurb use the word 'convenient'.

Negative and positive popular images of tinned foods co-exist. TV chefs (such as Nigel Slater or Yotam Ottolenghi in the UK) do not avoid but adopt them as shortcuts for items such as legumes which need lengthy preparation. Delia Smith, one of their TV predecessors, first published *How to Cheat at Cooking* in 1971. She used the same title in 2018 for another around the same time Jamie Oliver, far younger TV star also recommends a wide range of short cuts including using commercially prepared items. Both have come in for criticism, both defend themselves robustly echoing the positive images conveyed in Lola Milne's canned food book.

So, as the earliest of industrialized food packages, the tin can was also the first to attract both favourable and unfavourable public images to any extent. But in blazing a trail, the use of tins' capacity for preserving foods available year round is socially significant. And it both represents and is integral to a set of consequences in social relationships, among other themes pursued in the next three chapters that make up Part III.

Notes

1. It came from Rhitodi Chakraborty, who kindly gave permission to quote him.
2. Huntley & Palmer archive, HP185.

3. 'Taking the biscuit' by June Field, *Financial Times* Saturday 6 October 1979 H&P archive number HP 185.

4. George Palmer joined the company in 1841 when all the biscuits were still made in the back room of the London Street shop.

5. The typed copy in the archive carries the handwritten note that it is a 'Copy of Provisional Specification' that was filed, No. 8229 dated 13 May 1891. H&P archive number HP 680.

6. But Edward C. Barlow and Sons, 'one of the most successful in the industry' was set up in Hackney 1869, which became absorbed into Metal Box in the 1930s (Reader 1976: 8, 51).

7. Such arrangements continued well into the 1960s. Knowledgeable customers would ask for a bag of broken biscuits from those which tended to accumulate at the bottom of a nearly emptied tin.

8. Garside-Wight, G. (2015). 'History of the world in 52 packs: tin cans'. *Packaging News*. 13 August. Available online: https://www.packagingnews.co.uk/features/comment/soapbox/history-of-the-world-in-52-packs-part-4-tin-cans-13-08-2015 (accessed 6 April 2023).

9. Tin can used for the early preservation of food, Bryan Donkin and Co., London, England, 1812. Available online: https://collection.sciencemuseumgroup.org.uk/objects/co8097425/tin-can-used-for-the-early-preservation-of-food-tin-can (accessed 6 April 2023).

10. https://www.chalons-tourisme.com/decouvrir/nos-celebrites/nicolas-appert/ (accessed 29 April 2019).

11. The Society for the Promotion of the Nation's Industry (author's translation).

12. A good seal is critical and at the time difficult to achieve every time: 'so difficult was this that Appert resorted to manufacturing his own corks, laminated with the grain running in alternate directions' (Thorne 1986: 33).

13. The Advisory Office for the Arts and Manufacturing (author's translation).

14. He had been an active and generous participant early in the Revolution, despite being imprisoned for three months during the Terror for being too moderate.

15. (author's translation). 'J'ai tout sacrifié pour l'humanité, tout, ma vie entière', Barbier 1994: 7.

16. The Book for All Households, or The Art of Preserving All Animal and Vegetable Foodstuffs for Several Years (author's translation).

17. Endorsed by Bureau members on that date. https://gallica.bnf.fr/ark:/12148/bpt6k202755q.pdf (accessed 19 April 2019).

18. Facsimile in Bitting 1937: 23–4.

19. The site, now in the grounds of a school, is marked by a small sign high up on a wall http://bermondseyboy.net/viewtopic.php?t=133 (accessed 19 April 2019).

20. William Underwood, a Briton who had acquired some experience in the preservation of food before he left for Boston in 1818, set up first US cannery (Thorne 1986: 42).

21. The United States imported 'over 300,000 tons of tin plate-virtually its entire consumption and nearly three quarters of the Welsh product. Just ten years later America was herself producing nearly 400,000 tons, and the Welsh product had been driven from the domestic market' (Pursell 1962: 267).

22. Such as 'lightweighting'; a latex seal added by a Cryovac inventor; or the adoption of two piece cans.

23. Mennell, Stephen (2022), personal communication.

24. In 1906, the journalist, Upton Sinclair, had published his novel *The Jungle*, exposing the exploitative and punishing conditions in which immigrants worked in the Chicago meat

packing industry and the processing plants' grotesquely insanitary state. Ironically he intended his book to support campaigns for better working conditions, whereas the public reception focused on the scandalously unhygienic food handling.

25. Marion Familton kindly provided this information.

26. This book was on the point of submission when for the first time, the European Food Safety Authority reported that Bisphenol A was a health risk to all age groups. Available online: (accessed 20 April 2023). https://www.foodprocessing.com/food-safety/regulatory-compliance/news/33003716/efsa-says-bisphenol-a-in-food-is-a-health-risk?utm_source=FPRO+eNewsletter&utm_medium=email&utm_campaign=CPS230418074&o_eid=0735J0302267G1E&rdx.ident[pull]=omeda|0735J0302267G1E&oly_enc_id=0735J0302267G1EEFSA

27. A pseudonym.

28. Interview 2020.

29. The problem lingers even after that change, for lead-contaminated wine bottles, once empty, contaminated the ensuing cullet thereafter remaining in the recycling system.

PART III
HOW DID IT GET LIKE THIS?
INDUSTRIALIZED PACKAGING

Part three – introduction

This part of the book consists of three chapters. They tackle the main question posed in this book but from other perspectives. Where the chapters in Part Two started with a type of package which could contain any number of foodstuffs, Part Three's chapters revolve around three familiar 'consumer' packaged foodstuffs. One per chapter, these three are readily found in supermarkets across the world in the third decade of the twenty-first century.

The first is bottled tomato ketchup. This is a preserve of a type prepared in domestic kitchens for several centuries. Henry J. Heinz (1844–1919) and the early period of what became a multi-national company figure prominently in this chapter. There follows a chapter on a cooked item – a 'ready-meal', frozen or chilled. An archetypical instance is lasagne, an oven-baked pasta dish. In this incarnation it is comparatively recent, first put on the UK market in 1973, needing no more than heating and serving. The final chapter deals with raw, bagged salads – lettuces, watercress, spinach, etc. All can be found in clear plastic packed in a 'protective atmosphere'. That too is recent, by comparison with ketchup, though all three are industrialized food products in industrialized packaging.

Each of these three chapters chronologically tackles the question 'how has the relevant packaging landscapes for these three items become as it is now?' Each chapter examines the way precursors of that item were packaged now and at two earlier periods, mid-twentieth century and then a century ago (if, that is, they existed on the retail market at those earlier periods). The aim originally was, in principle, to examine the decision making that is involved, although in the event only occasional glimpses are evident. It will require different and much more detailed research approaches to get closer to those decisions.

In the process, many varying features are shown to be inextricably linked with whatever the package happens to be, the sauce bottle, the plastic tray or clear polypropylene bag, illustrating an additional view of transitions in the industrialization of the food supply. Some of these transitions are very recent – historically speaking, that is. Oblique evidence in advice to Britons during the Second World War about how best to manage under food rationing nods to frugality advising that "'Foods in packages generally cost more than the same food sold loose'" (Ministry of Food 1945: 6). *Inter alia* it illustrates the general position in mid-twentieth-century Britain (and elsewhere) when around half the foodstuffs available on the retail market was sold unpackaged.

This trio of chapters also contains Interludes. These largely self-contained sections briefly illustrate the range and variety of histories of other ideas or artefacts with which some of the packaging discussed is associated. In line with the STS orientation of the book, the emphasis is on the manner in which these other things coincided or co-evolved with innovatory packaging and/or innovatory uses.

Doing so helps counter widespread but misleading interpretations. Comments such as '(C)onsumer packaging *led to* marked changes in marketing and industrial organization in the staple-foods industries' are common (Mehren 1948: 336 emphasis added). So saying may well be a quick shorthand. But attributing to packaging the capacity for causing social change too infrequently gets challenged and risks lapsing into technological determinism.

At times, parts of these three chapters might seem distant from food packaging itself. But as components of answers to the question 'how did the modern food packaging landscape come to look as it does' the distance is less irrelevance and more illustration of the manner in which phenomena are joined together in persisting, complicated, mutually supporting links. The connections may be fragile – supply chains are readily disrupted at points distant from any reduced quantities of deliveries trucked to the supermarket shelves – but they are also components of the modern food systems crucially underpinned by food packaging.

As self-evidently industrialized foods, the manufacture of ketchup, ready-meals and bagged salad have nameable features in common securing their classification as industrialized. These include:

~ the foodstuffs for domestic consumption are produced somewhere other than the home – echoing the separation between home and work, hallmark of the industrial revolution.
~ they are eventually mass produced for a mass market, despite the modest scale of their beginnings.
~ their manufacture centres on increasingly automated assembly line principles.
~ procedures for cleaning, assembling ingredients and processing/cooking the foodstuffs plus those for manufacturing, filling, closing and labelling the package have increasingly merged into a single production line.

This last is an end-point of the logic prevailing since early industrialization, of trying to minimize the distance – and with it the costs of transport – when seeking to keep foodstuffs as fresh as possible between harvesting, processing and packaging. It takes propinquity to its logical conclusion, echoing Chapter 5's two independent companies' factories' occupation of a single building producing bottled milk.

The case of tomato ketchup illustrates the trajectory from kitchen preserve to mass-produced standardized sauce. This takes place over a good many decades but, via Heinz, a single company prominently responsible for this trajectory, can readily be traced. The founder, his view of business and his religious beliefs all play a part in the events that concern historians' accounts of the chronology and contribute to key characteristics of the tomato ketchup bottle. The second case is an item industrially cooked on a production line, far more recently developed from the domestic version than tomato ketchup, so much so it did not yet exist in this form in mid-twentieth century. The third case is of raw salads among other foodstuffs that are preserved in modified atmosphere packaging (MAP), a highly industrialized instance of modern food packaging. This last particularly well represents the manner in which the food package itself is integral – like the tin can – to the technology for foods' preservation. It exemplifies too the manner in which a widespread recent packaging technology is none the less based on several decades of research and development, especially in biochemistry and materials engineering. Further, it opens new lines of enquiry, e.g. seeking the thinking behind regulation governing labelling as well as investigating public response to MAP technology. At present, MAP continues to be ever more extensively used, a transition to something different seemingly not yet on its horizon.

CHAPTER 7
TOMATO KETCHUP AND TRANSPARENT BOTTLES

Tomato ketchup appears to be everywhere:

> The global tomato ketchup market size was valued at USD 20.90 billion in 2021 and is expected to expand at a compound annual growth rate ... of 2.8% from 2022 to 2028.[1]

> Heinz accounts for around 50 per cent of all the ketchup in American kitchens[2]

> Today, practically every home in the UK uses at least one Heinz product every week of the year.

> (Anon 1994)

Indeed, it is nowadays commonplace to walk into a supermarket in many regions of the world and find several shelves of bottles of tomato ketchup and similar sauces.[3] Not only are the sauces similar and not simply occupying a similar place in culinary use (intended, as one UK supermarket puts it, as food dressings)[4] their packages are similar too, no matter which company produced them. For a long while sauces were mostly preserved in rounded clear glass bottles of more or less similar sizes and shape. That the glass is clear not coloured is significant in the history of ketchups and sauces – an initiative, as will be seen, of Henry Heinz' in 1869.[5]

Describing it as a 'glass icon', H. J. Heinz Company's own online history records the introduction in 1948 of the 'octagonal shaped glass bottle now a globally recognized symbol of Heinz'[6] (Figure 10).

More recently PET (expensive but translucent, thus looking much like glass) or polypropylene (cheaper but 'milkier' with reduced transparency) are more widely used. Plastics are lighter and unbreakable, thereby providing savings and efficiency in transport from processing plant, to distribution centre and on to retail/food-service. The switch to plastics made it possible to devise a 'squeezable' bottle more rectangular than round, that stands on a widened plastic cap (Figure 11).

Heinz introduced that plastic ketchup bottle in the 1980s. After three years' work, a Heinz team pioneered it a year and half before competitors. In 2006, Dienstag reported that tomato ketchup in a 28 ounce plastic bottle 'remains the company's biggest seller' (1994: 177). The design of the squeeze package uses the simple device of retaining the bottle shape, but inverting it. Underlining the distinctiveness of the design, Heinz' version can be found online in the UK described as 'Heinz Top Down Squeezy Tomato Ketchup Sauce' (a counterpart in New Zealand is 'Pam's Upside Down

Figure 10 Heinz tomato ketchup visible in clear glass bottle.

Figure 11 Heinz tomato ketchup visible in PET upside-down squeezable bottle.

Tomato Sauce'). The design might plausibly be attributed to the wit of an advertising company charged with devising the new plastic bottle. But Foster and Kennedy explain that the 'upside-down pack' originated 'during visits to consumers' home where Heinz market researchers spotted folks storing ketchup in their refrigerators with the cap down' an innovation so popular that it quickly migrated to the United Kingdom and across Europe' (2006: 110).

This book's question as to how the food packaging landscape looks as it does can be interpreted in this instance in asking about the stages bottles of ketchup go through from the field, to the glass/plastic bottle-making factory thence to arrive on supermarket shelves. The question can be asked historically too – what was it like half a century ago, or a full century ago. Added to this is enquiring when and how ketchup moved from the domestic kitchen (where the annual tomato harvest from the garden was cooked into homemade preserves) to factory production on a mass scale to occupy so ubiquitous a market position today. This chapter pursues such questions by considering just one company, Heinz.

Perhaps it is Heinz tomato ketchup's extensive market penetration which is, on its own, testament to successful marketing. Certainly it takes no time to uncover all kinds of glowing testimonials currently available for Heinz tomato ketchup. Even supermarkets carry them under the heading of 'product description'. An example from France reads:

> Our sun-kissed tomatoes, combined with our passion and know-how, give our recipe such a unique and irresistible taste, Heinz Tomato Ketchup has an inimitable flavour that will delight young and old alike. The recipe for Heinz Tomato Ketchup, created more than a century ago and kept secret ever since, is imbued with its famous taste of tomatoes and spices. Vegetables, meat or fish, Heinz Ketchup complements all your dishes wonderfully. Our bottle is 100% recyclable, disposable plastic cap.[7]

The latter may include more information about the disposal of the package than a UK counterpart but the praise is very similar.[8] Marketing and advertising were two of the prominent business skills at which Henry Heinz excelled, contributing to the way tomato ketchup and its distinctive Heinz bottle have ended up as they are.

From fork to field today[9]

Where what happened in factories was once hidden from most people, another aspect of the secret lives not just of packaging but of packaging's contents is now far more available for viewing on TV.[10] Companies are also taking the opportunity to post videos of the manufacture of their products online. Heinz, describing itself as a market leader 'selling over 650 million bottles around the world every year', posted one showing the operations of one of their tomato ketchup factories in The Netherlands.[11]

Illustrated by the film, tracing the ingredients back to the factory where the ketchup was produced – or even further back to the field where the tomatoes were grown and harvested – is instructive. Starting backwards at the retail end with a labelled bottle of ketchup, it will have arrived by truck in a carton of, say ten or a dozen, one of about perhaps fifty such cartons in a cage or on a pallet packed automatically on a production line. At that final stage a full pallet would have been enfolded several times in stretch-wrap, transparent plastic film holding the consignment in place – replacing rope or similar still in use in the mid-twentieth century. These will have been loaded via forklift truck onto a lorry for delivery either to a regional distribution centre before being trucked to the supermarket or driven straight to the retailer. The cartons are examples of secondary- and the stretch-wrap, tertiary-packaging, most of which is entirely utilitarian – Figure 12 shows plain stretch-wrap part-removed from beer kegs for unloading.

Figure 12 Part-removed, stretch-wrap holding palleted beer kegs in place.

There is commonly minimal or even no colour printing, no eye catching designs, but plain labelling of bar codes and/or reference numbers that record the destination, order numbers, batch, relevant dates, etc. allowing traceability.

The factory producing the consignment may well contain two independent but symbiotic facilities in one building (see Chapter 5), with glass/PET bottles manufactured in one, ketchup in the other. Tomato paste is trucked into the factory in large, plastic lined boxes, while spices and other seasonings are delivered in plastic tubs or plastic bags to be added to it with vinegar, sugar, etc. Most of the ingredients are not secret, listed by law (in the UK in order of the largest down to the smallest proportion) on the label. A bottle of tomato ketchup on sale nowadays in the UK consists of:

(T)omatoes (148g per 100g Tomato Ketchup), spirit vinegar, sugar, salt, spice and herb extracts (contains celery) and spice.

Mixed together, cooked in giant vats, the bottles are filled, capped and labelled automatically. The equipment is large, complex, runs continuously and fast. Nowadays it is managed electronically, with what is happening where along the assembly line displayed on computer terminals. The familiar keystone-shaped self-adhesive labels on the bottles' front can readily be spotted in the film, attached to each bottle as it speeds past a section where the labels are ready, peeled from continuous reels.

In certain respects, then, the lives of some aspects of tomato ketchup packaging are no longer secret. But as with any video or film, intellectual property/commercial sensitivity, and editorial decisions shape what is included/excluded. Notably, for example, Heinz' film does not name the spices added to the ketchup mix in their Dutch factory, merely declaring they are 'secret'. Though ingredients are nowadays published, the exact proportions of each is not. What is explicit and often heavily stressed in such films and videos, however, is the scale of the whole operation. A common, prominent feature emphasizes the speed with which incoming ingredients are turned into the finished product. Similarly, the volume of everything – or so it can seem – is reported: from the size of the factory 'the biggest in Europe', the kilos of ingredients delivered, the rate per minute bottles are filled, to the number of boxes despatched to supermarkets 'all over the country'.

What is far harder to locate is the thinking behind the answers to 'how did it end up like that'. What lay behind the decision to bottle it in clear glass? Who invented the slogan '57 varieties' of which Heinz tomato ketchup is so popular an example? How is it that ketchup nowadays is less likely to be manufactured from raw tomatoes and more like to start with pasteurized tomato paste?

As noted, this chapter concentrates on the case of Heinz doing so for several reasons. One is tomato ketchup's status as 'America's National Condiment' as the culinary historian Andrew Smith puts (1996). Another is that the company's longevity allows the chronology of producing bottled tomato ketchup to be more easily followed. Furthermore, the reputed charisma of its entrepreneurial founder and subsequent success of the company makes a sufficiently good story for several commentators to have turned it into print. As a result, for just one company there are valuable sources.[12]

The case also helps underline Frolich's distinction between the respective focus of history and sociology – the former concerning itself with people and events, the latter with institutions – in a light-touch illustration of how the former may serve as forerunners of the latter. Henry Heinz' entrepreneurial genius for success later became institutionalized in the form of academic and other formalizations of marketing, branding and advertising. It did so not solely from the business success of the man referred to as 'The Founder' but as part of a general movement that accompanied the quickening of industrialization in America. Henry Heinz was not the only massively successful millionaire entrepreneur of his time, quite the reverse. Together with other Pittsburgh 'captains of industry' of the same period – Henry Frick, Andrew Carnegie, Andrew Mellon, George Westinghouse and others producing processed food such as Joseph Campbell – Henry Heinz was part of and contributed to the huge boom period of American industrialization at the end of the nineteenth and well into the twentieth centuries. The histories of the associated development of marketing and advertising represent additional histories with which the history of food packaging is inextricably linked. In the process, Henry Heinz – also Joseph Campbell – was part of the emergence of industrial foods, at the heart of which, making such foods possible, was packaging – Campbell's tomato soup in tin cans, Heinz' tomato ketchup in clear glass bottles.

From fork to field mid-twentieth century

Going back fifty years reveals that tomatoes' route from field to fork, and that of empty glass bottles to be filled, capped and labelled producing bottled ketchup, is not so very different from today's. But go back further to the mid-twentieth century and find that developments Heinz introduced in the 1960s show up how different processing and packaging ketchup was in late 1940s and 1950s. Before discussing those developments, sketching the background to the company's creation and above all illustrating the principles on which Henry Heinz established it helps understand those developments, even though its charismatic founder had died almost thirty years earlier in 1919.

****

Interlude: Henry J. Heinz, his ketchups, the company and his '57 varieties'

More than one commentator on the origins of the company writes of the world into which Henry John Heinz was born – in 1844 in Birmingham, an area now on the south side of Pittsburgh. He was five years old when in 1849 the family moved to the small, more rural community of Sharpsburg – where every household had a garden. In keeping with the customs of German émigrés such as the Heinz family, their garden was his mother's sole responsibility. Sufficiently well tended, it provided a surplus beyond the needs of the household of ten (Alberts 1973: 5).

An early biography (published just four years after his death) records it was a frugal way of life based on agriculture, entailing a necessary self-reliance, adding that work was a universal fact of life. 'Work' explains McCafferty – at one time private secretary to Henry Heinz himself – 'was drudgery or the reverse, according to the spirit with which it was accepted and done' (1923: 18).[13] 'Young Henry Heinz' was not one, he says, to make a drudgery of it, despite his having to begin sharing the family's work at the age of eight – the boy's upbringing was stern as was schooling under the Pastor of the Lutheran Church. Part of that daily effort was working in his mother's kitchen garden. 'When it expanded he sold its spare produce by going through the village with a basket.' At this point, McCafferty fastens on the shifts in the means of transport Henry Heinz used, as a way of signalling his precocity and success. 'When he was ten years old his industrial progress was marked by a wheelbarrow to displace the basket. Two years later his business had assumed the dignity of a horse and wagon' (1923: 18). Stephen Potter's popular history adds a handcart between wheelbarrow and horse-drawn wagon (1959).

As a boy, Henry Heinz had helped his mother harvest and turn home grown horseradish into a preserved relish – then in common use (Alberts 1973). Processing is an unpleasant task of washing, scraping and grating before packing in vinegar – hard on the hands, while the pungency of raw horseradish stings the eyes. Henry Heinz took to bottling horseradish for sale. Unlike the small local trade in pre-prepared horseradish sauce which used brown or green glass bottles, he bottled his in clear glass, selling it to housewives, grocers and hotel kitchens as the 'whitest and best-quality' (Alberts 1973: 7). Part of his sales pitch stressed that the transparent bottles allowed customers to see for themselves before purchasing that there were no unwanted fillers – such as turnip – and that the roots were well grated – without lumps. Sales rose. Alberts – a later biographer – suggests that Henry Heinz learned two lessons:

Housewives are willing to pay someone else to take over a share of their more tedious kitchen work.

A pure article of superior quality will find a ready market through its own intrinsic merit – if it is properly packaged and promoted.

(1973: 7)

Several notions and maxims were important in Henry Heinz' outlook, on life in general and equally in his business philosophy; he did not, it seems, make a clear distinction between the two. One, for instance, was 'prompt pay', described by McCafferty as 'an impulse of his character'. Apparently willing to bear some loss by paying on time which would have been avoided by a small delay, Henry Heinz recognized that paying promptly 'was one of the best business builders'. Maintaining 'spotless credit' was, he apparently said, 'the cheapest kind of good insurance' (McCafferty 1923: 120–1). Thus, sustaining good relations with clients stood him in good stead and contributed to the company's good name and success.

Not keeping creditors waiting was arguably part and parcel of his dedication to maintaining standards, which was fully expressed in his sustained pursuit of quality and championing purity. Another aspect, once his company became established, was not simply providing good facilities for his workforce – lockers, washrooms, uniforms – but also services, notably for those handling and packaging ingredients, manicures at least once a week, more for 'cleanliness and sanitation, rather than vanity' (Foster and Kennedy 2006). Hygiene – especially personal and domestic hygiene – was an increasing focus for 'sanitary scruples' towards the end of the nineteenth century which Henry Heinz incorporated into his commitment to purity in his company's products (Tomes 1998). Fully understanding the returns in terms of loyalty to the company as well as the economic, his treatment of his workforce may be fairly described as paternalistic but it was of a far kinder, humane, and some would argue Christian variety than his contemporaries among other industrialists. Further, his use of clear glass bottles was material expression of his commitment to honest, hygienic dealings with his customers, demonstrating that due care was taken when packaging the wares on sale. His was an object lesson for those selling ginger beer in an opaque stone bottle in early twentieth-century working-class Salford, which concealed the horror of discovering a drowned mouse (Roberts 1990: 119–20). Clear glass provides a contrast with the opacity of cans, which Zeide argues inhibited developing trust in canning. Petrick points out that '(B)y caring for products, talking about the virtues of Heinz pure foods … (these) examples of Heinz's commitment to purity encouraged the public to eat food made in a factory, ultimately relegating … poison(ing) by canned foods to the distant past' (Petrick 2009: 33).

The virtues of glass are extolled over a century later: '(A) glass bottle discharges extremely important functions … a common article of domesticity, an essential component of materials for the packaging industries … (I)t is prominently present in every urban supermarket and village grocery, invitingly displaying its contents to customers' (Meigh 1972: 1). Being able to see the contents is, incidentally, a major asset provided by cellophane as an early clear plastic – illustrated in advertising when newly on the market for the then novel wrapping (Tomes 1998: 34). In 1933 *Added Proof* was published, a pamphlet reporting '*how cellophane assists manufacturers in giving maximum sales value to their packages*'.[14] Hisano argues that the introduction of cellophane as transparent packaging for perishable foodstuffs represented a new way for shoppers for understanding food quality. As soon as foods are packaged, customers can no longer rely on taste, smell or touch to assess the goods on sale. Assessment can only be by sight. The 'new visuality' becomes prominent: as a 1945 advertisement for bread wrapped in DuPont's Cellophane declares that 'Cellophane shows what it protects' (original emphasis Hisano 2017: fig 1). Henry Heinz understood the sentiment in that slogan.

A feature of the world not so much into which he was born but in which he grew up was mounting suspicion of the safety of the expanding range of commercially processed foods on sale. Tinned and other commercially processed foods acquired a bad name through the nineteenth century, with justified wariness later spurred by the revelations of Upton Sinclair's *The Jungle*. Misleading advertising of adulterated foodstuffs had become routine. Henry Heinz alone – with his 'gospel' of purity and integrity – was different. There was nothing to hide.

Henry Heinz' faith did not compete with his entrepreneurship. Several sources tell the story of how, in 1896, he was in New York City travelling on the 3rd Avenue El railway (closed roughly half a century ago) when he spotted an advertisement for shoes, proclaiming "'21 Styles'". He pondered on how many varieties of foodstuffs were already in production (approximately sixty) and decided that fifty-seven had an appeal greater than, say, fifty-eight or fifty-nine. "'I got off the train immediately'" he records "'went down to the lithographers where I designed a street-car card and had it distributed throughout the United States. I myself did not realise how successful a slogan it was going to be'" (Potter 1959: 61).

It was one thing to be dedicated to purity in the products the company produced conveyed by the clarity of the packaging. It was another to convince potential customers that not only were those products of the best quality, they were also good to eat. Henry Heinz understood this well, and his sales techniques included regular free tastings, aimed at both retailers as well as the general public. He not only knew how to sell, he also understood to whom he had to sell. In addition to convincing the general public of the tastiness of his products, he also needed to persuade grocers. His very well-trained salesforce carried a Gladstone bag in the late nineteenth/early twentieth centuries, whose contents were listed for Potter by one of the thirty strong Heinz salesforce's recollection of fifty years before:

> Tomato ketchup, tomato chutney, horseradish, India Relish … Small meths spirit stove to heat sample tins of baked beans. Cardboard spoons to sample ketchup and chutney, Fancy serviettes to make the bottles on the counter look pretty. As you put them down you put your bit of fancy paper under them. Plain serviettes to clean spoons after sampling.
>
> (1959: 93)

Horseradish was his first commercially produced sauce in 1869, followed in 1876 by tomato catsup. Like his horseradish the tomato ketchups, visible through the glass of its bottle made with no adulteration or preservatives – are virtues springing, Petrick believes, from his religious faith and devotion to purity and quality (2011).

McCafferty admiringly reports Henry Heinz' maxims for successful labour relations in the company:

FIND YOUR MAN, TRAIN YOUR MAN,
INSPIRE YOUR MAN,
AND YOU WILL KEEP YOUR MAN

Apparently given to posting aphorisms for all to see Henry Heinz had stained glass windows made for the 'company auditorium, with their mottos exhorting employees to be prudent, loyal, temperate, earnest and hard working' (1923: 111).

A few months after Henry Heinz died (20 December 1919), a statistical reckoning of the company was produced which – along with a banquet given by the Directors for the employees – was to commemorate both his contribution and a half-century of conducting business. It did not count profits, turnover or even the growth in total sales (although it did include an entry for Carloads of Good Handled that year – a total of 17,011). Instead it enumerated the sheer scale of the enterprise:

Employees (6,523)
Branch Factories (including one each in Canada, England and Spain) (25)
Pickle Salting Stations (87)
Railroad Cars Owned and Operated (258)
Salesmen (952)
Agencies in all the Leading Commercial Centers of the World.
(McCafferty 1923: 106–7)

At the very end is the note: '(W)e own and operate our own Bottle Factory, Box Factories and Tin Can Factory, as well as our own Seed Farms' (McCafferty 1923: 106–7). The Heinz complex of factories in Pittsburgh already incorporated the company's own glass blowing operation by 1911. A photograph illustrates two men busy with their blow pipes with a wooden bucket – presumably of water – alongside (Foster and Kennedy 2006: 34).

During one man's lifetime, then, the company had grown from home-made horseradish sauce hawked locally door to door, to international success forming the background to Heinz with the clear glass bottle of tomato ketchup, central if not 'iconic' as one of its '57 varieties'.

****

From domestic to industrial foodstuff

Biographies and company histories paint a portrait of Henry Heinz as one of huge success fuelled by his conviction, if not religious faith, that products must be of the highest quality, preserved naturally by careful, hygienic processing, marketed and advertised with panache – and a dash of cunning. He is presented as charismatic, almost larger than life, a philanthropist, model businessman and benign employer. Biographers tend to attribute success to their subjects' personal qualities – or as McCafferty puts it of Henry Heinz to 'elements of his personality'. At the same time, McCafferty himself well understands that by the time of Henry Heinz' death, many of the principles according to which the company was run had become established, codified and taught to new generations:

(I)n his boyhood it had not occurred to men that the pursuit of the merchant might be made a branch of scientific public education … The majority of business men would have smiled ironically at the idea of a business training that involved academic study of basic theories and principles … if men did not actually assert that it was largely a matter of hit-and-miss, most of them assuredly conducted it on that basis.

(McCafferty 1923: 53)

In so many other ways too, Henry Heinz' methods foreshadowed what became established business principles. The catalogue of the company's assets illustrates what McCafferty's branch of scientific public education now taught to new generations of economists and students of management would call vertical integration. Rather than depend on a network of suppliers such as tomato growers who, in turn rely on companies breeding and selling seed, Heinz was able to control such stages upstream from ketchup production. Thus the company took charge of the quality of ingredients. As Petrick observes,

Heinz even specified the particular varieties of tomatoes and onions farm managers planted. Once harvested, these crops were partially processed in branch factories close to the fields, reducing the spoilage caused by transporting them almost 700 miles to Pittsburgh. In addition, this ensured that vegetables were processed as close to their peak flavor as possible.

(2009: 31)

She continues, citing an internal company document which declared: "'Perfect tomatoes for the purpose cannot be satisfactorily obtained on the open market, and therefore H. J. Heinz Company supervises the cultivation of its own tomatoes from the very selection of the seed and the preparation of the soil'" (Petrick 2009: 31). Harvey, Quilley and Beynon argue that such control allowed for the creation of that novelty, 'the mass-produced, globally distributed, standardised and industrially processed tomato' (2002: 160). Breeding was geared not to the taste or appearance of the raw tomato or one to be sold to the domestic cook, but to a tomato that was optimally suited to the mass production of ketchup (and soup) above all else, including ensuring the fruits matured at the same time allowing mechanical harvesting, thus replacing the need for seasonal manual labour. Similarly, the company was also able to make decisions about its own supplies of packaging, notably bottles and cans, by dint of ownership of the very factories that produced them.

In any case, Henry Heinz had pioneered other aspects of factory production that became established among manufacturers, including the assembly line. Foster and Kennedy also credit him with being 'among the few US food companies to employ professional chemists' noting that he is reported to have coined the term "'quality control department'" (2006: 37). Above all, Henry Heinz' pocket notebooks made it clear that he did more than merely pack fruit and vegetables into cans. He was 'a processor of *reciped* products' producing 'ready-made' items such as chilli sauce, tomato sauce, fruit butters as well as dishes such as baked beans with pork or macaroni with cheese (Alberts 1973: 41 emphasis added).

As noted, very broadly the stages from field to supermarket shelf have remained fairly similar for some four decades. Changes the company introduced in the 1960s contrast clearly with processing and packaging ketchup in the late 1940s and 1950s. Wartime and just post-war production was rather more like a mechanized version of the steps Henry Heinz, when young, would have followed, harvesting produce from his mother's garden, washing chopping and mixing in his mother's kitchen, bottling the high-quality mixture in those clear glass containers, originally stoppered by wax and string.

Heinz' agricultural research geared to maintaining its high-quality standards, increased yields, demonstrating, by mid-twentieth century, that regions hitherto deemed unsuitable for tomato cultivation could, after all, support commercial growing. As a result, tomatoes produced for processing were, by the 1990s, mostly Californian. For the first half of the twentieth century, production was seasonal both in the fields to bring in the harvest and in the factory to process it. Much of the work was manual, from planting to picking, packing in wicker baskets or those made, conical shape, of broad laths of wood, followed by hauling the baskets piled high with tomatoes for delivery in horse-drawn wagonloads to receiving stations. 'Heinz field men covered their territory by horseback, by buggy, or by bicycle' (Dienstag 1994: 157). Tomatoes were then processed by hand albeit on a scale far greater than the domestic: back at the factory, rows of uniformed women stationed in front of metal buckets and bowls would work at long tables checking and sorting. Those in charge of the cooking were men. Ogden Perry who started working in the fields during the summer (paying for his college education) and rose to oversee four Pittsburgh factories explained that the ketchup cooks '"had to be men of steel, because they were cooking in banks of open 350 gallon kettles. It was hard to breathe in those kitchens because of the vinegar vapor and general steam level. Basically it was a hellish job and the ketchup cooks were a revered bunch of people"' (Dienstag 1994: 158).

The reliance on fresh tomatoes harvested in season led, from an economist's point of view, to inefficiencies in the system, including high demand for a large temporary labour force, unpredictable demand for storage depending on the yield for any one year, large volumes of stock requiring storage space (idle for parts of the year) with corresponding high but fluctuating demand for bottles, labels and caps. Only a few years later, everything started to change: 'Heinz revolutionized the ketchup business – in the field and factory from packaging to marketing' (Dienstag 1994: 159).

Two other packaging changes were made during the later 1960s. The first revolves around the renewed attention to the food-service market in addition to retail. To get round retailers selling to restaurants and cafés, Heinz sought to sell direct. A new neckband for the bottle was added '"Served by Fine Restaurants Everywhere"' which clearly distinguished these packages from those on domestic kitchen tables. The other was far more significant, ironing out seasonal fluctuations in supply, involving Heinz' pioneering replacement of tomatoes with tomato paste thus allowing year-round production. Paste can be stored.

This innovation in the production of ketchup – by now Heinz' best selling line – posed a new question: in what was this novel ingredient to be stored and transported. The behaviour of this material had to be taken into account. While the process of turning fresh tomatoes into paste is faster than into ketchup, the result is none the less subject to spoiling without some further action. Vinegar and sugar are additional ingredients to tomatoes for ketchup, preserving the resulting sauce in the process. But tomato paste is destined only to replace the single ingredient of fresh tomatoes. For it to serve as an all-year round substitute for fluctuating seasonal harvests of fresh tomatoes, it must be safely preserved.

The earliest means of removing the high – and excess – volume of water in a fresh tomato was by adopting the domestic technique of boiling in saucepans, scaled up for commercial production in vats. This was replaced in the 1950s by Heinz Canada using an evaporator, originating in dairies, working on a vacuum principle. Once the paste was reduced to the required concentration, it was simple enough to use established canning techniques to sterilize it by heating to 200°F for storage in 100 ounce sterilized cans. Once again, the character of the tin can had to be reckoned with. Such cans are hard to handle, relatively expensive and their shape makes them awkward to store never mind being inefficient to dispose of when no longer needed. Anyway, good harvests put a strain on the system, requiring more paste than usual be stored.

According to Dienstag, no one any longer knows who first suggested replacing the cans with bulk storage tanks coupled with adapting a sterilizing procedure already used in the pharmaceutical industry. The upshot was the transformation of cans to bulk tanks. Although it was not straightforward, eventually effective aseptic processing was achieved with the added pioneering adaptation of filling railway cars with bulk paste – much like the movement of milk in bulk by rail (Chapter 5). In turn, storage was dramatically improved by packing paste in giant, flexible, sterile, 300 gallon, plastic bags. The bags were fitted with nozzles and in turn packed in a plywood box – whose straight sided shape allowed efficient packing without the gaps between the old cylindrical tin cans. Such boxes with a blue inner plastic bag can clearly be seen in Heinz' own film of ketchup production in their Dutch factory. Ensuring the bags are completely emptied is achieved by squeezing them through a system of rollers and screws dramatically reducing wastage. The squeezing technique is self-evidently afforded by the very character of the plastic.

Not only does the use of bulk packing of tomato paste dramatically increase the efficiency of ketchup production, a different version of secondary packaging is held, by Dienstag to be 'one of the key drivers of increased ketchup usage' (1994: 171). Once again it was packaging for the food service sector. And once again, a flexible plastic bag holding three-gallons of ketchup replaced catering size tin cans. Restaurant staff simply steadied the bag on a rack and then refilled the plastic 'squirt' bottles for the table via the bag's valve. Heinz' profitability continued to improve, helped by further developments in packaging – primarily forms of plastic pouches, large sizes for restaurant and café kitchens, single-serving size for fast food outlets.

Ketchup and its packaging: an industrial food

Petrick's succinct definition of industrial foods as those 'that are mass produced in a factory setting and require no or very little cooking to make them edible' inclines to seeing them from the viewpoint of the end-consumer, relieved of that cooking (Petrick 2012: 258). The assemblages illustrated in this chapter highlight the centrality of packaging by revealing the secret lives of mass production in factories. More than that, it demonstrates the successive shifts from domestic to industrial production and the key part packaging plays in those shifts.

The word ketchup's long pedigree also serves as a summary of such shifts. Occasionally a source claims that it is 'descended' from a vaguely specified Far Eastern region, the OED suggests the word is possibly derived from the Chinese via Malay. Treating catsup, catchup or ketchup as synonymous, the OED goes on to define it as '(A) liquor extracted from mushrooms, tomatoes, walnuts, etc. used as a sauce, more commonly ketchup', with written mentions in 1690 and 1730. Hannah Glasse is reported to have observed in the 1751 edition of her *The Art of Cookery* that the taste was 'like foreign catchup'. An earlier comment of 1721 cited in the OED explains it is a '"(S)auce comes in tubbs from and the best ketchup from Tonquin: yet good of both sorts are made and sold very cheap in China."' This suggests that commercially produced sauces were imported – at much the same time as soy sauce. But it continued to be made in British and American domestic kitchens for more than two centuries thereafter. Elizabeth Raffald's 1769 *The Experienced English Housekeeper* gives recipes for five catchups, with a walnut one which will keep for seven years (Raffald 1997), while ketchup of some sort seems well known enough to Dickens to talk of breaded lamb chops with plenty of it in his novel *Barnaby Rudge*.[15] Ketchup made from tomatoes is relatively recent: Catherine Esther Beecher has a recipe for one in her 1873 *Miss Beecher's housekeeper and healthkeeper*. Nowadays, however, the chances are that mention of 'ketchup' will automatically be heard as 'tomato ketchup' and although commercially produced mushroom ketchup remains on the market in the UK, it takes up a small fraction of supermarket shelf space compared to the tomato varieties. Henry Heinz is in large measure responsible for this assumption.

His ketchup is emblematic of industrialization in general no less than foodstuffs in particular. Henry Heinz started from domestically produced sauce stored in odd assortments of transparent containers happening to be to hand. He initiated the shift by making the first move to production on huge scales, produced by those who are strangers to anonymous consumers; mass production for mass markets – recognizing the significance for sales and reputation of bottling in clear glass. Heinz' type of marketing developed as that which concentrates on relationships between producer and consumer, knowing and wanting to continue to know what customers like and want (Berghoff, Scranton and Spiekermann 2012). Almost moving beyond the designation 'industrial food', tomato ketchup is readily described as a cultural icon of a whole nation's tastes, whose material and symbolic significance in plastic pouches, clear PET and glass bottles represents America both to consumers worldwide and Americans to themselves.

A small postscript to the significance of Heinz and that ubiquitous food package, the clear glass bottle, is a recent full-page advertisement in the 17 December 2022 issue of *The Grocer*.[16] It announced Heinz' launch of a new product, ready-made pasta sauce. The whole is an adroit blend of company history and the latest 'consumer trends', including:

> 2022 … the year we finally combined our unrivalled tomato expertise with natural ingredients to create award-winning sauce

After 150 years we have made a Heinz Pasta Sauce range that our founder, Henry Heinz, would give his seal of approval to …

Being late to the party we couldn't compromise on anything. So we added to our tomato expertise: 100% natural ingredients; Full range with no added sugar; Heinz tomatoes grown in Italy; New exploration recipes & favourites upgraded; Suitable for Vegans, Vegetarians … & Gluten Free

New Heinz Pasta Sauce
Ridiculously Late
Ridiculously Good[17]

Pasta sauce – a reciped product – provides everything needed to make a complete dish when added to nothing more than boiled pasta. It also serves as a neat link between a tomato ketchup, the bottled sauce and the subject of the next chapter, the ready meal.

Notes

1. https://www.grandviewresearch.com/industry-analysis/tomato-ketchup-market-report.
2. https://www.mashed.com/124899/the-untold-truth-of-heinz-ketchup/
3. Online digests of (presumably) market research testify to the size of the market. The dependability of the statistic remains unknown. https://www.statista.com/statistics/484809/tomato-ketchup-volume-sales-in-the-united-kingdom-uk/; https://www.statista.com/statistics/1304011/italy-production-volume-of-tomato-ketchup-and-other-tomato-sauces/; https://www.grandviewresearch.com/industry-analysis/tomato-ketchup-market-report
4. https://www.sainsburys.co.uk/shop/gb/groceries/table-sauces-dressings-condiments/tomato-ketchup#langId=44&storeId=10151&catalogId=10241&categoryId=231276&parent_category_rn=13208&top_category=13208&pageSize=60&orderBy=FAVOURITES_ONLY%7CTOP_SELLERS&searchTerm=&beginIndex=0
5. Usage here follows Petrick (2011); the terms H. J. or Henry Heinz refer to the founder and H. J. Heinz Company or Heinz to refer to the company.
6. Lingle, R. (2019). 'Evolution of a package: Heinz ketchup'. *Packaging Digest*. 8 July. Available online: https://www.packagingdigest.com/packaging-design/evolution-package-heinz-ketchup (accessed 6 April 2023).
7. https://www.carrefour.fr/p/ketchup-heinz-0000087157239 (author's translation) (accessed 6 April 2023).
8. https://www.sainsburys.co.uk/gol-ui/product/bigger-packs-/heinz-tomato-ketchup-800ml (accessed 6 April 2023).
9. The slogan 'from field to fork' has been widely repeated in food policy circles for a good twenty years. Paula Chin kindly offered the reversed version.
10. Inside the Factory BBC television. Available online: https://www.bbc.co.uk/programmes/b07mddqk (accessed 6 April 2023).

11. The factory reports producing 1.8 M bottles daily i.e. approximately 175,000 tonnes annually. https://www.youtube.com/watch?v=c1LePreHLY0 (accessed 6 April 2023).

12. The original intention had been to visit the Library and Archives of the Heinz Collection in Pittsburgh, made impossible during the COVID-19 pandemic.

13. Resulting in as much hagiography as dispassionate biography – and according to Alberts who some three decades later had access to private diaries and archives containing factual inaccuracies.

14. Hagley Museum & Library (nd). 'Added Proof: A new series of retail store tests conducted to show how cellophane assists manufacturers in giving maximum sales value to their packages'. Adam Matthew Food and Drink in History database. Available online: http://www.foodanddrink.amdigital.co.uk/Documents/Details/Pam_08035344 (accessed 6 April 2023).

15. Incorrectly given as Charles Rudge in Smith, with an incorrect attribution to Raffald's in claiming her ketchup would last for five years (2012: 23).

16. UK weekly trade magazine first published in 1862.

17. https://www.google.com/search?q=Advertisement+for+Heinz+pasta+sauce+The+Grocer+December+2022&rlz=1C1GCEA_enGB974GB974&sxsrf=AJOqlzW0PCtgq-kTUD1iePFAVhUaBOQS5g:1676823382331&source=lnms&tbm=isch&sa=X&ved=2ahUKEwiE0Lfw_aH9AhXGhf0HHUfTBmMQ_AUoAXoECAEQAw&biw=1407&bih=648&dpr=1.25#imgrc=8yLXSqrSUI3fNM

CHAPTER 8
READY-MEALS, MICROWAVES AND PLASTIC TRAYS

Ready meals are widespread: 88 per cent of people eat ready-meals/ready-to-cook foods.[1] Frozen or chilled lasagne is a suitable example of a ready meal with which to start. It too seems nowadays to be widespread for instance 'Lasagne is so popular here it could be considered a staple Irish food'.[2] Although the trend is not always welcome: '(I)t's a shame that so many bad versions of this popular Emilian dish (lasagne) are found in fast food restaurants and ready-made in supermarkets'.[3] For the industrial production of ready-to-eat lasagne is as far from the domestic production of the dish as could be imagined.[4] This is no mystery, for there are plenty of videos of each online.[5] The contrast is neatly encapsulated by simply listing the widely known names for the equipment used to cook it in the domestic kitchen – wooden spoon, gas hob, dessertspoon and glass, ceramic or enamel dish – compared to those even a non-specialist can start to name in its industrial counterpart – hopper, assembly line, silo, inspection panel and plastic tray.

That last is the second case of food packaging which is at the heart of an assemblage-like set of inter-related historical developments: the inventions of the microwave oven, the cold chain and convenience foods which co-evolved with plastic trays to produce the landscape of packaging for ready-meals nowadays. The plastic tray differs from the clear glass bottle which predates it. Bottles are in turn far older than Henry Heinz' glass selections which themselves date from an earlier mode of industrialization than synthetic polymer plastics. That earlier mode was based initially (in late eighteenth- and throughout the nineteenth-century England) on water- and steam-power, augmented by horse and cart (un)loaded by hand, thereafter followed by coal and petrol powered transport and on machines requiring human operators, displacing skilled craft workers.

By contrast, the plastic tray is emblematic of a later, twentieth to twenty-first century, mode of industrialization which revolves round electronics, IT, automation and the replacement of human machine-minders with electronic eyes and high-speed cameras built-in to massive factory equipment. Such factories manufacture the plastic packaging as well as those using that package[6] to contain whatever dishes are being produced, the chicken Kiev, the beef stew – and the lasagne.

Plastic occupies a singular position in the world of food packaging. It has been used to replace older materials such as glass and steel. But it has also been used to contrive new receptacles which can act as packaging, storage containers and cookware given the material's characteristic tolerance of extremes of temperature. Certainly some earlier aluminium containers also doubled as ovenware, but they are used in only a small proportion of ready prepared foods nowadays. Canned meat pies have been on the UK market in lidded pie-dish shaped steel for many decades labelled with the manufacturer's advice that the lid be removed using a 'robust' can opener for baking. But the scale, variety and general versatility and flexibility of plastic packaging that also acts not just as a baking dish but can be moved from deep freeze to hot oven without difficulty, far outdoes parallel qualities of steel.

Plastics are, in principle, extremely adaptable materials for food packaging. But a good deal of research & development (R&D) is commonly required to devise the optimum pack for whatever purpose it is to serve. *HeinzLine*, the in-house employee newsletter recorded: "'(I)t took 15 years of development and testing before Heinz found the right 'marriage' of technology in a multilayer plastic container that met the needs of the customer and maintained the quality and integrity of the product at the right price'" (in Dienstag 2006: 177).

Going back a century makes no sense for cook-chill ready-meals; they did not yet exist. So the chapter first traces the history of this archetypal form of industrial food – archetypal in that it is considered a meal in itself, unlike tomato ketchup of the previous chapter and the salad greens of the next which, though certainly ready to serve, are not. Ready-meals announce what they are. And it is to the history of their manufacture and packaging that the chapter now turns.

The invention of the ready-meal

Meals that are processed in a factory and sold ready to do no more than heat then serve date from the nineteenth century. A 'complete dinner' in a tin can was displayed at London's Great Exhibition of 1851 (Thorne 1986). Despite the huge crowds which attended, few would have known of such a thing at the time, let alone tasted any. But over a century later, a historian observed that '(T)he post-war era has seen the consumption of manufactured foods increase at an astonishing rate' (Johnston 1977: 40). Today journalists write about ready-meals from time to time and have dated them from the successful 1950s American TV dinner.[7] But the first frozen dinner – turkey, potato and vegetables sold in oven-ready aluminium compartmentalized trays which arrived in US grocery stores in 1952 – did not appear in that form as if from nowhere. As Laura Schapiro details, there was a good number of precursors – from fish sticks, which sold very well, to chicken sticks, ham sticks, onion flavoured poultry sticks which did not. These earlier examples were created not so much to test, as to *create* the market for ready-prepared foods, when the post-war US food industry sought to adapt for civilians frozen foods that had been developed to supply troops (2004). As for the package, the inspiration for the trays was their use for airline food, first military and then civilian, doing dual service as both pack and plate. The comparatively small domestic and retail ownership of a deep freeze in the early 1950s constituted a brake on growth of TV dinner sales – a limitation not, initially, relevant in the UK.

A common version of the chronology has ready-meals appearing on the British market at around the same time, but they were preserved by dehydration which can be stored at ambient (room) temperature rather than frozen. Also advertised as an accompaniment to sofa dining in front of the television, they were apparently marketed to young couples willing to be adventurous enough to try 'curry' and 'chow mein with noodles' at a time when a British 'cooked dinner' was widely regarded as 'the' archetype 'proper meal' (Murcott 1982, Charles and Kerr 1988). But noting that food rationing in the UK[8] (especially of meat) impeded their development, frozen food industry insiders, Davies and Carr, state that 'the first "documented" appearance of ready-meals in the UK came in March, 1953, under the Opulus brand belonging to the Australian firm, Cahills' – largely considered novelties, with slender demand. These authors also claim that it was Findus and Birds Eye 'boil-in-the-bag' products of the late 1960s which caught the public imagination as something akin to a ready meal (1998: 27–8). Trialled in 1971 in the Edgware Road (branch) Marks and Spencer's expansion of its range of foods was one of the very first, if not the first in the UK to make a firm and sustained move into the frozen market for ready-meals – expanded to 100 stores by 1973. Products ranged from peas and fish to foods such as lasagne.[9]

Alongside a photograph of a young woman adding a box of frozen lasagne to the supermarket wire basket on her arm, an article in the company's staff magazine for November 1972 announced that 'St Michael foods make it easier to put a good meal on the table quickly without sacrificing quality'. Their frozen range 'differs from most other well-known brands' for, as well as the 'usual frozen peas, it concentrates on high-quality dishes like lasagne and pizza which can be heated and served within minutes – *speciality recipes which normally only the most ambitious cook with plenty of time would attempt to prepare*' (emphasis added). The point the article makes is that according to their customers, frozen ready-meals – referred to as 'recipe dishes' – are no longer stored in the now more widely owned freezer against emergencies but are 'eaten within hours of purchase'.[10]

The company's next significant move is, logically, related to that last point. For in 1979, a 2013 news blog records, the first chilled, as distinct from deep frozen, ready meal was launched.[11] This was its chicken Kiev ready for heating and serving. 'By 2012 … chilled ready meal' comprised '57 per cent of the UK prepared meals market, according to business analysts Mintel'.[12] Mintel also reports 2011 market research data from Kantar World Panel on 'best selling ready-meals by type of cuisine' showing that Italian was by far the most popular – likely reflecting pizza's popularity. Through these decades of the growth in the ready-meal market, the plastic tray did two- sometimes three-fold duty as package, baking- and serving-dish. Market researchers continue to report massive growth in this market.[13] The UK ready meal market expanded during and since the pandemic lockdown.[14] Plastics of one kind or another are integral to this enormous expansion.

Many might think that plastics were a twentieth-century invention – and in key respects that is so. After all, the meaning of the word 'plastic' has become so familiar when referring to an item made of one or other synthetic polymer, that its earlier sense as 'pliable' tends to get eclipsed. What also gets eclipsed – or perhaps is not widely known – is that plastics industry insiders date the human use of a material now known as plastic to pre-industrial times, regarding the earliest examples as those occurring naturally: tortoise shell, horn, ivory.[15] Through the nineteenth century the range of naturally occurring items was extended, notably by chemical manipulation – the first being vulcanized rubber.[16]

All plastics are polymers, composed of a 'very, very large chemical molecule which has many repeating members just as a long metal chain has many repeating links'. A key distinction is between those that are 'found in nature, including cellulose (a component of wood) casein (in milk) silk and wool' and synthetics such as polyethylene, polypropylene, polystyrene, polyvinyl chloride (PVC), phenol formaldehyde resin (Bakelite), neoprene, nylon, silicone among a very large number of others. A further distinction is between those that are amenable to being shaped into different forms – thermoplastic polymers – and those which have other characteristics such as greater hardness or heat resistance – thermosetting polymers (Sacharow and Griffin 1980: 25–6). Most plastics used in packaging are made (primarily by applying heat) from fossil-fuels such as natural gas and petroleum, although there is a modest trend to replace them with renewable and biodegradable materials such as corn (maize) (see Chapter 10).

The packaging material needed for ready-meals – frozen in particular – has to have certain properties. It must keep the dish completely sealed from the filling stage to the removal of the covering film in the domestic kitchen – during which it has to remain impervious to rapid freezing, extreme cold and re-heating in either a microwave- or conventional-oven. As one frozen food science textbook puts it: '(T)he successful marriage of the product–process–package (PPP) elements is key in any food production process as are time–temperature–tolerance (TTT) considerations'. Once assembled and moved to the freezer part of the assembly line, the cooked and packaged meal is frozen fairly fast e.g. to achieve a 'core temperature of −20°C in 0.5 hr' then to be stored at −30°C, for which '(C)rystalline polyethylene terephthalate (CPET) trays' are best (Gormley 2008: 207). Containers for ready-meals are one of the trio of interrelated socio-technical phenomena already noted, described as assemblage-like. Attention in more detail must be paid to the other two, microwave ovens and the 'cold chain'. But more needs to be said about those plastic trays first.

Although it is possible to find online videos of factory production of plastic and packages made from plastic, it is hard to see exactly what goes on. So, the secret life, or rather the birth, of the plastic tray is described in the next Interlude, shedding a little more light on the question of the way the contemporary packaging landscape came about.

****

Interlude: how to make a plastic tray

Industrial estates nowadays are inclined to look the same and their factories built in the last decade or so also seem similar. Mostly windowless buildings, three or four stories high, maybe some silos at one side, roadways leading to covered bays at another and facing the road, a smaller block often like a glass box seeming to be separate, attached to the main building almost as an afterthought through which staircases running up a couple of levels can be seen. That smaller box is typically where Reception is housed, the main entrance for visitors who are provided with the inevitable label 'visitor' attached to a lanyard to be worn until surrendered on leaving the premises several hours later.

Upstairs those visitors are welcomed to the board room, invited to hang up their coats – this particular visit was in November – and warm themselves with coffee freshly made to greet them. The CEO and Process and Technology Manager gave up a good deal of time to introduce DAFA,[17] a company founded in a northern mainland European nation over fifty years ago still the location of its headquarters. Its main business is the global supply of 'quality packaging solutions' for the food industry aiming to do so sustainably. The company lays huge stress on moving to complete and 'true circularity', already taking back used tubs, pots and trays made of PET to recycle them not into different goods requiring lower standards but the same food grade packages preserving the same necessary characteristics such as heat/cold resistance.[18] This is a company which does not simply buy in plastic to manufacture trays and pots but makes their own plastic as well.

The company's plastic trays come in a variety of more than two dozen colours – except black. This is the company's response to the problem of recycling black PET trays, a problem which has nothing to do with the plastic or the trays. The difficulty arises from the design and nature of recycling plants in the UK. [19] These involve reliance on optical recognition of plastics which use the reflection of light to identify the type of plastic as part of the sorting procedures.[20] Black does not reflect light, so the scanners cannot 'read' black. Recycled PET (rPET) includes any number of colours reflecting the nature of the items included. A way of achieving consistency has been to add carbon black to obliterate the colour variation, thereby reducing the overall recyclability of PET items. DAFA's solution is to make a virtue of the resulting variety of colours of the rPET – each recycling stage could produce some difference. DAFA carefully controls the combination of colours of the recycled feedstock – patenting their recipes.

The process of making their own plastic starts with reception of the feedstock – the output of recycling (done in a separate plant where heating, among other processes, assures it is food grade) processed into small pellets or flakes – such as those in Figure 13.[21]

Packed in big bags – like those in Figure 14 – they arrive by truck and are stored in stainless steel silos visible from the road.

The feedstock is then melted, mixed well to ensure the colours, etc. are evenly distributed throughout, thereafter extrude through a very fine aperture to spread out on rollers to be pressed into desired thickness, widths, etc. The process works to a tolerance measured in a few μm each side of the sheet. The edges are differently formed to strengthen the sides (reminiscent of a selvedge on a bolt of fabric) in order to reduce tearing during manufacture/ · handling. The resulting sheets are continuous, warehoused on very large rolls on racks, floor to ceiling, each fully labelled enabling, among other things, full traceability.

At all stages, the temperature of the material is critical. Too low and it does not hold its shape, too high, and it becomes brittle, breaking like glass. A feature of processing is to heat and then cool – the speed and duration at each stage is also critical.

Figure 13 rPET flakes, feedstock in circular, thermoformed food packaging for ready meals.

Figure 14 Large white bags containing rPET flakes.

When it comes to thermoforming, the sheet is fed into the machine, heated to 320C, rolled over a mould to form the desired shape, cooled to 280C and then blast frozen at −53°C before being moved to the end of the machine for packing. The trays (tubs or pots) are moved along the line by vacuum from one stage to the next.

The freezing stage removes excess moisture producing some 1,000 litres per line per week. It also includes some oils. This by-product is collected in a large plastic tank with about 9 inches of water at the bottom with a thinner, darkish blue layer above. Classed as hazardous waste it goes to power generation. Thermoform machines use 2.5 tons of sheet per hour and there are 1,000 tons i.e. two weeks' supply in store. Reel changes are semi-automatic. When a reel runs out, an operative has to open a cage at the end of the machine, just before the platform (at waist or even chest level) on which the completed batch of trays emerges. They remove the reel onto which the sheet now full of regularly spaced holes left behind as the material for the moulded trays has been removed (much like pastry from which a series of biscuits has been stamped). The reel of leftover sheet is tossed into a cage which is later wheeled to the area where the sheeting is ground into a powder and returned into the process as feedstock.

An operative picks up the batches of trays and packs them then and there into cardboard boxes, slaps onto its side the printed label that emerges from the machine, ready for moving into the store of plastic-wrapped boxes awaiting despatch. Older machines still need manual packing, etc. But newer machines are robot controlled – robots located at the end of the line wait for a batch of formed trays to arrive, pick up a flat bed with banks of suction cups that, by vacuum, lift the batch of trays, swivel round, sleeve them in blue slightly translucent plastic and place them in cardboard boxes. Some robots also assemble the flat-packed cardboard box.

The whole operation is controlled electronically. At intervals on the factory floor, there is a bay with a few screens. At the touch of a finger, the display can be changed to show different details of what is happening where in the plant. The main servers for the coordinated IT system are in the headquarters in Europe where what is displayed in the English factory (including in the Process and Technology Manager's office) can also be monitored.

It is evident that making rPET ready-meal trays is, in this particular company, not just a highly industrialized process. It is also at the forefront of the relevant segment of the food packaging industry, in that it is aiming for 'complete circularity' in its operations. For now the chapter turns to consider the conjunction of ready-meals, microwave ovens and the cold chain.

****

Co-evolution: 'convenience foods', microwave ovens and the cold chain

Although deriving from completely separate origins, the advent of two socio-technical processes – creating microwave ovens and frozen foods – converged in the late 1970s and early 1980s in the UK (later than the United States). Around then a far older difference of opinion became focused on those ready-meals at the centre of this convergence – a disagreement as to the virtues/vices of prepared foods found in many countries. Indeed they are not limited to criticizing ready-meals but spill over into a range of other factory prepared food items under a heading of 'convenience foods' – a third socio-technical entity. Factory produced foods – such as lasagne on its plastic tray, under plastic film enveloped by its cardboard sleeve – are at the heart of the those three socio-technical processes to which is added a fourth, namely, the very idea of convenience foods. Together they have emerged to occupy a massive place among foods purchased worldwide nowadays.

The emergence of 'convenience' foods – socio-technical aspects

Insider accounts repeatedly refer to 'convenience' as the reason for the huge success of industrial foods especially frozen and chilled ready-meals – a view echoed by some historians of twentieth-century eating (e.g. Oddy 2003). Discussing the various spurs to innovation in food packaging, a now retired director of an industry research division was clear. Though, he explained, 'food safety is always at the centre of some innovation' and 'product quality' is another important reason for new inventions, 'the real major reason in packaging … has been convenience. Take cans: the easy-open ends, the ring pulls on drinks cans, the use of plastic materials for microwave heating of foods and things like that'. Insider views of what lies behind convenience tend to couple it with other broader social trends, including in particular the increase in women's employment outside the home since the end of the Second World War.

By the late 1960s a US business research report held marketers understood too little of changes in 'consumer behaviour'. 'The changing life style of the American family is influencing consumer value-attitudes, with a shift from products and services to the saving of time as the high-priority value' (Anderson 1971: xv). The problem was identified in its foreword 'A new interpretation of convenience orientation is needed by marketers' for there was a 'dearth of scientific studies analyzing convenience-oriented consumer behaviour'. This was limiting 'the marketer in his efforts to meet the needs of the rapidly expanding convenience-goods market' (1971: xv). The study's key finding recorded it was a combination of 'socioeconomic status and stage in the family life cycle' which helped identify the 'convenience-oriented consumer' against a backdrop of increasing affluence (1971: 117): cost of convenience purchases influences consumer behaviour more than stage in the family life cycle among the less affluent, whereas the reverse is the case where cost is less of a concern. That the behaviour of consumers vis à vis 'convenience' foods is even deemed a problem requiring new research a half-century ago underlines the significance for marketing of the notion of convenience, at least in the United States. Such accounts, however, tend to side-step the differences of public opinion about the virtues and vices of using factory produced foods, focusing more closely on trends and attempts at developing new markets for novel products – i.e. supporting supplier-induced demand. And it is in this fashion that they fasten on the value of convenience for modern families.

Those differences of opinion are typically aired elsewhere, among food writers and nutritionists in particular. Views are familiar: some condemn ready-meals and their ilk as nutritionally inferior; some regard manufacturers responsible for the 'loss of cooking skills'; some regard them as tasteless and unappetising; others argue their adoption is part of the so-called de-structuring of meal patterns, supposedly accompanied by a decline in sociability; others simply seek to account for the changes (Poulain 2002). Most arguments are interlaced with more and less explicit condemnation of those who buy and serve convenience foods as lazy if not guilty of some other form of moral failing.

Opinions of this type, however, predate the invention and common use of the specific expression 'convenience foods'. In 1934, *The Scotsman* newspaper reported an address to Peterhead fishermen given by an MP for East Aberdeenshire. He was bemoaning those who shunned fresh food – particularly herrings – leading him to

come to the sorrowful conclusion that it is to a large extent due to ignorance and laziness on the part of the women, and particularly the young women of this country. The reason we consume more canned and tinned food than any other country in the world is that our womenfolk don't know how to cook, and won't be bothered to learn'.

(cited in Lyon and Kinnear 2013: 133)

A second example is from the United States, representing a broader view of the matter. An elderly member of the Board of Heinz interviewed by Stephen Potter for his 1959 book observed that

when I was a boy it was considered almost disgraceful not to have food which had been made in the home kitchen. To give you an example of what I mean, when it was my mother's washing day, I remember as a boy (I'm talking of about 1900 now) if she wanted to buy a loaf of bread from the baker's, she would send me around to the back door so the neighbours wouldn't see me.

(Potter 1959: 67)

At the same time, Thorne, reporting the 'complete dinner' displayed at the Great Exhibition, is unabashed about publishing his views on its use as '(T)hat product of twentieth century lethargy' (1986: 56).

When recognizing the longevity of such condemnatory views, it is important to keep them separate from tracing the history of foods dubbed 'convenience' and the history of the very name and evade relying on commentators who view the history through an evaluative lens. The origin of the designation 'convenience foods' is elusive, but one historian reports that it arrived in Britain from the United States in the early 1960s (Moseley 2020). By the 1970s its use was sufficiently common for a British food scientist to provide a definition in his Dictionary: 'processed foods in which a considerable amount of the preparation has already been carried out by the manufacturer, e.g. cooked meats, canned foods, baked foods, breakfast cereals, frozen foods' (Bender 1975). This chimes with the remark by historians Daniels and Glorieux that convenience foods 'constitute one of the most important changes in today's food consumption habits and are one of the most important bases upon which the modern food industry is built' in the opening of their study seeking to discover how far convenience foods have become a fixture of modern eating patterns in Belgium (2015). Other historians treat its meaning as self-evident, and do not even discuss definitions (Johnson 1977, Burnett 1989, Levenstein 1993, Oddy 2003).[22]

Coming far closer to making the combination of social with technical evident, the historian Frank Trentmann's, however, harks back two centuries in his history of consumption. 'Comfort, cleanliness and convenience – to use an eighteenth century phrase – were dynamic drivers of consumption'. The phrase referred to the manner in which goods (and some services) made things easier and more enjoyable for the people concerned (2016: 4). In like vein, some sort of notion of convenience in the domestic kitchen is not new. It turns up in nineteenth-century household manuals and recipe books, first cousin to, thrift and economy, often in the name of labour-saving (Bose 1979, Murcott 1983).

Neither Trentmann nor the geographer Peter Jackson *et al.* (2018) explicitly refer to the socio-technical. The latter adopt a different approach to convenience food, 'reframing' it for their investigative purposes to focus not on the food but on associated activities which make the use of a one or other food, style of cooking or other set of procedures more convenient from the user's point of view. Both Trentmann and Jackson provide reminders that it is more fruitful to think in terms of the introduction of factory-prepared foods not as an event but as a socio-technical process, in which both social activities *and* technical invention are intertwined.

Cast in those terms helps reflecting on public and political responses to technical innovation. Sometimes, it seems far easier to identify hostility to technical inventions in foods, but so doing risks eclipsing recognizing any welcome.[23] For instance, after the Second World War, once recovery was under way, some mood of optimism and welcome for new technologies was evident in both the United States and Europe. A particularly graphic comparison existed across the Cold War divide (1945–89) between East Germany (GDR) and West Germany (FRG). The historian Alice Weinreb reminds her readers that, at the time, communism versus capitalism was caricatured: the former the 'unfree' and the 'starving', the latter the 'free' and the 'satiated' (2017: 6). In the GDR, the prevailing ideology expected all adults be employed, a goal that 'encouraged the state to take an aggressive approach toward regulating domestic labour' reducing women's work at home by organising feeding family members elsewhere' e.g. children in school (2017: 177). Thus convenience food was the subject of energetic promotion, part of a scientific and rational approach to domestic kitchens. By contrast, Weinreb observes that, with a shorter school day eliminating a need for lunch, 'West Germany continued to distinguish itself through its continued opposition to school lunches' (2017: 191). Absent was an expectation that all adults would be in full-time employment, with no corresponding official promotion of convenience food – rather the opposite, women were to prioritize homemaking. As Weinreb observes, in the

FRG, reliance on home-cooked lunches appear as 'definitional to its identity – and to its difference from the GDR' and with it, a dramatically different view of labour-saving and convenience foods in the home (2017: 193).

The emergence of microwave ovens – a socio-technical process

The microwave oven is the most recent technology of the domestic kitchen to have reached a mass market worldwide. John Burnett used the speed and extent of its 'market penetration' as evidence of England's increasing prosperity in the 1980s (1989). As far as can be discerned, however, a good deal of the technology's history has been written by industry insiders, with a few exceptions (Cockburn and Ormrod 1993).[24]

Several accounts of their origins credit an engineer Percy LeBaron Spencer, as 'best known as the inventor of the microwave oven'.[25] At the time he was employed by Raytheon, a company that had successfully supplied radar, etc. to the US military during the Second World War. Those accounts tell a story of his standing close to a magnetron (often a key component of radar) one day in 1945/6 when he noticed that a chocolate bar in his pocket melted, prompting the thought that microwaves could be harnessed for cooking. At the time, the company – like Swanson, creators of TV dinners – was having to switch from military to civilian markets in order to stay in business in peacetime. The possibilities of a microwave oven held out the promise of effecting the change.

While Spencer may have been the one who pursued the potential application of magnetron technology to make an oven 'the possibilities of using microwave tubes for heating were already quite well known' and other companies were also pursuing similar enquiries, as Hammack (a chemical and biomolecular engineer) observes.[26] A similarly more nuanced view of the history is taken by J. M. Osepchuk (after he had retired from Rayethon where he had been involved with microwave research and development) sceptical of the 'founding father' approach to history (2009). In any case, there is a longer pre-history of the invention of radar – originating in Britain and taken in secret to the United States as part of a war-time deal between the respective governments.[27]

Although patents were taken out at the time, a good deal more technical work was required to design an oven safe enough to put on sale. Initially, the main market was the commercial food service sector, notably airlines [28] and restaurants, which in turn put safety in the spotlight. 'Operation had to be as automatic as possible, for many users would be short-order cooks' and engineers had to expect that many would experiment i.e. play with it (Hammack 2005).[29] There was a good bit more work to be done too before thoughts turned to creating a domestic market; the rugged looks to which Rayethon engineers were used for military products, had to change to the sleek, with finishes that could embellish a home. Moreover, launching a virtually unknown and dramatically different home appliance meant mounting full-scale sales drives, right through to regiments of demonstrators drilled in appropriate attitude, smiles and baked potatoes to show off the speed with which cooking can be done. The move was reflected in news coverage – such as 1972 report in the *New York Times* of two of Litton Industries Inc.'s new models of 'home microwave ovens' anticipated as the nucleus of a drive 'to tap new markets potentially estimated at $750-million by 1976'.[30]

All this work was first developed in the United States, but enthusiasts in the UK for microwave ovens picked it up in the 1970s/80s, notably Gordon Andrews and Lewis Napleton.[31] As Burnett implies, the microwave oven 'took off' in Britain during the 1980s. As part of the early promotion work, Leatherhead Research Institute[32] put on a day conference on 16 October 1987, for those in the food industry, introducing aspects of the then novelty.[33] As the final presentation of the day, a home economist demonstrated how to cook using a microwave oven instead of a hob or conventional oven. Extracts from contemporaneous notes made at the time reveal a wholly original way of cooking was required, complete with a novel vocabulary.

Verbs and adverbs describing well-established styles of cooking which tend to summarise the position of the foods in relation to the heat source coupled, perhaps with indicating the medium in which they are placed would seem not to apply that easily to preparing foods in a microwave oven. Words such as bake, roast or grill, boil, fry or steam are, it would seem, rendered inapposite by the use of microwaves to heat food. Indeed, even the verb 'to cook' did not serve the demonstrator well. Instead she referred to '*passing through* 2 kilowatts of energy'; describing how to prepare chicken satay she explained that you had to heat the satay from frozen and 'then *pass* the sauce'. As she worked her commentary included: 'one of the things I want to do is *to cook out* some of the vegetables … ' 'if you're putting on a selection of veg, you risk wastage because they've got *to cook off* extra … ' 'We can warm our accompaniment *through* the microwave' 'Just *lift* the potato' by which she meant lift the temperature, i.e. heat it.

(emphasis added when writing the notes during the demonstration)

What was noticeable about the mode of preparation required was a repeated placing an ingredient or a mixture in the oven, waiting for the specified brief time, removing it and replacing it with some other item, waiting once more, maybe pausing the timer to stir the foods being cooked before continuing. This succession of activities may need repeating six or seven times before the final dish can be assembled. The procedures reflect the way that a major use for the microwave oven which manufacturers imagined was to replace the use of earlier, slower technologies of hob and oven with the speed of the new one.

Thinking in such terms does not take into account the frequency with which items have to be taken in and out, stirred, replaced by different ones, timed, repeated and so on. Each stage is quite short, 2 minutes here, 7 there. The demonstrator sometimes held on to the door while waiting, as if unselfconsciously displaying how quickly a stage was completed. The total time may be much reduced, but the new oven required methods of cooking which made doing other tasks simultaneously far harder. Compared to the use of earlier cooking techniques where items could be left unattended in the oven for an hour or more with only an occasional stir, rather than minutes in a microwave oven, could seem unduly laborious and at odds with the way domestic cooks typically use their time.[34]

While sales of microwave ovens on both sides of the Atlantic soared, from the start they were increasingly commonly used for (re)heating, baking a potato in 6 minutes instead of 45, warming baby food and perhaps de-frosting separate ingredients for conventional cooking. Such use far outstripped adoption as a replacement for cooking even one dish let alone a three course meal in a conventional oven or on a hob. In addition, the use to which microwaves ovens were actually being put did not need special microwaveable packaging. Microwave-safe dishes and plates already available in most kitchens served as containers.

More to the point, this part of the history of microwave ovens adds another case to the STS literature where intentions of inventors are not adopted by purchasers whose main use of the novelty turns out to be something originators regarded as subsidiary. In the same way that inventors of the mobile phone did not anticipate public enthusiasm for texting rather than using it as a moveable replacement landline so inventors of the microwave oven did not seem to have anticipated a preference for heating ready-meals rather than as a replacement for a hob or what is now called a conventional oven. After all, Napleton – that career-long enthusiastic proponent of the microwave oven – entitled his memoir *Look! It Cooks*. The cover illustration shows a smiling, aproned woman behind a table laden with roast turkey, four dishes of vegetables, soup tureen, tart and a plateful of biscuits. More to the point, the item visible through the glass door of the microwave oven is not a manufacturers' pack but a conventional casserole dish, a design centuries old (2001).

No history of microwave ovens in Britain can ignore an especially memorable microwave oven, on the market around 2008 – the *Beanzawave*. It was considered both the world's smallest and probably least successful – enjoying minimal 'take-up'. Heinz market research had already reported that people were less likely to stop for lunch during the banking crisis recession – a finding credited with prompting the innovation. Coupled with that was helping 'time-pressured Brits' in tougher economic times.

(M)icrowave expert, Gordon Andrews, MD of GAMA Microwave Technology Ltd, and Technical Officer of the Microwave Association, has teamed up with Heinz to create a prototype of what is believed to be the world's smallest portable microwave perfectly sized to fit a Heinz Snap Pot .... Can be plugged into the USB port of a standard laptop.[35]

So runs the press release to mark its launch.[36]

While the *Beanzawave* was designed specifically to accommodate the pre-existing packaging of a single portion of baked beans,[37] much work went into designing the most appropriate packaging and containers for use in microwave ovens as the realization emerged that ready-meals were ideally suited for microwave de-frosting/ heating. Not all pre-existing packaging materials were suitable – metals, for instance cause arcing. Instead, new materials were being trialled. *Microwave News*[38] carried a small item[39] about a 'Cygnet range of disposable table ware'. This was a new range of bowls, dinner places, platters, etc. made from 'a totally new process involving the lamination of solid to expanded polystyrene'. '(R)esistant to temperature up to 98°C ... it can be used in a microwave oven straight from the deep freeze.' The same issue reported 'a new method of packaging food for micro-wave' [*sic*] being produced in the UK but invented in Sweden.[40] This was specifically designed for ready-meals as well as snacks used by the pub market, the take-away market and institutional catering.

Manufacturers seemed to be seeking new markets for instance – that issue of *Microwave News* reports moves for microwave ovens to be adopted by hotels providing food service at night when the kitchens are closed. Research developing and refining packaging for use in microwave ovens has continued since, evident in technical contributions to the scientific literature (Alexander 1993, Lorence 2020).

The archives contain much detail on the sales drives, the refinements of specialized packaging as well as novel market niches into which microwave ovens could be inserted. They fill out what is no more than glimpses of what was involved during the exponential growth in sales during the 1970s and 1980s. They reflect not just in the effort to sell products or meet demand, but enlarge on what was needed to *create* demand.

The development of the cold chain – a socio-technical process

The novel, *East of Eden*, has the protagonist Adam Trask suffering a disastrous 1915 venture. A load of refrigerated lettuces he transports by rail from California to New York arrive as a malodorous, rotten mess after delays to the journey. John Steinbeck's book helps date an early stage in the creation of the 'cold chain', although, as Rees observes, Steinbeck sets Trask's misfortune more than a decade after the first successful longer distance transport of iceberg lettuce had been developed (2013: 94). In any case, it is not as if preserving food by using very low temperatures was even new in 1903. Samuel Pepys' Diary for 11 December 1663 records stories from East Prussia he heard in a coffee house of very similar techniques as theirs for freezing fish solid.[41] In later centuries, those in lower latitudes where the climate was still cold enough in winter for ice to form on fresh water ponds, the wealthy English aristocracy of 1600 and 1700s, continued to build semi-underground brick-lined houses on their country estates to store the ice their servants harvested in the depths of winter.[42]

What marks out Steinbeck's fictional business failure is that Adam Trask had already bought an icebox for his household, making him a relatively 'early adopter' to use today's marketing expression. The very first ice boxes were simply storage cupboard-like containers about the height of a kitchen stove kept cold by ice blocks delivered door to door twice a week by the ice man – a system still in use in Southern California in the 1920s. Experiments with refrigeration, i.e. devising a device to make ice artificially instead of relying on naturally occurring ice, had begun in the later part of the nineteenth century. But though the beginnings of the modern cold chain can be dated from a good deal earlier than that, its development overall was not only very slow but tended to fluctuate.

It is 'refrigerating engineers (who) refer to the infrastructure that makes paths of trade for perishable food possible as cold chains' (Rees: 3). Such chains are interlinked refrigeration technologies that preserve perishable foods at an optimum low temperature that keeps them stable between the points of production and purchase, and, ideally, thence to the eventual store (refrigerated as appropriate) ready for commercial- or domestic-kitchen preparation.[43] This description makes it sound simple and indeed self-evident. Getting it to work effectively is what is complicated. Cold chains are integral to lengthy food chains and make their extent possible. And here if anywhere, what the foodstuffs are transported *in* is central. If nothing else, despite the successful preservation of foods at very low temperatures, cold can also cause damage e.g. freezer burn, requiring suitably stout packaging for protection.

A set of historical stages in devising the cold chain is discerned by Rees. The first has already been mentioned, namely procedures devised to generate cold, using naturally occurring ice. People learned that packing everything – both ice and foods – very tightly allowed transport of perishables from New England as far as India – a route used in this way from the 1830s. The second stage was not simply using cold but managing it. It is one thing to invent means of refrigeration, quite another to ensure it is reliable, given foods' perishability. More than that, the new machinery had to be practicable and affordable. Once making smaller more manageable machines (both refrigerators and deep freezers) was accomplished, the next task required working out technologies for controlling the temperature precisely. While an embryonic cold chain was emerging, with different foodstuffs transported along it, being able to alter the temperature at one or other stage was essential, given variation in rates of perishability. Only on reaching such a point could a new phase of expansion take place, the volume of foodstuffs transported grow, the distances lengthen, and a number of separate chains develop.

An earlier stage could arguably be interpolated when in 1923 Clarence Birdseye – inspired by his observations of pre-historic Inuit exploitation of freezing temperatures in Labrador – introduced 'quick freezing' at his newly formed company's fish freezing plant in New York, recorded as the first (Williams 1963: 2). Quick freezing is the process used ever since. As Birdseye had discovered, reducing the temperature rapidly preserves the nutritional quality as well as the structure of the foods (large ice crystals which form during slow cooling that break down the structure do not have time to form) never mind the economic advantage since it all runs faster (Johnston 1977: 60).

Rees' discussion deals primarily with the creation of the cold chain in America – where each stage of the cold chain's development was initiated. While today cold chains run worldwide, other countries developed their home-grown versions in America's wake. By the 1930s, there were some twenty packers and not quite so many distributors, primarily institutional, in the United States. This was large enough, however, for E. E. Williams to publish the first issue of *Quick Frozen Foods*.[44] But it was not until that decade, he records, that freezing began in England, only to be halted completely when war broke out. By contrast, in 1942 the US military required frozen food packers 'set aside a minimum of 35–60 million pounds of vegetables' of the following year's production – with 2,000 tons of metal allocated to the industry by the War Production Board (Williams 1963: 26).[45]

For a cold chain to develop, a wide range of associated technological devices have to become involved. It is not just requirements for appropriate controllable storage at all points along the chain after production, although that is essential. Examples include specialized very low temperature areas in distribution centres/warehouses, where palleted supplies are moved to and from racks, floor to very high ceiling, by forklifts, driven by staff huddled in outdoor winter wear, who statutorily are allowed a maximum of 20 minutes per stint before moving to a warm area for a break.[46] It also requires suitable equipment in retail stores – resulting nowadays in rows of deep freeze cabinets in supermarkets and stand-alone chest freezers in small convenience stores as well as storage equipment in homes – fridges and freezers. Above all, it requires means of transport that hold the supplies in the perfect temperature and humidity.

It also needs the support of the public who had to learn to regard refrigerated food as 'fresh' i.e. no different from newly harvested. Suspicion of fridges is recorded to have been that much greater in France than elsewhere, for two reasons. Those who typically shopped daily did not consider they needed home refrigeration – and could not see it was necessary for commercial uses either. Second, if merchants had refrigerated facilities, there was nothing to stop them from selling days old stock as if it were newly acquired (Freidberg 2009: 29).

More than that, the cold chain is not just a technology that consists of that string of devices linked by the very idea of itself, it is also dynamic; things move along it. And this in turn has to be managed successfully. Those concerned are experts in the relatively new specialism of logistics. An industry insider explained something of the responsibilities involved. Everything is geared, he said, to 'making sure that we as consumers get a quality product that is fit to eat and fit for purpose'. This requires focusing on efficiency and the safety of the product the length of the supply chain. This means he and two colleagues' getting involved with several others in their customers' companies: 'the marketing people, as well as the quality people and the distribution people' to deal for instance with the way changes in packaging box sizes evolved and solving whatever problems arose. 'What may suit the market, may not suit the product. It's how you actually get that right on the basis of "is the packaging robust enough for the product itself?" You need a different style and a different specification of packaging for, let's say, a box of two gross of chocolate bars as against a box of toffees'.

The range and variety of matters to be thought of was considerable: 'because we had air conditioned warehouses, and of course insulated vehicles with specific specification to ensure (a) that there was a thermodynamic content to it, but also that, for example, (b) floors were not made of wood like most trucks. They were made of aluminium planks because there could be the possibility … of a splinter sliding into a case and penetrating the product. There's simple and there's complex … being a logistician doesn't just mean you run trucks and sheds, it's actually thinking about the product itself; the quality of the product while it's in your care; how you want to make sure it gets to the final destination in good order and there was no possibility of it being infiltrated or penetrated in any form, and so you could put it straight on the shelf'. He continued, ruminatively.

It's all about materials handling and packaging, and that's what it's all about. To me, packaging is probably more about the way in which you can produce the most efficient materials handling solution, most cost-effective, and assuming that the food technologists have done their work, and have the right packaging spec for the job that is required, and the environment through which the product is being transferred from farm to fork effectively.

Rees among others may have thoughtfully identified historical stages in the development of the cold chain, but he does not mention that suitable packaging is essential for its success. As frozen or chilled foods move along the chains, they have to be contained in something that preserves their desired cold state.

Packaging and ready-meals, microwave ovens and frozen foods

Packaging, then, lies at heart of the assemblage-like trio of ready-meals, the microwave and frozen/chilled foods. Without it, everything would have to operate very differently. As already observed, the kind of package needed for frozen/chilled foods, ready-meals in particular, must have specific properties. From very early on, retail packaging for frozen foodstuffs tended to be cardboard boxes. Preparation would involve little more than removing the contents and using a household ceramic or enamel dish for heating in the oven. But by the late twentieth century, the distinctive features of the microwave oven appeared 'to dictate' packaging requirements. Jenkins and Harrington's textbook is based on the clearly stated premise that to 'an overwhelming degree' plastics best meets them (1991: 4). Moreover, their position bears out (the engineer) Hammack's contention that '(T)he microwave oven has achieved the status of a primary technology, meaning that other technologies adapt to it instead of vice versa' (2005). For not only did the aluminium of TV dinners have to be replaced, the 'challenge of dual ovenability' had to be met; materials would have to withstand microwaving and the 400°F (200°C) of conventional ovens as well as 0°F (−18°C) required for quick freezing. A range of factors affect the selection of plastics including resistance to deformation at different temperatures; being food-safe on contact; cost. They concluded that either PET or CPET was the most suitable.

In describing the co-evolution of the cold chain, microwave oven and frozen/chilled ready-meals, this chapter has introduced a notion of 'assemblage-like' to describe their convergence in the last few decades. The whole illustrates the complexities of the industrialization not just of that trio, but of cooking itself. In so doing, the discussion has relied on invoking something near to an inevitability of food packaging's – notably the plastic tray – being integral throughout. In addition, the industrialization of packaging materials themselves, reflecting in particular the manner in which science and technology has been harnessed, is shown to be part and parcel of ever more complex versions of twentieth- and twenty-first-century industrialization.

Notes

1. Mintel (2022). Available online: https://store.mintel.com/report/uk-ready-meals-and-ready-to-cook-foods-market-report (accessed 6 April 2023).

2. Costello, R. (2019). 'What's really in your lasagne ready meal?' *The Irish Times*. 9 April. Available online: https://www.irishtimes.com/life-and-style/food-and-drink/what-s-really-in-your-lasagne-ready-meal-1.3845595 (accessed 6 April 2023).

3. Genaro Contaldo, an Italian, UK-based chef. https://www.citalia.com/gennaro/how-to-make-lasagne/?infinity=ict2~net~gaw~cmp~17620392662~ag~~ar~~kw~~mt~~acr~38494 14225&gclid=Cj0KCQiApb2bBhDYARIsAChHC9s0tvbDsMFmw-0ndO5nk9Ym9yWeFehE qXkHS1JH26UrOqlfWPDV7FUaAgP-EALw_wcB (accessed 6 April 2023).

4. Lasagne is a name for both the dish's wide sheet pasta and the dish itself (Larousse Gastronomique 1988). Despite its Italian name in the ready-meal market, its origins are considered Mediaeval – a version was recreated on TV by food historians Ruth Goodman and Polly Russell. BBC Two, Inside the Factory, Series 3, Pasta https://www.bbc.co.uk/programmes/b08zjhj4 (accessed 6 April 2023).

5. https://www.google.com/search?q=how+to+make+lasagne+video&rlz=1C1GCEA_enG B974GB974&oq=how+to+make+lasagne+video&aqs=chrome.69i57j0i22i30l9.8552j0j1 5&sourceid=chrome&ie=UTF-8#kpvalbx=_hQptY-OJDruVhbIPp_G02As_30; https://natashaskitchen.com/lasagna-recipe/; https://www.youtube.com/watch?v=YNQM8ifqMy0; https://www.tiktok.com/@jaylfc86/video/6907435482951519490?is_from_webapp=v1&item_id=6907435482951519490 (accessed 6 April 2023).

6. For want of space the discussion ignores ready-meals' plastic film and cardboard sleeve, branding, etc.

7. https://www.bbc.co.uk/news/magazine-21443166; https://www.independent.co.uk/news/uk/this-britain/the-rise-and-rise-of-the-ready-meal-so-what-s-for-tv-dinner-tonight-5346532.htm (accessed 6 April 2023).

8. It only ended in 1954.

9. https://archive.marksandspencer.com/timeline/food/ (accessed 6 April 2023).

10. Lasagne, SMN, Nov 1972. JPG.

11. '(S)tored at temperatures at or below 8°C'; https://www.chilledfood.org/the-history-of-uk-chilled-foods/ (accessed 6 April 2023).

12. https://www.bbc.co.uk/news/magazine-21443166 (accessed 6 April 2023).

13. https://www.smh.com.au/national/heat-and-eat-ready-meal-sales-surge-as-time-poor-families-opt-for-convenience-over-home-cooking-20220728-p5b59t.html;

14. Jimmy Nicholls. 'Simmering down'. *The Grocer*. 8 January 2022, 43–4.

15. https://www.bpf.co.uk/plastipedia/plastics_history/Default.aspx; https://www.horners.org.uk/the-company/overview/

16. https://plastiquarian.com/wp-content/uploads/2015/06/plasticbook.pdf (accessed 6 April 2023).

17. An invented name preserving the anonymity of both staff and company.

18. As much as possible is re-used. For instance heat produced as a by-product of the operation is re-used, representing a financial saving into the bargain.

19. At the time of the visit, pre-pandemic.

20. Recycling plants elsewhere in Europe do not rely on optical recognition for sorting which means black does not pose a problem. But optical recognition systems are less expensive than alternatives.

21. As near weightless as used to be the soap flakes for washing 'delicates' before laundry liquid was introduced.

22. But Scholliers (2015) calls for an agreed definition.

23. As Shapiro notes (1986: 8), enthusiasm for science and technology lay at the heart of the domestic science movement and its espousal of Taylorism in the kitchen, at the turn of the nineteenth/twentieth centuries in America, with counterparts in the UK, New Zealand, Finland Sweden, etc. (Ekstrom 2013).

24. More recently detailed discussions have been taken up by academics in engineering.

25. https://www.atomicheritage.org/profile/percy-spencer and see also https://www.aps.org/publications/apsnews/201510/physicshistory.cfm; https://spectrum.ieee.org/a-brief-history-of-the-microwave-oven; https://ethw.org/Microwave_Ovens; https://www.enchantedlearning.com/inventors/page/m/microwaveoven.shtml; https://www.massmoments.org/moment-details/percy-spencer-inventor-of-microwave-oven-born.html (accessed 6 April 2023).

26. https://www.inventionandtech.com/content/%E2%80%9C-greatest-discovery-fire%E2%80%9D-0?page=full (accessed 6 April 2023). Hammack, W. (2005). 'The Greatest Discovery since Fire'. *Invention & Technology* 20 (40).

27. https://microwavemasterchef.com/microwave-oven-history/ (accessed 6 April 2023).

28. A 1995 flight-catering textbook refers not to a microwave oven but 'the regenerating oven… usually us(ing) a system of forced air circulation' (Jones and Kipps 1995: 127).

29. https://www.inventionandtech.com/content/%E2%80%9C-greatest-discovery-fire%E2%80%9D-0?page=full (accessed 6 April 2023).

30. https://www.nytimes.com/1972/07/14/archives/litton-introduces-microwave-ovens.html (accessed 6 April 2023).

31. Archival material about both men is held in London's Science Museum. https://collection.sciencemuseumgroup.org.uk/people/ap28359/andrews-gordon; https://collection.sciencemuseumgroup.org.uk/people/ap28360/napleton-lewis (accessed 6 April 2023).

32. https://www.leatherheadfood.com/about/Leatherhead (accessed 6 April 2023).

33. During a Q&A session after one of the talks, the speaker admitted that nobody knew whether or not microwave ovens were safe for users in the long term.

34. Experienced domestic cooks routinely deal with additional things simultaneously – from washing up, laying a table, tidying the kitchen to say nothing of feeding the dog or dealing with a crying two year old: see https://www.food.gov.uk/sites/default/files/media/document/818-1-1496_KITCHEN_LIFE_FINAL_REPORT_10-07-13.pdf (accessed 6 April 2023).

35. 11S/2.29/04 Science Museum Archive: for accompanying photograph, see https://www.beanzawave.co.uk/ (accessed 6 April 2023).

36. https://www.dailymail.co.uk/sciencetech/article-1191606/Beanz-meanz-microwaves-Heinz-create-gadget-heat-snack-60-seconds.html; https://www.gadgetreview.com/beanzawave-the-worlds-first-usb-powered-portable-microwave-oven https://www.fastcompany.com/1291762/beanzawave-worlds-smallest-microwave (accessed 6 April 2023).

37. Still on the market in the UK at the time of writing is https://www.heinz.co.uk/beanz/product/100185200051/no-added-sugar-beanz-snap-pots (accessed 6 April 2023).

38. Summer 1975 2(2:1). *Microwave News*. The publication 'is produced on behalf of Litton Microwave Cooking Products Ltd (gives Sutton address). It is devised and published by John Shanahan & Associates Ltd (gives address, Poland St) naming the editor as Greg Tingey'. A magazine of the same name is still published, now online. https://www.microwavenews.com/about-us (accessed 6 April 2023).

39. It is unsigned, but has no manufacturers' contact details although the name Swan Mill Paper Company Ltd is included, making it uncertain as to whether it is a news report or advertisement. The Company still trades: http://swantex.com/#aboutus (accessed 6 April 2023).

40. Spelling was not yet stable. 'Micro wave' was another variant.

41. https://www.pepysdiary.com/diary/1663/12/ (accessed 6 April 2023).

42. The ice house at seventeenth century Aynhoe Park in Oxfordshire was still intact in 2004.

43. As an industry insider, observed: '(T)he people who abuse food, more than anybody else, is the consumer. They used to call it the hatchback factor. You or I would go to the shop, get all this stuff, put it in the back of the hatchback, and think, "*Ooh, I think I'll get my haircut now*", and the car sits outside in ambient in the middle of summer, and then you start thinking about campylobacter and *E. coli*'.

44. E. E. Williams was already publisher of *Butchers' Advocate*, a meat trade weekly of which he had become owner in 1934 (Williams 1963: 1). His book is based on the complete run of *Quick Frozen Foods*. This is an instance in which cognate enterprises are developed close to one another until grown sufficiently large to 'stand on its own feet'. A further example is illustrated in his recording that early exhibits of frozen food packs were mounted at the 1938 National Canners' convention in Chicago (Williams 1963: 7).

45. Shortage of metals and other raw materials for the packaging industry during the Second World War as noted was widespread in addition to the shortage of other items such as bottles – despite increased demand for bottled beer for troops as well as orange and milk for civilians (Penn *c*. 1948: 55).

46. An industry insider explained that forklift trucks in the UK are reported to have originated during the Second World War when the US military brought them across.

CHAPTER 9
SALAD LEAVES AND PROTECTIVE ATMOSPHERES

Photographs of supermarkets in Singapore or Cape Town, Melbourne, Oslo or Santiago show that their fruit and vegetable aisles look strikingly similar despite their geographic dispersion. Classified into cucumbers, tomatoes, apples – some misted to help retain the crispness of a lettuce or to heighten the colours of red and green cabbages side by side in a bin – the foods are piled up, uncovered. It is tempting to suppose this is intended to give the immediate impression of foods straight from the farm, garden or orchard. Compare those photographs with those of street market barrows of today in Bordeaux or London, or of farmers' market stalls in Santa Cruz or Dunedin. The style of presentation is much the same: banks of fruits, salads and vegetables displayed to look as fresh as if they had just been harvested. Go back to the 1950s not long after the Second World War; the street markets and market halls of Lisbon, Swansea or Helsinki look little different – there are apples and cabbages raw, uncovered. In turn, these look little different from their counterparts before both world wars, for some features of selling salads, vegetables and fruit have not changed for well over a century.

Concentrating on the bins and shelves of raw cauliflowers, leeks and onions, piles of apples and oranges, neat rows of sweetcorn and peppers, it is, however, easy to overlook two major differences in the way fruit, vegetables, salads and herbs are sold today compared to those mid-twentieth century and before. It is not just that, on closer inspection, apples, carrots or potatoes are in plastic bags and oranges, limes and lemons are three, six or seven to a net (the yarn is plastic). It is not only that soft-leaved salads, lettuces and watercress are washed, then enclosed in plastic bags, so too are vegetables, ready-prepared for the pot, handfuls of sprouts, 'batons' of carrots, chunks of swede (rutabaga) ready to add to a stew. It is also that they are *sealed* into their plastic bags. Further, it is that some bags seem slightly puffed up, an inflated effect noticeable when handled.

'Fresh' – watercress, bunched or bagged

Look closely at one UK instance, on sale in a few shops – more expensive supermarkets and 'all good foodie outlets' as its marketing has it. Eight different leaves might be contained in one of Steve's Leaves' transparent bags, along with very finely sliced carrot or shreds of raw beetroot. This part of Vitacress, the parent company,[1] is based on a farm in St Mary Bourne, a village about 70 miles (approximately 110 km) south west of London, near the town of Andover, Hampshire. The village has been called the 'watercress capital of the world' by another commercial grower.[2] Watercress, which grows in water, whose taste is often described as peppery, is as often talked of as widely used to make soup. Steve's Leaves, however, sell it as a salad, to be eaten raw. Signalling their devotion to the plant, they declare:

> Now 100% recyclable bag. We take extra care of our babies. Our unique 'pillow-bags' are filled with nothing but fresh air, cushioning our leaves so they won't get squished in your trolley or fridge. Packed in perfect portion sized packs for no waste.[3]

This description adroitly conveys the virtues of these pillows. Not only is the plastic bag recyclable, stopping it polluting the environment still further, but the number of leaves each contains is managed to do away with left-overs. This catalogue of virtuous selling culminates in support for reducing the problem of gargantuan amounts of edible food wasted annually (Evans, Campbell and Murcott 2013). As significant, those small leaves are packed so each has space around it, protecting them all from being bruised or crushed by any contact either with each other or the bag itself.

Elsewhere on the brand's website is a further declaration as to '(W)hy we love watercress':

> Watercress is part of our DNA – we've been growing watercress for over a century. Eliza James, the so called 'Watercress Queen', created the watercress beds at St Mary Bourne in 1908 and we are still growing watercress here today.

The geographic location of the farm and the identity of Eliza James are significant for unravelling the history of watercress packaging – or as will be seen, its lack of wrapping.

Unlike ready meals or ketchups, in many parts of the world foods classified as salads are typically eaten raw. So too are most fruits, as are many vegetables, although both are cooked, the latter widely so – simply boiled or as an accompaniment to, or ingredient in, more intricate dishes.[4] This has not, however, always been the case. In Mediaeval England eating raw fruit was largely considered unhealthy, with cooking the solution (Wilson 1976: 299). Nowadays, selling fruits, vegetables and herbs ready to be eaten raw commonly means that all concerned – producers, retailers and customers – share an interest in their being fresh, not merely this side of rotting.

For producers and retailers, freshness is a virtue that makes it an important selling point which, if not commanding a premium, certainly seeks to evade depressing the price. For shoppers, freshness is widely understood to signal as short a time as possible between harvest and arrival in a kitchen and, thereby, regarded as a sign of goodness in both the nutritional and gastronomic sense. Yet frozen peas are advertised as fresher than any sold in the pod, sitting stored in rows of supermarket freezers alongside courgettes and spinach, carrots and edamame beans, their freshness literally frozen in time. And at one stage, a London wet fishmonger, presumably thinking the word had sufficient marketing potential, used to add 'fresh' to every label – sardines, line caught tuna, Cornish crab – as well as fresh kippers and fresh smoked haddock, despite, by definition, their being preserved.

Freshness is not so innocently self-evident. Its meaning has varied historically, as Susanne Freidberg shows. Partly, she explains, this derives from nineteenth-century city dwellers' memories of the dangers of perishable foods – milk carried tuberculosis, dirty vegetables dysentery (2009: 6) – coupled with increasingly widespread public knowledge of twentieth-century discoveries about bacteria. It also, however, resulted from unregulated advertisers' use of 'fresh' to capitalize on public interest in quality to sell their wares. Until

> eventually it became profitable for processors to trim, slice and package all kinds
> of refrigerated foods, and to market them as convenient *yet still fresh*. 'Fresh cut'
> fruits and bagged salads are among the more familiar examples.
>
> (2009: 7 original emphasis)

Indeed, she cites a representative of fruit growers who declared that freshness is 'the cornerstone of our industry' (2009: 2).

Regulators, she points out, have to try and determine when the term 'fresh' can and cannot be used as to describe/advertise some food or other. The Food Standards Agency (FSA), regulator for England, Wales and Northern Ireland, has to grapple with parallel questions, concluding that in the case of fruit and vegetables:

> The term 'fresh' is now used generically to indicate that fruit and vegetables have
> not been processed (e.g. canned, pickled, preserved or frozen), rather than that
> they have been recently harvested. This is acceptable provided it is not used in
> such a way as to imply the product has been recently harvested (e.g. 'fresh from the
> farm'; 'freshly picked') if this is not the case (see paragraph 31 above).
>
> (2008: 12)

Paragraph 31 turns, be it noted, on a different meaning of the word:

> Expressions such as 'freshly cooked', 'freshly prepared', 'freshly baked', 'freshly
> picked' should have no other connotation than the immediacy of the action
> being described. Where such expressions are used, it is recommended they be
> accompanied by an indication (e.g. of the date or time or period – 'freshly prepared
> this morning') of when the action being described took place.
>
> (2008: 11–12)

Even so brief an extract from the FSA document signals that their attempts at defining freshness can only make a start; the expression does not remain stable.

In the process of arriving at the current packaging landscape of salads, fruit and vegetables, an array of socio-technological innovations has been pressed into service, including refrigeration, irradiation, ultra-heat treatment, 'upstream' plant breeding or harvesting unripe fruit that is stored during transport in controlled temperatures/humidity to prompt optimal ripening timed for pre-planned distribution schedules. In addition, transport too has to be understood as one of these technologies, now that the food industry has shaped consumer demand to expect year-round availability of fruit and vegetables. These are often air- rather than sea-freighted to assure as short a time as possible between harvest and arrival on retailers' shelves.

On one hand, this well meets industry's understanding of consumer demand; on the other are those who condemn such industrialized production of freshness, pointing to the damaging environmental consequences that include using 'throwaway' plastic bags. Evans *et al.* (2020) examine the combination of the designation 'fresh' and such novel technologies, adopting a rather different analytic viewpoint from either of those positions. Instead of regarding freshness as a self-evidently virtuous quality of foodstuffs, they by-pass such evaluation to regard freshness as something to be 'unsettled' in a way different from those who want to 'expose' the baleful realities of the food system. It is not that they are unconcerned about adverse effects – quite the contrary for they suggest that 'freshness' has multiple realities. Their point is that their approach allows by-passing unduly simple black/white, pro/con positions on the use of plastic to the more even-handed discussion of the range of advantages and disadvantages to help decide the trade-offs which achieve the optimum results while minimizing adverse unintended consequences. Their overall position is one this book shares, namely of looking at a topic about which views are in conflict in a fashion that accommodates nuances otherwise ignored in simplistic good/bad characterizations. So doing can contribute to improving efforts by *all* concerned to reduce adverse consequences of current usage.

Questions of the meaning of 'freshness' were not on any regulator's horizon in the mid-twentieth century, certainly not for nations still in the midst of reconstruction after the Second World War. Food rationing in the United States ended in 1945 (with the exception of sugar which continued to be rationed until two years later). In the UK, however, food rationing did not end completely until 1954. Fruit, salads and vegetables had never been rationed in the UK, but their supply was uncertain, especially for imports.

Fruit, salads and vegetables were sold unwrapped, neatly stacked in boxes, piled up in greengrocers' shops which, in Britain's temperate climate, were (and sometimes still are) commonly open-fronted straight onto the street.[5] Packaging at that time was unlikely routinely to be brown paper bags – paper was in short supply throughout the war. Greengrocers wrapped potatoes or carrots, a head of celery or a fat cabbage in old newspaper to catch the soil that still clung to them. Others simply picked up the brass scoop from the scales, using it as a chute to slide the carrots or potatoes just weighed straight into the customer's shopping bag, dried-on soil and all. Even when supplies of brown paper bags improved, the habit of being served by the greengrocer themselves or an assistant persisted, with each customer waiting their turn. It was the shopkeeper who selected, picked up, weighed and, when it happened, packaged the shoppers purchases, handing them over only at that stage. A minor tension could – and still – be found between customers wishing to touch, smell or squeeze an orange or melon to determine its ripeness and greengrocers who did not want their stock bruised or the carefully perched displays disturbed. Mostly, shoppers contented themselves with just looking – sometimes peering very closely indeed – to assess the state of the goods on sale.

Vegetables were not only sold at greengrocers. They were also available at street markets on certain days of the week and from barrows pitched in the gutter or at the edge of a wide pavement at a strategic point in a town centre where most people passed by, on other days of the week. Both these arrangements continue today. To these outdoor sales in the last couple of decades and more are added farmers' markets typically specializing in the provision of organically grown produce, commonly at higher prices but sold directly to the shopper largely by growers themselves. They are not, of course, nowadays the main places for buying food. What all had and have in common, however, was personal service coupled with the scant use of packaging. That pairing had prevailed for a good couple of centuries and more but was to change first in the United States and then, imported to the UK after the Second World War, with the introduction of self service – the history of which is detailed in the next chapter.

Selling in the street – as distinct from a fixed building – is particularly long established, especially for foodstuffs which perish rapidly. Hawkers and food sellers are recorded plying their trade in ancient Rome (at whose height was the largest pre-industrial city in Europe) and across the rest of the continent thereafter (Holleran 2016). Major eighteenth century cities, such as London and Paris, were probably very well served by street sellers to the sound of their familiar, rhythmic cries (Taverner 2003). By mid-century, artists, poets and composers had adopted and adapted those cries, thereby both making them both more popular and helping preserve them.

Contemporary engravings survive, one set, *Kirks' London Cry Pack* of *c.* 1754, issued as a pack of playing cards, is held in London's Guildhall Library (1978). Somewhere between a shout and snatch of song, these cries' words had become standard, the intonation and lilt helping potential, mostly illiterate, customers recognize from some way off what was for sale. The range of items sold was very wide, but most of the smaller number of foodstuffs reproduced on the playing cards are noticeably highly perishable – especially fish, shellfish and offal, fruit such as melons, strawberries and cherries, also herbs such as mint and sage.[6] No items are shown individually packaged; instead they are transported in quasi-domestic containers of several styles of baskets, trays and a wheelbarrow.

Vegetables and fruits continued to be sold in the streets of major cities into the nineteenth century, persisting during the period when shops as they are recognized today were increasingly being established. Foodstuffs continued to be sold unwrapped, transported in containers compact enough to be manageable by one or maybe two people.[7] The London-based journalist Henry Mayhew (1812–87) provides vivid accounts of the lives and activities of those on its streets day and night. The doings of costermongers and barrow boys, prostitutes, swindlers, pickpockets and shoplifters, beggars, vagrants and musicians, clowns, sword swallowers and more are described in considerable detail – including street-sellers of 'eatables and drinkables' (Mayhew 2012).

He talked to two watercress sellers, a man in his 60s and an eight-year-old girl. The man explains that most of his fellow sellers used to have some other trade, but have become too old or infirm to continue. But there are also small girls, he says, no shoes, feet blue with cold. The eight year old is a thin, rusty-haired child, in a light cotton gown and threadbare shawl, who, although she is still young, responds to Mayhew's questions about toys and games with a 'look of amazement' and asks wonderingly whether 'the likes of me' would be allowed just to look at a park. Unlike other mostly barefoot children observed at the Farringdon market, this girl has something to put on her feet – a pair of oversized carpet slippers. She had to shuffle to keep them on, Mayhew observed.

There were two London markets where watercress was sold in season. Covent Garden – the main fruit and vegetable market – where it was on sale, ready bunched. And Farringdon market where women presided over their hampers crammed with watercress and small girls bargained with them, ready to pay no more than a penny for a 'market hand' as the eight year old called it. She might walk to the pump to freshen the leaves after they had been squashed in the hamper, and would then pause somewhere suitable, put her basket down and organize tying the stalks into 'as many little bundles as I can. They must look biggish or the people won't buy them, some puffs them out as much as they'll go'. Then she began the work of hawking them round the streets. She described her cry: 'Creases, four bunches a penny, creases'.

Although Mayhew does not say anything about the route via which the watercress reached London, it is very likely that by the time he published this account in 1861 it was already being carried by rail from Hampshire. It was a growing trade. Construction began on a new railway line in the same year – one that connected to an existing line between London and the south west of England, opening in 1865 as the 'Mid-Hants Railway'. Locally grown watercress was thus carried direct to London, continuing for a good many decades, hence the nickname 'The Watercress Line'.

There is also earlier evidence of transporting watercress by rail between St Mary Bourne and London. And it was St Mary Bourne where Eliza James established her watercress beds.

James rose from poverty stricken beginnings in Birmingham where as a child she sold watercress in the streets. Her business acumen helped bring considerable success – by mid-life reportedly the wealthiest woman in the UK. Widely known as the 'Watercress Queen', via James and Son, the company she founded, she handled as many as fifty tons of watercress per weekend. Living into her seventies, so famous was she that 'Her death, in 1927, received international attention and the *New York Times* described her as the "oldest and best known of the characters of Covent Garden," who arrived at her market stall each day on a watercress cart driven by her son.' Recounting her continued working 'like a Trojan', the report continues: '"(I)n the evenings she goes around the railway stations to meet the afternoon consignments of watercress, and sells them at once to the barrow men, to be retailed all over London"' (Lane 2017: 29). She trademarked the name 'Vitacress' which – coming full circle – is the name now used by the company producing Steve's Leaves on the very watercress beds Eliza James created.

Transported by rail, washed under a pump in the street, packed in Steve's Leaves pillows or some variant, all are carried out with an eye to keeping the watercress as fresh as possible. The very activities enact that aim. And buried in the midst of the different enactments of keeping them fresh is food packaging, one form in particular. This is modified atmosphere packaging (MAP).[8] The inflated pillows allowing Steve's Leaves space around each other are promoted as filled with nothing but 'fresh air'. Implicitly, the air in those pillows is contrasted with that of bags of salads 'packaged in a protective atmosphere' presented as keeping the contents fresh. How did leaves get to be sealed in that protective atmosphere that Steve's Leaves proudly eschew? The Interlude that follows provides a chronological background to the use of this form of food packaging.

****

Interlude: modified atmosphere packaging

A passage appears in the abstract of a 1988 article published in the *International Journal of Food Science & Technology*:

> An equilibrated modified atmosphere containing 1–3% O_2 and 5–6% CO_2 was established with 35 um low density polyethylene film after flushing with 5% O_2, 5% CO_2 in N_2. This resulted in a shelf-life of approximately 14 days at 5°C, almost double that of the controls.
>
> (Ballantyne, Stark and Selman 1988: 267)

The article reports the results of a study demonstrating an extension to the shelf-life of iceberg lettuce packed in a modified atmosphere. The quotation illustrates well the manner in which the technique is squarely identifiable as 'science and technology', primarily an application of both biochemistry and materials science to the preservation of foodstuffs. Some readers will understand all the technical references, most may only recognize some (an um is the same as a micron). Some readers will also be able to date the study as necessarily later than 1933 when low density polyethylene (LDPE) – invented 'by accident by scientists working for ICI' – was created half a century before the article was published.[9]

Turning to ask 'how did MAP get this way' reveals disagreement about its precise origins in the various literatures. Food science textbooks published several decades ago present chronologies stretching back to the late nineteenth century (Davies 1995, Blakistone 2012) while more recent commentaries by industry insiders push the timeline back even further to the 1820s.[10] Food scientists were clearly familiar with the basics of MAP by the 1930s. A 1939 general popular science book illustrated the links between science and industry with a feature titled 'science keeps our food'. Apples kept in 'gas storage' can be 'preserved for a great length of time at comparatively small expense' (Low 1939: 30).

A broader perspective on the scientific development of MAP from its inception was presented by a US economist in a 1967 report. The author explained his purpose. 'Although much has been written about CA (controlled atmosphere) storage, it is nearly always of a relatively narrow technical nature. This bulletin seeks to provide a broader historical perspective; where possible, it brings in economic and social considerations' (Dalrymple 1967: 2). The author drew several conclusions. One was to point out that while many think of CA storage as relatively new, its history is long, involved and international, with the science only 'taking off' (mostly) in the UK in the 1920s–30s, followed by commercial development in the United States in the 1950s–60s. Another picks out the way that consumers of apples – the foodstuff on which he concentrates – benefited from higher-quality fruit throughout a longer season while growers received higher net prices. 'Seldom', they reflected, 'have both groups been so clearly benefited by a new agricultural technology' (Dalrymple 1967: 2).

Further commercial development seems to have happened in the UK. The retail chain Marks and Spencer (M&S) is credited with an innovation that initiated '(T)he rapid growth in MAP products in the United Kingdom' (Parry 1993: v). M&S successfully launched a test of MAP packaged meat in 1979, quickly followed by the other major high street food retailers, such that by 1993 Parry confidently claimed: '(T)oday the United Kingdom leads the world in terms of market size and range of MAP products' (Parry 1993: v).[11]

Shorn of either boast or even marketing evaluation, an internal M&S report from the company's Packaging Department entitled 'Packaging Technology: Projects and Activities 1977–78' confirms that date. 'Shelf Life Extension' is a short sub-section of 'Reduced Store Handling'; it states:

> To reduce merchandising waste and increase turnover in the U.K. and in Europe, new techniques are being examined to maintain quality for longer periods. Gas flushing of meat, special packaging of poultry – gas flushing of bread has been examined and work will continue in 1978.[12]

If a report of M&S's next step is archived, it has yet to be located. But a reference to MAP surfaces later in a 1985 document on priorities for the packaging department which requires 'introduc(ing) a further source of supply of controlled atmosphere packaging materials' followed by a plan to extend the modified atmosphere principle to 'tomatoes, mushrooms, brussels [sic] sprouts and apples'.[13] Further note of continued work on MAP appears in a report dated August 1985 that '(W)ork is in hand … on bulk controlled atmosphere packaging of poultry'.[14]

The appeal of MAP is rooted in the industry's concept of shelf-life. Shelf-life is one of the technical terms used in the quotation heading this section, but the only one likely to be known to all readers, for it spills over from technical food industry use, probably via marketing and journalism, to become a widely understood expression.[15] For most day-to-day purposes, people need no careful definition to indicate that some food has a limited life. In the 1988 article in question, however, it has a technical meaning not least as the outcome measure for the study, thereby requiring operationalization and specification for experimental purposes.

Technical term or not, there is, however, no single, agreed definition in the food technology literature, although formal versions approximate one another (Khetarpaul and Punia 2017). A simple contrast can be drawn between a general public concern with the length of time a food item can be kept before it is unfit for use, and that of retailers who are 'particularly interested in the length of time a product can stay on its shelf in order to maximize sales potential' (Man 2015: 1). And, notwithstanding Dalrymple's conclusion for the 1960s, it is to this second interest that the use of MAP now seems most closely geared.

Certainly, a retailer would point out that a longer rather than shorter shelf life is in consumers' interests – and might add, that, as an industry viewpoint has it, it makes a 'significant' contribution to reducing food waste.[16] But thus far, exploration of the matter suggests that there is a greater volume of attention in the technical literature paid to the methods, applications and utility for using MAP for an ever-wider variety of foodstuffs among food scientists – and thereby presumably the food industry – than there is research attention to public opinion about MAP. Indeed, a study has yet to be found which investigates people's awareness of the term or knowledge of its meaning.

Perhaps the next twist of this history will turn on the extent of public awareness and knowledge about the technology – leading to a question of labelling. In the UK there remains a regulatory requirement that MAP be labelled: '(I)f a product has been packaged in a protective atmosphere, include the words "packaged in a protective atmosphere" on the label or packaging'.[17] The word 'modified' does not appear. Instead it is replaced by the adjective 'protective', connoting something more positive, valuable even. It originates in the UK's erstwhile membership of the European Union (EU) whence the requirement and wording come. But in the United States (and, apparently Australia and New Zealand) MAP preservation technology is, according to an article in the US online trade magazine *Food Safety*, 'invisible' to the consumer, since labelling its presence is not typically required.[18] This may account for the absence of public reaction even if there was inclination to object. Either people do not know about it or they do not recognize MAP via the wording on the back of their bags of supermarket ready-to-eat salad or hand-cooked potato crisps (chips).

Those last observations must, however, remain hypotheses. Much more exploration is required including systematic examination of mass- and social-media coverage, whether or not the technology has ever been the subject of adverse criticism by an NGO or pressure group. It appears thus far, however, that it is the plastic, not MAP, that is being noisily, publicly condemned.[19]

****

That Interlude documents one version of an answer to 'how did it get like this' by sketching the emergence of MAP. It details another instance where the food package itself is integral to the technique/technology for food preservation. It exemplifies too the way in which a widespread packaging technology understandably considered recent, is based on several decades of research and development. Furthermore, it opens new lines of enquiry, including seeking the thinking behind the EU regulation governing the label's wording that omits the word 'modified' and unpicking how MAP is, apparently, unnoticed, when single-use plastic food packaging is widely publicly condemned. For now, however, MAP continues to be ever more extensively used, a transition to something different not yet on its horizon. Not all have adopted it. Steve's Leaves packed in 'fresh air' stand half way between unwrapped bunches of watercress at farmers' markets or organic shops and the supermarkets bagged in that 'protective atmosphere'. All three co-exist.

The next Interlude illustrates the chronologies of packaging and of shopping serving as background to their convergence of twentieth-century food packaging in the disruptive advent of self-service food retailing.

****

Interlude: on the convergence of the histories of food packaging and of shopping

As noted, the history of food packaging is also the history of a long list of other innovations. These are multiple, co-evolve, but they are also non-linear and certainly are not invented in a smooth chronological trajectory. This Interlude focuses on the case of shopping and its history as well as its connection to the history of packaging. It is not, though, possible to talk of the history of shopping without also investigating the invention of the shop – along with considering its interior organization – and its precursors. To this must be included not just the mode of shopping, but also the very idea of it, plus its implications for associated social relationships.

Shops are (initially) urban phenomena. It is as if their emergence depends on the invention of towns and cities, a matter of economies of scale, with a certain concentration of population underpinning the survival of each enterprise. Although ancient Rome had its shops, much food was still provided there by itinerant hawkers (Holloran 2016) on a scale not matched till nineteenth-century London (Mayhew 2012). Indeed, until the last couple of centuries in Britain (if not Europe and many of its nations' colonies) most food for most people was not acquired by shopping in shops. Peddlers occasionally carried olives, anchovies or spices but in the nature of their activities could not readily carry fresh/raw foods (Fontaine 1996). Those able to acquire a surplus to sell – direct from a farm, perhaps – took fruit or vegetables from door to door. But it was the regular markets in even small towns which were especially important from the early Mediaeval period. Many were set up in market halls (Schmiechen and Carls 1999), often two storey buildings, with space at ground level protected from the worst of the weather but with neither doors nor windows where stall holders trade, visible to their patrons in as much light as possible. And, of course, even the very poor may have been able to grow some of their own supplies of root crops or cabbages. As for salads, herbs and some fruits, gathering from the wild supplemented what little could be bought. Until at least the early-modern Period, however, the circulation of coins especially in remote rural areas was limited, replaced by exchange or barter. Predictably, in so fluid a set of circumstances, prices were barely fixed; bargaining was prevalent.

All these arrangements were temporary – relying on baskets, hawker's packs or trays, market stalls collapsible for storage. Shops by contrast are fixed, an indoor space, with doors and windows, allowing the creation of a certain organization of the interior: a space eventually divided into sales area for customers and assistants with others for staff and assistants only such as stock rooms. A swift chronology of the creation of the shop summarizes successive inventions as a background for highlighting the significance of the connection between the history of shopping and that of food packaging.

Inventing the shop – a brief chronology (mostly England)

During the Middle Ages, selling food to the public was open air – the market square and, as noted, the market hall. What initially were temporary stalls were gradually made semi-permanent, all under the scrutiny of market officials.[20] In parallel, fixed places for making sales were ground floor rooms of a private house, with the goods sold through the window. Increasingly, sales were being moved indoors, with a 'shewying borde' on which to display goods. Mediaeval markets continued through the early-modern period, being the mainstay for selling provisions to townspeople. Country people would make the trip into town to buy and sell where an element of haggling was assumed.

It was during the seventeenth century that shops as interior spaces grew steadily – developed first in cities and towns but increasingly in villages. Gradually a shop came to mean a room within a house, open fronted, with any window space left unglazed, shuttered when needed by a grille. As gradually shops were expanded, glazed windows began to be introduced, albeit very costly and thus fitted only in élite shops in cities. At the same time, the interiors' organization became more elaborate – increasingly counters replaced 'shewying bordes' as standard, above, alongside or in front of, nests of drawers. City centres' scale made it possible to develop specialization among shops, but small towns and villages retained their general shops, carrying a large variety of goods, both durable (turpentine, candles, soap) and foodstuffs (spices, dried fruits). Such trends in the invention of shops generally continued through the eighteenth century, although much everyday food shopping remained in the open-air markets and hawked through the streets.

By contrast, it is the nineteenth century when retailers introduced innovations in the nature, organization and design of shops in general. Multiple shops (chains), larger shops and department stores are all creations of this century. In the process, fixed prices became more prevalent, associated with the innovation of marking the asking price on the goods themselves. Two further aspects were devised too: one was a style of active selling sufficiently energetic to generate complaints about 'pushy sales methods'. The other was the promotion of browsing as a pleasurable/leisure activity.

None the less, the whole venture was, ultimately, about selling. The form of social relationship between shopkeeper(s) and customers was in part expressed by the manner in which they greeted customers and then escorted them to a chair where they remained whilst an assistant brought goods to them. The shopkeeper's provision of a service was made visible in the etiquette of waiting on their customers. At the same time so doing controlled their customers' gaze, confining them to the chair, thereby discouraging any from having a look round on their own. Although the shopkeeper was a servant of sorts, it was they who knew where and what the goods were, as repositories of such specialist knowledge. In this they were superior to their customers who thereby depended – more or less sceptically, it can be supposed – on their advice. All the same, the very business of looking became more prominent, for shopkeepers were making good use of the newly available plate glass for their windows. Certainly that may not have applied to food shops as much as to the new department stores, but the general idea of 'having a look round' could still become familiar.

Packaging was used in the grocery trade in the eighteenth century: 'bags in which a wide variety of goods might be stored and the smaller paper packets in which they were often sold' (Stobart 2013: 114). They also appear in witnesses testimony in trials for shoplifting 'in such a way as to suggest they were the norm. Thus we see three separate thefts of a bag containing 17lb of tea, another with 14 lb of ginger and a sack with 56 lb of rice' along with '"a paper of nutmeg" and "a parcel of almonds"' (2013: 116). Containers that increased the recognizability of the foodstuffs inside, afforded by e.g. the packaging of tea in tin boxes turned up in the eighteenth century. But it seems that by the early nineteenth century, 'packaging increasingly took the form of bags. Around 1816 one shop's held various grades of paper (including blue paper, generally used for wrapping sugar), but also 109 lb of paper bags sold in seven separate lots' (2013: 141). Grocers were still selling two pounds' weight (approximately a kilogram) of sugar in distinctive blue paper bags in 1950s London. Wrapping foodstuffs their customers bought was a central element of their work (Chapter 3). This was integral to the distinct relationship between grocer and customer, carrying implications for the length of time the latter remained in the shop, but also for their opportunity to inspect, smell and possibly even taste goods before they were packed, opportunities eclipsed by pre-packaging. Such food packaging arrangements persisted well into the twentieth century. In any case, as noted earlier '(I)n Western Europe and North America until the 1920s most foods were sold unpackaged' (Lummel 2007: 173).

It is, then, that one of the most significant part food packaging has played – and continues to play – in the modern food system was initiated. And it happened at the very point where production and consumption intersect, retailer and customer meet. And it is at this point of convergence in the histories of food packaging and shopping when self-service is invented.

Food packaging and the invention of self-service in the United States

By the 1920s, shopping in many nations worldwide entailed some or all of the following: shops were indoor, fixed spaces; customers had become used to a habit of looking for and at what was on sale, carrying the implication of being able if not to select one item over another, certainly one shop over another. A specifiable etiquette and well understood relationship between shopkeeper and customer was routinely enacted without the need for either party having to think much about how to accomplish it. Prices were fixed and advertised, ruling out both an implicit invitation to bargain and avoiding the need to ask. The idea of one shop not merely selling a multitude of items, but very different types of item, both packaged and unpackaged had become familiar – Figure 15 shows a typical general store of the period.

Figure 15 Exterior, 1920s general stores, packaged and unpackaged food visible through the window. Mrs Oliver stands in the doorway.

This broad state of affairs was the background, against which Clarence Saunders, a grocer, opened a new store in Memphis, Tennessee. In the summer of 1916, he gutted the old store on a site he owned and on 6 September 1916 opened 1,125 square ft. (approx. 104 square m) using his Piggly Wiggly Self-Serving System.[21] In October, Saunders filed a patent for his invention – duly confirmed in 1917.

The main immediately visible novelty of his creation was completely rearranging the layout with most of the space thus cleared turned into lanes lined with shelves on which groceries were ranged. In particular, he specified the almost maze-like routes customers were to take, clearly marked with arrows on the diagram that is included in the patent application.[22] Thus the customer was led to pay at one place, at the end of the prescribed path.

In the process, the counter, direct descendant of the shewying borde, interposed between customer and shopkeeper, completely disappeared. Disappearing with it was the part played by shopkeepers and their assistants as guardian of the goods over which they presided, authorities on their quality or desirability. Gone was the shopkeeper who knew the customers and what they preferred or could afford. Gone with it was that personal relationship that develops when people interact on a regular basis. Shop assistants lost their authority and were 'reduced' to the less skilled status of operators of tills and check-outs. And instead of goods being out of bounds, customers could now handle them, look more closely, pick up two to compare different manufacturers' products.

What makes self-service possible is packaging. Certainly customers can (Chapter 10) serve themselves from bins, tubs or canisters of loose goods, but it can be impracticable, slow and, whether by the standards of the 1920s or the 2020s, may be regarded unhygienic. While packaging by the grocer in the back-room of the shop persisted until after the Second World War in the UK at least[23] (Chapter 3), it overlapped with packaging by manufacturers which was already well established by the time Saunders patented his invention.

As Susan Strasser remarks, packaging that much further up the supply chain paved the way for nationwide trademarked brands and their advertisement, both key elements in the creation of mass markets (1989). Gail Cooper's discussion of the development of the American chocolate industry adds that the new locus of packaging meant that companies could begin to 'compete on the basis of reputation rather than price' (1998: 77). Primary packaging now undertaken by the manufacturer replaced shopkeeper's packaging on the premises. Indeed, this shift made the major change in the relationship between grocer and customer even more visible. No longer did the customer have to rely on the shopkeeper to fetch or lift down the item wanted; shoppers' earlier reliance for advice on the grocer was supplanted by the information supplied directly from by manufacturers themselves on the package. Grocers and their authority were pushed out of the way as a new direct, if virtual, relationship between manufacturer and customer took its place. Now the customer could decide independently of the intermediary of the shopkeeper.

A wholly new assemblage is created. Gone is the one consisting of a foodstuff, a grocer and a customer. Introduced is an assemblage in which packaging itself is newly a 'player', an actant, shopkeepers side-lined as the manufacturer is introduced creating a novel relationship directly with the shopper.

The adoption of self-service in the UK

It was not until after the Second World War that shops in the UK rearranged their shops for self-service.[24] Commentary of 1961 illustrates that it was still novel:

> The post-war years have seen ... the appearance of numerous self-service stores and supermarkets, which in their turn are a direct result of the post-war shortage of labour. In such stores, the only salesman is the package itself.
>
> (Harrison 1961: 822)

> For all its flaws, self-service selling will oust older methods of retailing in many areas. As it does, package design becomes more important to business men.
>
> (Pilditch 1961: 11)

Pilditch's calls his book on packaging *The Silent Salesman*. War-time arrangements required shoppers to register with a named grocer, butcher and dairy in order to buy their rations until 1954. Without such arrangements, supervising the tasks involved would have been harder to organize – one reason for the delayed introduction of self-service arrangements. A further reason revolved around tight wartime and post-war building controls, limiting alterations to the internal layout of existing shops and/or building new ones. The first self-service shop in the UK is held to be a Co-op in London in 1942 (Shaw, Curth and Alexander 2004) which initially duplicated its stock by running self-service side by side with counter service so that customers could opt in or out of self-service (British Market Research Bureau (BMRB) 1950). Others were very slow to follow suit. Among the several reasons was the variation in advantage to shops between the large multiples and independent small traders (Usherwood 2000: 114–15). All the same, the government seems to have considered the innovation valuable, for its sponsorship enabled retailers to visit the United States on fact-finding missions.

In 1950, a market research report could still refer to self-service as a 'new method of retailing' ((BMRB 1950: iv).[25] It sought to review the 'the advantages and the various problems of this new form of retailing, with special reference to the grocery trade' (1950: 1). The results show that traders who had switched to self-service reported positive results:

(i) sales increased – more a result of impulse buying than at the expense of other shops

(ii) wage costs were lower in relation to sales

(iii) net profits increased

(iv) 'leakage', i.e. losses due to pilfering, had not increased

(v) most customers preferred the system, for it was quicker.

Sales staff's fears lest their expertise become redundant were also reported to have been allayed. Customers answered surveys signalling preferences for the increased speed of shopping as well as for not having to talk to assistants, instead just picking up what they wanted. In sum the report concludes that the retailer finds that 'his turnover increases, wage costs per £ sales fall, net profits are bigger, the appearance of his shop is improved, the problem of shop congestion at peak periods is solved'. Customers 'find shopping time is reduced', queues disappear and 'they can see the whole range of goods in stock'. As one interviewee is quoted as saying:

> You get to learn what to get and not get as you go. When I first went I bought more than I should but now I usually get what I want and only sometimes buy an extra. Most people seem to believe you spend more and it is easy as everything is laid out and it's so easy to pick up packets and tins of things because they look nice and tempting and make you want to buy. (Lower middle-class housewife. Aged 20.)
>
> (1950: 21)

Significantly the report adds: the '(M)anufacturer finds that packaging becomes of greater importance' (1950: 50).

Summarizing the observation that the history of food packaging is also the history of food shopping, some seventy years ago, the then President of the Federation of British Industry, (FBI) Sir Robert Sinclair, is reported to have observed that

> Packaging is the last phase of manufacture and the first of selling and nowadays, with the advent of self-service stores, where the pack must literally sell its contents to the shopper, it is often the final phase in selling as well.
>
> (BMRB 1950: 30)

****

Sinclair's sage remark underscores the actants in that new assemblage to which needs to be added marketing and advertising, branding and design, all centred on the packaging. That 'bunched or bagged' continue side by side in the current packaging landscape of raw fruits, salads and vegetables may limit the opportunity for branding. Marketing has been attempted via a spray direct on to the skin of salads, avocados, etc., but the extensive use of MAP in clear plastic coincidentally provides not just visibility of the contents but also a medium for branding – shrewdly summarized as already noted by Pilditch's *The Silent Salesman* (1961). The chronology portrayed in this chapter can only convey the barest of outlines and in the process is an unduly simple account. It misses out the position in, say, 1940s California, where the commercial feasibility in expanding sales of such perishable foods to more distant markets was impeded by limitations in the state of packaging techniques at the time (Mehren 1948). Similarly the account does not come completely up to date, for despite the difficulty of automating picking fruit, vegetables and salads the San Francisco Chronicle reported that developments in robotics suggest workable mechanization may soon be successful despite noting that at the time (2013) most harvesting was still done by hand – once more, the first not the last word.[26]

Notes

1. https://www.vitacress.com/ (accessed 6 April 2023).

2. https://www.watercress.co.uk/growing-watercress-faq (accessed 6 April 2023).

3. https://www.stevesleaves.co.uk/ (accessed 6 April 2023).

4. As is widely known, some such as the legume, commonly known as red kidney beans or the tuber, cassava, need to be cooked to render naturally occurring toxins inert, while fruits such as quince or perry pears are too tart enjoyably to eat raw.

5. https://www.iwm.org.uk/history/what-you-need-to-know-about-rationing-in-the-second-world-war (accessed 6 April 2023).

6. Among the items men are depicted as selling are beef, gingerbread cakes and Newcastle salmon, with four of women, one each hawking eels, 'sheeps Hearts Livers or Lights to Day', periwinkles and crabs from the basket on her head and live lobsters. The woman selling lobsters is unusual in this pack. Everyone else is carrying their wares in baskets perched on their head, strapped to their back or over their arms, whereas she has contrived a tray with short legs at each corner to rest down on the cobbles. In it she has two wide shallow baskets displaying rows of lobsters. As numerous among the foodstuffs are fruit, herbs and vegetables: four men, one selling potatoes from a wheelbarrow, one with what is possibly a misshapen basket of turnips perched on his head, a third with a basket covered by a cloth selling 'Strawberries Wood Strawberries Hautboys. Cherries, Large Duke Cherries' specifying the variety in the process and a fourth with a huge fairly deep basket on his head with another five, handled-baskets slung from his arms selling bunches of sage, thyme and mint. Finally a further four women are depicted; one selling damask roses – widely used in the kitchen at the time as demonstrated in Margaretta Acworth's Georgian Cookery Book (1987) – bunched in her basket slung over one shoulder, with one bunch held out in her hand, two more each with those wide shallow baskets on their head – of peaches, apricots and 'fine Ripe Necturns' a third with a basket on her head and a handled basket on her arm of musk melons while a women in hat and cloak pushes a barrow full of cucumbers neatly ranged in rows.

7. A series by Francis Wheatley who exhibited them at the Royal Academy towards the end of the century is shown at https://spitalfieldslife.com/2011/01/26/wheatleys-cries-of-london/. Accessed 6 April 2023. Scrolling down to the strawberry seller will clearly show her holding two pottles – small, cone-shaped handled baskets specifically designed for strawberries. The price would be per pottle.

8. https://www.propac.com/packaging-equipment/modified-atmosphere/ (accessed 6 September 2019).

9. http://plastiquarian.com/?page_id=14332 (accessed 23 March 2021).

10. https://www.campdenbri.co.uk/blogs/modified-atmosphere-packing.php (accessed 26 March 2021).

11. Note *Meat Science* carried a 1977 article on the preservation of refrigerated meats with controlled atmosphere (Silliker *et al.* 1977).

12. M&S Company Archive, reference Q/Q13/15/12/5/1, 3.

13. Ibid., 5.

14. M&S Company Archive, reference Q/Q13/1/5/12/5/9, 2.

15. Although it does not appear in the 1971 compact edition of the Oxford English Dictionary, it is now found in online dictionaries and as well as having a Wikipedia entry.

16. UK Advisory Committee on Packaging: http://www.packagingfedn.co.uk/images/reports/Packaging%20in%20Perspective%20-%20November%202008.pdf (accessed 7 April 2021).

17. https://www.gov.uk/guidance/food-labelling-giving-food-information-to-consumers#history (accessed 25 March 2021).

18. https://www.foodnavigator-usa.com/Article/2005/11/17/FDA-asked-to-rescind-use-of-carbon-monoxide-for-meats#. The use of carbon monoxide which preserves the red colour of meat and of tuna is banned in the EU and Canada, but was debated in the United States in 2017. https://www.ag.ndsu.edu/foodlaw/processingsector/packaging-labeling for note of US food law. (both accessed 29 August 2019).

19. https://www.food-safety.com/articles/4209-opportunities-in-modified-atmosphere-packaging (accessed 26 March 2021).

20. Other than foods, more permanent wares – leather saddles, chests or furniture – were sold in this period, direct from the tradesman's workshop, often the ground floor of his house in town.

21. A photograph of the first store two years after its opening is found at https://commons.wikimedia.org/wiki/File:Piggly_Wiggly_1918.jpg (accessed 6 April 2023).

22. https://patents.google.com/patent/US1242872A/en (accessed 6 April 2023).

23. And observable in a New Zealand supermarket in 2019 where, in a backroom whose open door made it visible from the customers' side of the fresh meat counter, large vacuum packs of lamb chops were opened and the contents repacked into smaller sizes designed for barbecuing.

24. Although Switzerland, Belgium and Sweden were thought of as pioneers (BMRB 1950).

25. The report refers to the debate current at the time as to how a super-market on one hand and self-service on the other may or may not be differentiated. See also Shaw, Curth and Alexander who note that the discussion was reflected in *The Grocer* at the time (2004: 574).

26. San Francisco Chronicle 'Robot Lettuce Pickers in Salinas Point to Future of Farming', 14 July 2013.

PART IV
WHERE NOW?

Introduction to Part Four

The question 'where now' faces various directions; one could refer to the future of the food packaging landscape, aspects of which are briefly examined in the next, final, chapter. The question, second, can just as importantly be asked of directions for the study of that landscape. Future investigation must improve on this book, not least, third, by inspecting the long list of topics omitted in the foregoing chapters. Only some include:

- ~ pursuing the book's main question about how the food packaging landscape came about, which needs to be extended to ask about the relation with histories of cuisines, eating practices and cultural conventions associated with meals and menus.[1]
- ~ redressing this book's Anglocentrism to develop a worldwide grasp of the food packaging landscape and its histories, examining the position in Japan in particular (Hendry 1995, Cwiertka 2020).
- ~ focus on smart/active/intelligent food packaging (Risch 2009). Not new, it was used in the Second World War US aircraft industry. 'Bags of silica gel are tied to the metal parts before wrapping to absorb any moisture from the air which has been trapped within the plio-film package. Silica gel is used because it is too inert to start up any chemical reaction with the metal finishes. An ingenious color indicator enclosed in the package is used as a signal' (Parkinson 1944).
- ~ detailing the history and sociology of the role of food packaging in branding, marketing, advertising and commercial promotion of products and its complex infrastructure. Investigations need to get down to fine details such as: the frenetic pace of working in a brand strategy agency for a commemorative re-launch of, say, Heinz-baked beans; the itinerant life of packaging designers temporarily moving to work in clients' offices to be 'in the thick of it all'; novice copywriters' bafflement at what one calls the 'argot' when a client declares they need FOP splashes, SOP standouts, and a BOP romance copy (front-of-pack, side-of-pack, back-of-pack).
- ~ studying the emergence of the packaging industry itself. This needs to cover the history and role of trade associations, of the trade press, of the size, value and structure of packaging manufacturing, the education, training and the establishment of university departments, of which the earliest is that of Michigan State University.[2] It is there that 'packaging as an academic discipline' was created, as Twede says in an interview (Anthony 2016). In support of such training, there

are a good many textbooks and handbooks whose readership is also geared to practitioners in the industry.

~ examining the history and role of regulation of food packaging, nationally and internationally.

~ identifying food packaging's historical development in respect of innovators' conception of gender – 'the housewife' has been widely regarded as the key 'consumer' (e.g. Cockburn and Ormerod 1993).

CHAPTER 10
FOOD PACKAGING: A TRIO OF FUTURES AND A PROVISIONAL ENDING

It is rarely a good idea to conclude one book by starting the next. In this instance, however, something like it is inevitable. Partly it is a reflection of the way this whole book is far too big for itself.[3] In part it is also because a major purpose of the preceding chapters – as the first not last word – leads to such an ending, however temporary it must be. This book was always designed to be superseded.

Its final chapter is much the same as the previous nine in that it is to do several things. Certainly it ends, as may be expected, with reflection on the preceding chapters. But before then, it considers transitions and conversions once more. This time it is three that have been planned, their overriding purpose being actively to change the food packaging landscape itself. Located at retail level, they originate, however, on the supply side, but with a particular sensitivity to changing public attitudes – where 'changing' refers to reporting secular trends, but also to an active intention to alter everyone's attitudes and activity. All three have primarily been spurred by efforts to reduce single-use plastic in food packaging.

Single-use plastic, solutions

Declarations by giant corporations foreswearing plastic packaging are plentiful.

> Our mantra and framework: Less plastic. Better plastic. No plastic.
>
> (Unilever)[4]

> We've used the three-pronged strategy of use less plastic, recycle more, and support system-wide improvements to set sustainable packaging goals that we continue to work toward globally.
>
> (Walmart)[5]

> In April 2022 South Australia became the first state where our supermarkets introduced compostable fruit and vegetable bags, available in all 67 stores across the state.
>
> (Woolworths)[6]

The background to such moves is global. They run from the 'top': the United Nations announced that '(I)t has become abundantly clear that the issue of single-use plastics has led to a global crisis, the scope and scale of which is only now becoming evident'.[7] Individual nations have their own policies. Some are very recent, such as India or New Zealand both in 2022,[8] some elements of US policy rather earlier,[9] the EU has been implementing its plans since 2021,[10] Chile was congratulated by the UN,[11] while some are pending, e.g. for Wales.[12] But even if policies for reduction of single-use plastic food packaging are widely being put in place, implementation, evaluation and any ensuing action deemed necessary were found in 2017 to vary considerably (Xanthos and Walker 2017).

Research on 'consumer attitudes' to single-use plastic indicates much concern that single-use food packaging be reduced (Walker *et al.* 2021; Weber Macena *et al.* 2021). The picture, however, tends to be patchy and varied; some seek alternatives, others simply avoid buying any. Data from one study record that participants are willing to pay for what they judge to be sustainable packaging, but not for any they consider unsustainable or about which they are not certain. The authors summarize their work by observing that since there is no general agreement about what kind of packaging actually is sustainable, their study raises a question:

> (I)f neither theorists, nor companies, nor government agree on the sustainability of different types of packaging – how are consumers supposed to make correct assessments?
>
> (Herrmann, Rhein and Sträter 2022: 106,219)

So, it would seem that from even a limited inspection of the position, beneath the general sentiment enshrined in international and national policies lies a mixture of attitudes and practices, plus lack of agreement about so much of the necessary detail.

Single-use plastic, solutions 1: Beeswax food wrap

The first of the three cases of a deliberate transition is the invention of a completely new, long-lived form of food packaging. This is an instance at one remove, for rather than being concerned with pre-packed manufactured goods on retail sale, it is an example of food packaging designed for domestic use – as storage in the kitchen or for carrying food 'on the go'. Initially, it took the form of a simple, single, sheet of wrapping material – typically of a cotton cloth coated with beeswax. After a decade or so on the market, however (suggesting sufficient demand), bags and other shapes and sizes are now included.

How such an innovation came about leads to a distinctive answer. Initial instances appear to result from just one or two individual's entrepreneurial energy and pioneering zeal. A rough-and-ready online exercise first carried out in 2018 was repeated in December 2022. Where in 2018 only two very small companies could be identified, the repeat yielded seven manufacturers in three different countries. Three more similarly small enterprises were now added, also founded by one or two people. Two more sources are also now available, from pre-existing, well known, commercial, domestic kitchen accessory suppliers.

What the five small manufacturers have in common is not simply their scale or the 'kitchen table' origins, but also the way they describe the motivations of their company's originators. These include phrases such as: a passion for doing something positive for the environment; a family want to reduce plastic food packaging; our founders are husband and wife; already with a background in selling sustainable products.

Parker Johnston's[13] start was very similar to these. She dates her thinking about devising her beeswax food wrap to the 2000s, launching her company towards the end of that decade. She reflected on those ten years and more of her increasingly successful small company and described the original impetus. Initially, she explained, her starting point was less environmental, more worrying about safety. As she pointed out, looking back, the concern about plastic in the environment had not really started. What prompted her thinking was reading about Bisphenol A and other endocrine disruptors. Her fears had grown about the risks from the plastic itself. This led to her searching for something that was as close to the natural as possible. As a result she spent a good deal of time in libraries and museums, looking for information about likely, naturally occurring materials.

Shrewdly (she described herself at the start of the conversation as entrepreneurially minded), Parker narrowed down her list of likely candidates to include only those which had already received regulatory approval. Equally shrewdly, one of her criteria was that her product had to mimic the behaviour of plastic, with the same character as cling wrap, serving the same purposes as plastic. Thus it had to be mouldable to its contents or covering a dish – to have the 'plasticness of plastic'. Unlike plastic, it had to be readily cleanable and storable ready for re-use. That way people would already know what it was for and how to use it. Parker displays considerable doggedness, describing how she sought as many different shapes and sizes of dish, bowl and likely contents for her novel wrap as possible in order to start determining its optimum size and shape.

An increase in the significance of debates in the mass media about the environment and about food waste, that were barely started when she founded her company in the 2000s, is reflected in her company's sales records. Around 2018, the pace picked up and more new companies in many other countries were putting such wraps on the market. Parker is pretty sure that those developing debates are responsible for spurring both the production of other wraps in addition to her own and consumer readiness to consider non-plastic wrap.

The upshot is that Parker Johnston's enterprise, undeniably 'niche' when it began, found its time had come once the reduction of single-use plastic moved up public/policy agendas. Hers is, of course, not the only innovation which can stand as a response to that topic. Also designed to replace oil-based packaging is the second case to be considered – that of bio-based plastic, typically used to bag foods.

Single-use plastic, solutions 2: manufactured biodegradable polymers

Researchers at VTT,[14] a long established institute in Espoo (near Helsinki), were among the earliest to develop techniques for demonstrating biodegradability, and were involved too in pan European work on associated standardization. Commitment to sustainability led to seeking ways of converting by-products from waste and/or lower- to higher-value uses. Resulting from starch production for the paper-making industry are quantities of potato peelings, prompting their experimental use in the creation of greaseproof food-wrapping (Figure 16).

At least two decades later (3 November 2022), an English newspaper reported a study emanating from 'The Plastic Waste Innovation Hub' of University College London, directed by Mark Miodownik, materials scientist and engineer (Purkiss *et al.* 2022). The conclusion was that '(M)ost plastics marketed as "home compostable" don't actually work'.[15]

While it is unsurprising that the work was reported for readerships beyond the academic, what is striking is that an organic vegetable box delivery company, Abel & Cole, altered its policy on the basis of this (and other studies). Before Purkiss *et al.* published, *The Grocer* carried an article by Hugo Lynch of Abel & Cole explaining their thinking in 'ditching "compostable" plastics'.[16] Almost immediately, a notice appeared

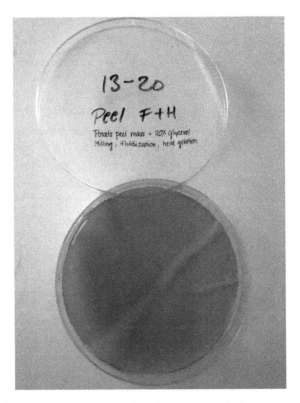

Figure 16 VTT's experimental, greaseproof food wrapping made from potato peelings.

on that company's website: '(I)t turns out that compostable plastic only breaks down under certain conditions. And unless your local waste collector has exactly the right kit, compostable plastic behaves a lot like regular plastic'. The company reports its solution – stopping using compostable plastics. The text continues to detail what additional measures are being taken to reduce and/or reuse packaging, citing the 'research behind our decision'.[17] Without a working technical solution to the automatic separation and sorting of compostable plastics in an 'entirely unregulated sector', the company's decision is based on the view that such packaging must be prevented from ever entering the system.

Strikingly, Riverford, a slightly older organic vegetable box delivery company, made plain its own position.[18] Less than a week later, its founder Guy Singh-Watson wrote of his surprise at their 'fellow veg box business' announcement.[19] Riverford's reading of research findings, coupled with their own experience of successfully composting bio-based plastic bags, led them to continue usage. Singh-Watson conceded, however, that 'differences between various "sustainable" plastic alternatives is complex, and nightmarishly hard to communicate', adding that 'it is impossible for any business to implement a well-managed cradle-to-grave lifecycle for our packaging when there are over thirty different kerbside recycling systems across the country'. The upshot, he concluded, 'is confusion and chaos'. Although diverging in their policies, these two organic vegetable box companies share a view of the market and regulatory position. It echoes WRAP's[20] new guidance issued two years before which addresses 'the *confusion* over compostable plastic packaging giving retailers and manufacturers the tools to make the right decisions when considering using compostable plastic' (emphasis added).[21]

At the time of writing, the strong impression is of a transition still in progress. This is a stage when the basic research effort is no longer so young but regulation (at least in the UK) of compostable packaging remains limited – in the view of some, unpardonably so. This prompted Miodownik *et al.* to declare that the public is confused. It is hard to tell yet, though it is possible, whether this instance is more far reaching than the other two cases considered in this chapter. Answering questions about what place biodegradable plastic takes in the packaging landscape lies in the future; only beginnings are currently visible.

Single-use plastic, solutions 3: unpackaged

'Unpackaged' food shopping is contemporary and positive, or at least it could become so early in the twenty-first century. It has, however, taken fifty years to happen. Certainly, the advent of self-service is key in the co-evolution of shopping and industrialized packaging (Chapter 9). But the latter's introduction did not take place all at once. Even if packaging, in industry insiders' view (Chapter 2), originated in the late nineteenth century, it probably only accelerated towards what is recognizable today after the Second World War. So, documenting FGR supermarket innovations from their post-war beginnings, Lummel records their investing in packing machinery, 'especially for fruit, vegetables and cheese, which was concentrated within an area outside the sales floor', aiming to 'avoid both time-consuming and expensive wrapping behind the counter' (2007: 173). Again, around 1960, the laborious tasks of selling coffee beans, weighing and bagging were replaced by coffee-roasting companies' marketing of their beans 'in vacuum-sealed packs and with a pre-printed price recommendation. With an attractive design the packs were then delivered by the industry in standardized cartons which could be easily placed on to the self-service distributor's shelves' (2007: 166).

Underlying these shifts were changes in the organization of the supply chain which also saw the beginning of the centralization of warehouses. From the late 1950s onwards, 'distribution companies began either setting up packing centres or outsourced wrapping to a packaging company' (2007: 172). The point was to optimize sales space. By the mid-1960s this had shifted, with almost all goods reaching the supermarket pre-packed. He adds a neat point that it took some time before packaging was standardized; in 1961 there were over 400 different cylindrical tin can formats. But further efficiencies could be gained once all foodstuffs arrived at the shop 'standardized, stackable and on pallets' to European standards.[22] As he observes, food innovations of that period were also innovations in packaging.

A similar shift from less- to more-fully packaged is recorded by Roger Horowitz' discussion of meat distribution, especially in retailing, in the United States. Shoppers 'snapped' up the new 'convenient sliced bacon package', for which investment in labour and machinery was needed. Equipment for quick-curing belly pork was introduced in the 1950s, with 'speeds doubling within a few years'. The quick-cures were, however, ineffective against a new difficulty of a deterioration in colour and loss of flavour when slicing bacon in advance. 'Better packaging was the answer to this new problem.' As Horowitz observes, the initial use of cellophane (almost from its introduction in the United States by DuPont) underwent a transition to vacuum packaging. 'Refrigerated bacon could now be stored for six weeks' (2006: 66–7). Summarizing some of the changes in Europe, Trentmann offers a sketch:

In 1950(s) West Germany, peas, lentils and rice were mostly sold loose. By the end of the decade, they all came pre-packaged …. In Berlin and Paris, half the rubbish was now packaging, mostly paper and cardboard: plastic still made up only 3 per cent of waste in 1971. In Canada, beer continued to be served in returnable bottles but, elsewhere a new culture of convenience took over …. In West Germany, the number of one-way bottles doubled in the course of the 1970s to reach 3 billion.

(Trentmann 2017: 635–6)

All the transitions look to be from unpackaged to packaged.

Packaging can, visibly, mark social status. The sociologist Jukka Gronow examines what could be an oxymoron of Soviet consumerism of the 1930s. This was a period of Soviet Union history when it was just becoming possible to aspire to an improved lifestyle without risking condemnation as 'dangerously petit-bourgeois' (2007). First-class eating-out became possible and luxury-food stores could be found in the major cities. A shop's inferiority, however, could be detected by the *absence* of food packaging. Some seventy years later, the exact opposite is evident. Another sociologist, Isabelle Téchoueyres, reports that for the denizens of the City of Bordeaux's open-air street markets, it is the *absence* of packaging which is held to announce their superiority over the industrialized provision of food. The 'freshness of products is a quality widely granted to market goods because they appear closer to their natural state: free of packaging, fruits and vegetables seem to arrive directly from the soil to the stalk; the complex commercial process which takes the products through successive hands is denied' (2007: 246).

It is only after the invention of packaging, with its plethora of connotations, especially those which are negative, that the word 'unpackaged' can start to make a newly positive sense. In turn, this allows a specific version of 'unpackaged', a novel form of retailing food to make sense. 'Zero waste' shops sell virtually no foodstuffs that are packaged by manufacturers, but instead they are sold loose, unpackaged – not necessarily a simple change (Fuentes, Enarsson and Kristoffersson 2019). It is undoubtedly a tiny shift, historically speaking, even if its publicity looks far larger. It will be an unknowable time before anyone could talk of 'from unpackaged to packaged and back again' if that ever happens.

Catherine Conway[23] is credited with setting up the first modern zero-packaging shop in the world in 2006 in north London, then in her twenties.[24] Customers at such shops either bring their own containers or can borrow or buy reusable ones on the spot to serve themselves from duly labelled bulk containers with rice, nuts, dried fruits, etc. Conway explained that she had always tried 'to live an ethical life' and had long sought refills rather than newly packaged household cleaning products. What seems in retrospect to have been key in precipitating her towards zero packaging more broadly was a mouse who had proved difficult to deter (but which she had not the heart to kill) in her east London flat. To protect her store cupboard food supplies, she decanted foods into glass jars because 'it was just practical'.

> And I remember very clearly one day putting the stuff into Kilner jars and having all of this packaging my hands and thinking, if I can refill (household cleaners) – which I consider to be quite a difficult product in terms of health and safety and information that the customer needs and things – then why can't I refill rice and muesli.

Her further thought was 'well, why don't I have a go at doing something?', one which coincided with her being frustrated in her then current job and looking for something interesting. She found herself getting 'involved in the concept of social enterprise' and an associated organization which provided modest short-term funding.

> So I just thought, 'well what would happen if I just set up a whole shop where everything was refillable, and would that be quite an interesting campaign?'

Initially she had a single stall in a street market, then a second at which point, despite family help to drive supplies to and fro, it all became too difficult. 'It's just impossible to carry that much heavy stuff … You know … 10 kilo sacks of dried goods and things'.

Her history of those early days exposes the complete absence of a supply chain for bulk unpackaged goods. In her 400 sq. foot shop she carried 700 products 'about 80% of which were refillable'. She bought from a retail cheesemonger, a European delicatessen, and could negotiate deals such that, from the latter, she could

> buy extra virgin olive oil … and they would give it to me in a 25 l drum. Now it was much, much cheaper for them to put it in a drum (you know … they bottle it in Italy) than it was for them to put it in 50 fancy 500 ml glass bottles. So, at that point, I got it much cheaper, the producer saved money, I could get a bigger margin on it, and I could pass it on cheaper to the consumer.

But it was difficult to make money in such a small store where London rents were high and when a separate larger enterprise failed, she had to start all over again.

> When I sort of came up for air, I realised that I still hadn't really made a dent. Still, packaging wasn't – so we're up to 2013 now – on the agenda in the way that I wanted it to be.

She described her continued work of publicizing the idea – the thinking behind what led to her shift of focus (in July 2022), including developing collaborations with larger retailers, is detailed online.[25] Conway's early beginnings and commitment are parallel to those early ideas of Parker Johnston's and others who set up companies to sell beeswax food wrappings: a strong personal dedication to environmental improvement, reduction in waste, coupled with determination and entrepreneurial flair.[26]

Growth in the zero food packaging shops since Conway's first shop in 2006 seems to have been considerable. Initially, their viability was fragile: around 2008, hearsay had it that there was a fairly rapid rate of closure among such small enterprises that were known to have been started in the Netherlands, Germany or the UK. Today, in the UK alone, a blog which includes a directory of zero waste food shops declares there are more than 100 of them in all four of its nations.[27] This pattern is reflected in a pan European Union (EU) study of the nature and extent of zero waste retailing. Graphs for dates of opening, forecasts of total number of packaging-free shops per million people, all record a steady increase (Beechener *et al.* 2020: 7). It reports 'very strong growth in the sector over the past 10 years, in terms of shop numbers, job numbers, and total turnover growth', estimating an average of EU total turnover from bulk good sales in 2030 of approximately €1.2 billion and a 'best case scenario' of over €3.5 billion (2020: 15).[28]

Single use plastic: coda

Tempting as it might be at first sight, the discussions of the three cases just presented are neither to be construed as an example of permanent transitions, nor a 'return' even to the position of packaging in food retailing of the early twentieth century or even the nineteenth. They represent a set of novelties in the landscape of twenty-first-century food packaging whose persistence remains unknowable. It is, however, striking that the great number of websites, reports and videos of zero packaging shops and their proprietors not only illustrates a remarkable similarity in the latter's autobiographies, motivations and commitment, but also in the very look of such shops. And zero food packaging shops are, for the most part, concentrated in industrialized nations. Possibly this form of practical response to 'overpackaging' is growing. Now there is a detectable impetus, a rejection of industrialized trends and forms of consumerism, replaced by an explicit valuation of commitments to ethical alternatives and pared-down living. Makers of beeswax and similar alternatives to single-use plastic domestic food wrappings evince a parallel sensibility. Indeed, the demographic/social milieu commonly associated with such rejection is sagely recognized in the choice of retailers whom Conway advises on moves to zero waste aisles in larger shops – an organic-only retailer and branches of an 'up market' supermarket in a well-heeled suburban area of a city.

Those three cases of reaction against single-use, oil-based plastic are likely still to represent a tiny element of the whole contemporary food system. That their fate remains unknown is obvious and, indeed, beside the present point. Given that they are current – whether by chance in a state of flux as might be the case of compostable plastic packaging, or tentatively shown to be increasing as in the case of beeswax wrapping or zero-packaging food shops – enables a different view on the decision-making behind their adoption. Where so much of decision-making about the early lives of food packaging established centuries ago was either incomplete, never recorded, or lost, and where much of twentieth-century thinking may remain in archives (no-one will know until much more investigation has begun), some of the thinking behind the institution of these three cases is available, precisely because it is both current and also emanates from individual zeal and dedication. [29]

A provisional ending

It is not just seemingly recent technological innovation which has its origins earlier than some expect – so too are thoughtful observations about the social place of food packaging:

> The packaging industry can be represented as an undesirable and unrighteous manifestation of the 'consumer society', adding unnecessary frills and expense to the process of distribution, using scarce materials extravagantly, disfiguring the landscape with litter and contributing, especially in the food industries, to the debasement of taste with products cultivated and processed by unnatural means.
>
> (Reader 1976: 214–15)

With Reader's comment in mind, this chapter rehearses the raison d'être for persisting with this book's multitude of disparate angles and directions. Asking how did the current food packaging landscape come about has led to different types of answer. Much of the book has answered the question chronologically. A good deal has answered it in terms of the way a food package is made, how its very material is manufactured, the invention of a packaging-making machines, barrels, paper, Owens' bottle making machine. Other answers have been far more fine grained: devising a successful metal beer barrel, cataloguing the dramatis personae involved in patenting canning. Still others have illustrated the co-evolution of a food package with the development of other major inventions, such as plastic trays of ready meals that can go directly into a microwave oven.

Asking how the modern packaging landscape came to look as it does today is intriguing in its own right for those with that quirk of curiosity. But there is more that propels writing about the various types of answer presented in the previous chapters. A key purpose rests on the (sociological) truism that the way people see something shapes their thinking and what they do, or do not do, with it, to it or about it. The book's intention turns on ways of looking at and thinking about food packaging and its myriad features. It tries to reveal things unnoticed, unknown and 'hidden in plain sight' (at least in industrialized, consumerist societies).

Only beginning the task, able to do no more than scratch innumerable surfaces, this book is, to repeat, a first, not the last word on the matter. None the less, it strives, in the process, to stress the materiality of food packaging together with the materiality of the foods they contain, as well as the materiality of the people who pack, carry, buy and eat them. Attention to the materiality of food packaging is not to replace study of the associated social or economic histories or to by-pass the cultural and political. They are to be put on a par with one another and their intricate interrelation highlighted.

The notion of assemblage was introduced early on, to be borne in mind when reading more of the historiography of food packaging inventions and innovations. It was never intended – and no space has been made for it – to serve as a slavish analytic exercise for every case introduced. Technical terms such as assemblage, along with transition, conversion, or come to that detailed discussion of materiality are only occasionally mentioned in favour of seeking to display the expanse of empirical answers to the question about the origins of the current packaging landscape. Those terms appear now and then through the book by way of underscoring this interconnection between the material and the social, for now, aiming to emphasize their parallel importance. Such allegiance to STS thinking, adopted in deliberately light touch fashion, does not aim to make an intellectual contribution to that specialist literature, but instead is to underpin a particular and less common orientation to thinking about food packaging.

The reason for doing so is simply that there is a potentially catastrophic problem. The world is in trouble. Unless effective, global measures are taken, as all the most authoritative commentaries confirm, the planet will become uninhabitable. And dealing with food packaging as it has become in so many versions is among the tasks needed. It may be that all the environmental scientists' predictions are wrong and the worst may not happen. But acting as if those scientists are right has not, as far as is known, been shown to do the planet any harm, rather the opposite. And while the economic and other costs may be high, may reduce profitability, may require currently well-off nations to sacrifice more than those less well off, the costs are comparatively short-lived compared to irreversible planetary damage that ultimately renders all life extinct. The planet will survive whatever happens, just that all life that it once supported will be dead.

Adopting STS attitudes in thinking in terms of assemblages, co-evolution, transitions and conversions is to help see the several sides to the inventions and innovations, the promise and the drawbacks, that make up the way the current food packaging landscape has come about. Seeing the kaleidoscope of facets and angles of which the landscape is composed instead of undemanding divisions into 'good'/'bad' is to do no more than shed more light on the current state of affairs. Without, however, a secure understanding of how the food packaging landscape comes to look as it does, policies and good intentions are unlikely to succeed.

This book's conceptual attitudes allow side-stepping deterministic interpretations that treat technologies as responsible for 'altering' society. It is not microwave ovens as such which change kitchen practices and are not, despite Hammack's assertion, responsible for altering women's roles. Those technologies are undoubtedly actants, players on the stage of change. But it is the *combination* of the technologies, from the magnetron to the provision of a stable domestic electricity supply, with the uses to which people do or do not put them, which are responsible for changes. Technology and society are not independent of one another. Technology does not somehow exert influences external to society – any more than do people manipulate components of technology with no 'obstruction' from the materials. Technology is part of society and the social is integral to the technological.

Further, that STS approach is adopted to help set aside seeing food packaging as the sole outcome of some singular flash of inspiration by a 'father' of an invention or a great man (rarely a great women, *pace* Margaret Knight). The history of technology makes plain that one invention has to be understood as the successful outcome of several precursors, its earlier trials and errors in the plural. Such an approach helps play down human motivations as a source of taming things, conquering them to serve human purposes. Adopting it is to put technology and society together, to be sure of recognizing they are interrelated if not interlocked with both having a form of agency, both are active not passive, actants not actors. It is to deploy the approach as a resource for evading the analytic drawbacks of whig history, technological determinism or a separation between technology and society, thus supporting a move towards a clearer-eyed view of the food packaging landscape.

At the outset, it was firmly stated that the book's discussion does not intervene in discussions about food packaging and the environment. In like vein it very firmly side-steps calls for action to limit environmental damage (but Zeide 2018, Mah 2002). Thus it neither commends buying from an unpackaged food shop nor does it argue against it. It neither promotes reducing, reusing or recycling, nor does it wish them scaled back. It does not urge alignment with one or other anti-plastic campaign, with 'eating local' or shopping at farmers' markets but neither does it recommend evading engaging with them. It barely mentions alternative food networks or one or other food movement, but that is not to say they are unimportant. Nor does it advocate widely publicized practices of eating which would reduce the use of processed and pre-packaged foodstuffs, as promoted by journalists like Michael Pollan (2008) but neither does it suggest they are not important. In any case, this book's coverage cannot – and is not designed to – provide appropriate evidence to support any of these actions, significant though they may be. This book neither recommends nor condemns those actions. Others are already recommending all these activities and more. This book is to complement their efforts not duplicate or supplant them.

Yet this book is not the least indifferent to the damaging environmental effects of food packaging and does not ignore them. On the contrary, it must refer to them. Indeed, a key raison d'être for putting this book together is the idea that should anything need to be changed, it is as well to acquire an understanding not just of what it is, but also how it came about. Centrally, it seeks to make the lives of food packaging more visible. Accordingly, it aims to prompt closer inspection of what food packaging is and what it does, *for good and ill*. It aspires to prompt questions along the lines of: if one or other type of food packaging were to be abolished, what would the gains and losses be? Could any losses be made good in other less damaging ways? If nothing else, this book urges anyone, moved to complain of the volume of food packaging they are obliged to discard, to do two things. One is to discover if that same packaging served any useful purpose before discarding it. The other is to ensure that any proposed alternative neither reduces the utility of the packaging it replaces nor introduces new problems.

So the book tries to support more nuanced thinking when contemplating food packaging's virtues and vices. It seeks to make it easier to notice that black/white views, however beguiling, can often be too simple. A PET bottle littering a gutter that ends up in landfill may well be an example of 'plastics bad' but how do rPET bottles, duly recycled and returned as feedstock for new bottles, compare? Does that become an example of 'plastics good' or is it a case of 'plastics not quite so bad'?

The book illustrates the manner in which histories of food packaging do not exist in isolation from the histories of other technologies – of transport, retail or storage, of the cold chain, types of oven or ideas about convenience or the ease of use. It tries to encourage recognizing the co-evolution of food packaging's invention and use with that of those other technologies revealing the manner in which they all become intertwined. They may even be locked together in such a way as to create huge difficulties for anyone trying to imagine where to start to untangle them. Picturing counter-intuitive alternatives may be the best answer, but failure to recognize the nature and extent of the entanglement in the first place could lead to costly blunders.

Overall the book intends to provide ways of looking that help far clearer appreciation of both the food packaging landscape's history and its current nature. It seeks to help knowing that landscape in greater depth and detail, as well as supporting wider recognition of the way packaging locks the food system together. If the food system needs a major overhaul then it is essential, when working out where to start, to grasp how extensive is the underpinning role of food packaging in its persistence.

Notes

1. A point underlined by the anonymous reviewer of draft one of the ms.

2. School of Packaging (nd). 'History: packaging beginnings'. *Michigan State University.* Available online: https://www.canr.msu.edu/packaging/about_the_school/history_and_mission (accessed 6 April 2023). Note that the dates recorded on the MSU website and those listed by Diana Twede, one of its most eminent researchers (Anthony 2016), are out by a year.

3. Primary material enough for a book three times the length was collected – an unavoidable consequence of the strategy adopted for amassing it. Given how little previous work could be located more material than could be used was deliberately gathered in order to have an extensive volume against which to make decisions about what to select.

4. Unilever (nd). 'Rethinking plastic packaging'. *Unilever.* Available online: https://www.unilever.com/planet-and-society/waste-free-world/rethinking-plastic-packaging/#:~:text=Our%20plastic%20goals&text=Ensure%20that%20100%25%20of%20our,recycled%20plastic%20in%20our%20packaging (accessed 6 April 2023).

5. Walmart (nd). 'Sustainable packaging goals'. *Walmart.* Available online: https://www.walmartsustainabilityhub.com/waste/sustainable-packaging/goals (accessed 6 April 2023).

6. https://www.woolworthsgroup.com.au/au/en/sustainability/Product/sustainable-packaging.html (accessed 6 April 2023).

7. General Assembly of the United Nations (nd). 'Plastics'. Available online: https://www.un.org/pga/73/plastics/73rd session of the UN 2018-19 (accessed 6 April 2023).

8. Ministry for the Environment (NZ). (2022). 'Plastic and related products regulation 2022'. Available online: https://environment.govt.nz/acts-and-regulations/regulations/plastic-and-related-products-regulations-2022/#:~:text=Banned%20items%20as%20of%201%20October%202022&text=The%20following%20products%20are%20no,subset%20of%20plastic%20type%207) (accessed 6 April 2023); https://static.pib.gov.in/WriteReadData/specificdocs/documents/2022/jul/doc20227169001.pdf (accessed 6 April 2023).

9. Office of the spokesperson (2022). 'U.S. Actions to Address Plastic Pollution'. Fact sheet. 28 February. Available online: https://www.state.gov/u-s-actions-to-address-plastic-pollution/ (accessed 6 April 2023).

10. Anon (nd). 'Single-use plastics' European Commission' Available online: https://environment.ec.europa.eu/topics/plastics/single-use-plastics_en (accessed 6 April 2023).

11. Anon (2018). 'Latin America and the Caribbean bids good-bye to plastic bags'. UN Environment Programme. June. Available online: https://www.unep.org/news-and-stories/story/latin-america-and-caribbean-bids-good-bye-plastic-bags (accessed 6 April 2023).

12. Senedd Wales (2022). 'Plastic Free July'. *Senedd Research.* 14 July. Available online: https://research.senedd.wales/research-articles/plastic-free-july-breaking-up-with-plastic-across-the-uk/ (accessed 6 April 2023).

13. A pseudonym.

14. Anon (nd). 'What is VTT'. *VTT*. Available online: https://www.vttresearch.com/en/about-us/what-vtt (accessed 6 April 2023).

15. Weston, P. (2022). '"It's greenwash"'. *The Guardian*. 3 November. Available online: https://www.theguardian.com/environment/2022/nov/03/greenwash-home-compostable-plastics-dont-work-aoe; 'Frontiers' (2022). 'Startling Discovery: 60% of Home "Compostable" Plastic Doesn't Fully Decompose, Contaminating Our Soil'. *SciTechDaily*. 29 December. Available online: https://scitechdaily.com/startling-discovery-60-of-home-compostable-plastic-doesnt-fully-decompose-contaminating-our-soil/; Anon (2022). 'University College London Study: The Big Compost Experiment'. *Circular for resource and waste professionals*. 3 November. Available online: https://www.circularonline.co.uk/research-reports/university-college-london-study-the-big-compost-experiment/ (accessed 6 April 2023).

16. Lynch, H. (2022). 'Why Abel and Cole is ditching "compostable" plastics'. *The Grocer*. 28 October. Available online: https://www.thegrocer.co.uk/plastic/why-abel-and-cole-is-ditching-compostable-plastics/672866.article (accessed 6 April 2023).

17. Abel & Cole (2022). 'Why We're Moving Away From Compostable Plastics'. October. Available online: https://www.abelandcole.co.uk/blog/post/why-we-re-moving-away-from-compostable-plastics (accessed 6 April 2023).

18. Abel & Cole was founded in 1988, Riverford (1987).

19. 'Riverford (2022). 'Plastic: Recyclable does not mean recycled'. Available online: *Wicked Leeks*. 2 November. Available online: https://wickedleeks.riverford.co.uk/opinion/plastic-recyclable-does-not-mean-recycled/ (accessed 6 April 2023).

20. A UK based charity established in 2000 geared to sustainability via e.g. improving the plastics economy and reductions in food waste. They are responsible for overseeing progress on The UK Plastics Pact. WRAP (nd). 'A roadmap to 2025'. Available online: https://wrap.org.uk/resources/guide/roadmap-2025-uk-plastics-pact (accessed 6 April 2023).

21. WRAP (nd). 'Compostable packaging guidance'. Available online: https://wrap.org.uk/resources/guide/compostable-plastic-packaging-guidance (accessed 6 April 2023).

22. As Jakob Klein observes, the welcome Lummel implies that was accorded standardization is the reverse in post-socialist China, where the new variety of shapes and sizes is a welcome relief from socialist standardization (2019).

23. Interview 2019.

24. Anon (nd). 'Cath Conway'. Available online: https://www.rivercottage.net/festival/2019/cathconway (accessed 6 April 2023). This is the second instance of only two where an interviewee is not given a pseudonym, since what is publicly available online is part of the discussion.

25. Anon (nd). 'Plastic Free July–Interview with Unpackaged's Catherine Conway'. Available online: https://www.onegreenbottle.com/plastic-free-july-interview/#:~:text=Catherine%3A%20We%20started%20off%20as,consultancy%20working%20with%20other%20stores (accessed 6 April 2023). See also for her work towards a zero packaging supply chain Anon (nd). 'The Refill Coalition'. Available online: https://www.refillcoalition.com (accessed 6 April 2023).

26. For similar autobiographies: Greenfield, R. (2022). 'The First Zero-Waste Grocery Store in San Diego, California!' Available online: https://www.youtube.com/watch?v=4nHK3B3LCrs; https://www.youtube.com/watch?v=6lxp6MUjeV4; 'Ocean Spirit' (nd). 'GoodFor: New Zealand's First Zero Packaging Store'. Available online: https://www.youtube.com/watch?v=KnX7OmxSiJI (accessed 6 April 2023).

27. Morrison, Z. (2021). 'Over 100 zero waste shops in the UK'. Available online: https://ecothriftyliving.com/2019/10/over-100-zero-waste-shops-in-the-uk.html (accessed 6 April 2023).

28. Estimates of such shops' longevity must always be set in the context of shop closures generally. In the UK at the end of 2022, total store closures were reported by to be 17,145, an increase on 2021 (Centre for retailing research nd).

29. That some is online, must always take into account in just the same way that a historian always has to ask themselves about how the document they are looking at came to be created, who created it, how and why did it survive and more, so parallel questions have to asked about material that somebody places online. Equally, sociologists know to be cautious about interviews. This is less to worry about leading questions or courtesy responses (where people are held to give answers they think are wanted). More it is to recognize that interviews are very particular, definable instances of social interaction which need to be analyzed as such, notably recognizing them as co-productions by each party (Hammersley and Atkinson 2007, Silverman 2019). So the search for underlying thinking about innovation in food packaging cannot be straightforward, examining current instances opens up different opportunities.

REFERENCES

Acworth, M. (1987). *Georgian Cookery Book*, eds. Prochaska, A. & F. London: Pavilion Books.

Adrosko, R. (1992). '"The Fashion's in the Bag": Recycling Feed, Flour, and Sugar Sacks during the Middle Decades of the 20th Century'. *Textile Society of America Symposium Proceedings* 557.

Agustina, E.W. & Susanti, V.E. (2018). 'Natural Wrapping Paper from Banana (Musa Paradisiaca Linn) Peel Waste with Additive Essential Oils'. *Journal of Physics: Conference Series* 1022: 012032.

Alberts, R.C. (1973). *The Good Provider*. London: Arthur Barker Limited.

Alexander, G.A. (1917). 'Machinery and Labour-Saving Devices in the Glass Bottle Trade – The Owens Devices'. *Journal of the Society of Glass Technology* 1: 105–8.

Alexander, G.W. (1993). 'Preformed Containers in a Carton and Paperboard Setup Containers for Microwaveable Food'. *Tappi Journal* 76(1): 164–8.

Anderson, A. (1997). 'Historical and Archaeological Aspects of Muttonbirding in New Zealand'. *New Zealand Journal of Archaeology* 17: 35–55.

Anderson, A. (1981). 'Barracouta Fishing in Prehistoric and Early Historic New Zealand'. *Journal de la Société des Océanistes* 37(72): 145–58.

Anderson, W.T. (1971). *The Convenience-Oriented Consumer*. Austin Texas: Bureau of Business Research, Graduate School of Business, The University of Texas at Austin.

Ángel-Bravo, R. (2021). 'The Banana Leaf Approach: An Appreciation of Utilitarian Handcrafted Artifacts in the American Context'. *Sociedad y Economía* 42: e10248.

Anon (1994). *The Complete Heinz Cookbook*. (place of publication unknown): Coombe Books.

Anthony, S. (2016). 'Interview: Professor Diana Twede, Ph.D'. *Packaging World*. https://www.packworld.com/article/interview-professor-diana-twede-phd (accessed 6 April 2023).

Atkins, P.J. (1991). '"Sophistication Detected": or the Adulteration of the Milk Supply 1850–1914'. *Social History* 16(3): 317–39.

Atkins, P.J. (2010). *Liquid Materialities: A History of Milk, Science, and the Law*. Farnham, Surrey: Ashgate.

Atkinson, P. (2013). 'Blowing Hot: the Ethnography of Craft and the Craft of Ethnography'. *Qualitative Inquiry* 19(5): 397–404.

Ballantyne, A., Stark, R. & Selman, J.D. (1988). 'Modified Atmosphere Packaging of Shredded Lettuce'. *International Journal of Food Science & Technology* 23(3): 267–74.

Banning, J.L. (2005). *Feed Sack Fashions in South Louisiana, 1949–1968: The Use of Commodity Bags in Garment Construction*. Doctoral dissertation: Louisiana State University and Agricultural & Mechanical College.

Barbier, J.P. (1994). *Nicolas Appert: Inventeur et Humaniste*. Paris: C. C. B. Royer.

Barnes, S.J. (2019). 'Out of Sight, out of Mind: Plastic Waste Exports, Psychological Distance and Consumer Plastic Purchasing'. *Global Environmental Change* 58: 101943.

Barrett, H (1967). *Early to Rise*. London: Faber.

Bean, R.N. (1977). 'Food Imports into the British West Indies: 1680–1845'. *Annals of the New York Academy of Sciences* 292(1): 581–90.

Beard, M. (2016). *SPQR: A History of Ancient Rome*. London: Profile Books.

Beaton, S. (2007). *A Contemporary Maori Culinary Tradition—Does It Exist? An Analysis of Maori Cuisine*. Masters dissertation: University of Otago.

Beechener, G. *et al* (2020). 'Packaging-Free Shops in Europe: An Initial Report'. *Zero Waste Europe*.

Beecher, C. (1873). *Miss Beecher's Housekeeper and Healthkeeper*. New York: Harper.

Bender, A.E. (1975). *Dictionary of Nutrition and Food Technology*. London: Butterworth & Co, (4th ed).

Berger, K.R. (2002). 'A Brief History of Packaging'. *EDIS* 17 (1–5): ABE321/AE206.

Bernas, B. (2011). 'The Evolution of Jar Machine'. *Fruit Jar Annual*. https://vdocument.in/the-evolution-of-jar-machine-society-for-historical-evolution-of-jar-machine.html?page=1.

Betzig, L.L. & Turke, P.W. (1986). 'Food Sharing on Ifaluk'. *Current Anthropology* 27(4): 397–400.

Bevan, A. (2014). 'Mediterranean Containerization'. *Current Anthropology* 55(4): 387–418.

Bijker, W.E. (1997). *Of Bicycles, Bakelites, and Bulbs: Toward a Theory of Sociotechnical Change*. Cambridge, MA: MIT Press.

Bitting, A.W. (1937). *Appertizing or the Art of Canning; Its History and Development*. San Francisco, CA: The Trade Pressroom.

Bix *et al* (2009). 'Packaging Design and Development'. In Yam, K.L. (ed), *Wiley Encyclopedia of Packaging Technology*. Hoboken, NJ: Wiley.

Blakistone, B.A. (ed) (2012) *Principles and Applications of Modified Atmosphere Packaging of Foods*. Gaithersburg, MD: Chapman Hall, (2nd ed).

Blumer, H. (1954). 'What is wrong with social theory?' *American Sociological Review* 19(1): 3–10.

Bose, C. (1979). 'Technology and Changes in the Division of Labor in the American Home'. *Women's Studies International Quarterly* 2(3): 295–304.

Bowen, S., Brenton, J. & Elliott, S. (2019). *Pressure Cooker*. Oxford: Blackwell.

Boyd-Orr, J. (1966). *As I Recall*. London: MacGibbon & Kee.

Brandes, K. (2009). 'Feed Sack Fashion in Rural America: A Reflection of Culture'. *Online Journal of Rural Research & Policy* 4(1): 1–23.

British Market Research Bureau Limited (1950). *Self Service in Great Britain: A Study of the Latest Method of Grocery Retailing*. London: BMRB.

Brody, A.L. (1993). 'The Market'. In Parry, R.T. (ed), *Principles and Applications of Modified Atmosphere Packaging of Foods*. Boston, MA: Springer Science & Business Media.

Buechler, H.R. (2016). 'Field to Bag, Bag to Field'. *Textile Society of America Symposium Proceedings*, 962.

Burnett, J. (1989). *Plenty and Want*. London: Routledge.

Burnett, J. (1999). *Liquid Pleasures: A Social History of Drinks in Modern Britain*. London: Routledge.

Byrne, A.L. (1999). *Guiness Times*. Dublin: Town House.

Cable, M. (2001–2). 'The Mechanisation of Glass Container Production'. *Transactions of the Newcomen Society* 73(1): 1–31.

Cable, M. (2005). 'The Centenary of the First Automatic Bottle-Making Machine'. *Glass Technology* 46(3): 255–62.

Cahn, W. (1969). *Out of the Cracker Barrel*. New York: Simon & Schuster.

Callon, M. (1984). 'Some Elements of a Sociology of Translation: Domestication of the Scallops & the Fishermen of St Brieuc Bay'. *The Sociological Review* 32(1): 196–233.

Callon, M. (1986). 'The Sociology of an Actor-Network: The Case of the Electric Vehicle'. In Callon, M., Rip, A. & Law, J. (eds), *Mapping the Dynamics of Science and Technology: Sociology of Science in the Real World*. Basingstoke: Macmillan.

Carlisle, R.P. (2004). *Scientific American Inventions and Discoveries*. Hoboken, NJ: Wiley.

Centre for Retailing Research (nd). 'The Crisis in Retailing: Closures and Job Losses'. https://www.retailresearch.org/retail-crisis.html (accessed 6 April 2023).

Chadwick, P. (2022). 'Details emerge of government policy'. *Packaging News* (June): 3.

Charles, N. & Kerr, M. (1988). *Women, Food and Families*. Manchester: Manchester University Press.

References

Cinotto, S. (2013). *The Italian American Table*. Urbana: University of Illinois Press.

Claudio, L. (2012). 'Our Food: Packaging & Public Health'. *Environmental Health Perspectives* 120(6): A232–A237.

Cochoy, F. (2014). 'Trojan Cans'. https://limn.it/articles/trojan-cans/ (accessed 23 June 2015).

Cochoy, F. & Grandclément-Chaffy, C. (2005). 'Publicizing Goldilocks' Choice at the Supermarket: The Political Work of Shopping Packs, Carts and Talk'. In Latour, B. & Weibel, P. (eds), *Making Thing Public: Atmospheres of Democracy*. Cambridge, MA: MIT Press.

Cockburn, C. & Ormrod, S. (1993). *Gender & Technology in the Making*. London: Sage Publications Ltd.

Coles, R. (2003). 'Introduction'. In Coles, R., McDowell, D. & Kirwan, M.J. (eds), *Food Packaging Technology*. Oxford: Blackwell.

Coles, R., McDowell, D. & Kirwan, M.J. (eds) (2003). *Food Packaging Technology*. Oxford: Blackwell.

Cooper, G. (1998). 'Love, War, and Chocolate: Gender and the American Candy Industry, 1890–1930'. In Horowitz, R. & Mohun A. (eds), *His and Hers: Gender Consumption and Technology*. Charlottesville: University Press of Virginia.

Cowell, N.D. (1994). *An Investigation of Early Methods of Food Preservation by Heat*. PhD thesis. Reading, Berks: Department of Food Science & Technology, The University of Reading, September.

Crockett, A.W. (1985). 'Injuries from Tin Cans in Patients Presenting to an Accident and Emergency Department'. *British Medical Journal* 291(6511): 1767–8.

Cronon, W. (1991). *Nature's Metropolis – Chicago & the Great West*. New York: Norton.

Curry, A. (2005). *Agincourt: A New History*. Stroud, Glos: Tempus.

Cwiertka, K.J. (2020). 'Packaging of Food and Drink in Japan'. In Meiselman, H.L. (ed), *Handbook of Eating and Drinking: Interdisciplinary Perspectives*. Cham, Switzerland: Springer.

Dalrymple, D.G. (1967). 'The Development of an Agricultural Technology: Controlled-Atmosphere Storage of Fruit'. *Technology and Culture* 10(1): 35–48.

Daniels, S. & Glorieux, I. (2015). 'Convenience, Food and Family Lives. A Socio-Typological Study of Household Food Expenditures in 21st-century Belgium'. *Appetite* 94: 54–61.

Davidson, A. (2006). *The Oxford Companion to Food*. Oxford: OUP.

Davies, A.R. (1995). 'Advances in Modified-Atmosphere Packaging'. In Gould, G.W. (ed), *New Methods of Food Preservation*. Boston, MA: Springer Science & Business Media.

Davis, D. (1966). *A History of Shopping*. London: Routledge & Kegan Paul Ltd.

Davis, D & Carr, A. (1988). '*When It's Time to Make a Choice*': 50 Years of Frozen Food in Britain. Grantham, Lincs: The British Frozen Food Federation.

Den Hartog, A. (1998). 'Serving the Urban Consumer: The Development of Modern Food Packaging with Special Reference to the Milk Bottle'. In Schärer, M.R. & Fenton, A. (eds), *Food and Material Culture*. East Linton: Tuckwell Press.

Densmore, F. (2012). *How Indians Use Wild Plants for Food, Medicine & Crafts*. New York: Dover Publications, Inc.

Dienstag, E.F. (1994). *In Good Company*. New York: Warner Books.

Dixon, M.J. (2010). 'The Sustainable Use of Water to Mitigate the Impact of Watercress Farms on Chalk Streams in Southern England' Doctoral dissertation: University of Southampton.

Drummond, J.C. & Lewis, W.R. (1939). *Historic Canned Foods*. Greenford, Middlesex: International Tin Research & Development Council.

Ducos, L. (2014). *Importance of the Traditional Land-Use and Land-Tenure Systems of Waraka, Seram Island, Maluku, Working Paper 144*. Bogor, Indonesia: CIFOR, Centre for International Forestry Research.

Dunn, M.E., Mills, M. & Veríssimo, D. (2020). 'Evaluating the Impact of the Documentary Series Blue Planet II on Viewers' Plastic Consumption Behaviors'. *Conservation Science and Practice* 2(10): e280.

Dungworth, D. (2009). 'Innovations in the 17th-Century Glass Industry: The Introduction of Kelp (seaweed) Ash in Britain'. *Actes du Deuxieme Colloque International de l'Assocation Verre & Histoire*. https://www.verre-histoire.org/colloques/innovations/pages/p004_association.html.

Ekström, M.P. (2013). 'Carin Boalt and Her 27,000 Meals'. *Food & History* 11(1): 107–22.

Elkington, G. (1933). *The Coopers: Company and Craft*. London: Marston & Co Ltd.

English, S. (1923). 'The Ashley Bottle Machine'. *Journal of the Society of Glass Technology* 7: 324–33.

Enock, A.G. (1943). *This Milk Business*. London: H.K. Lewis & Co. Ltd.

Enock, A.G. (1974). 'Fifty Years Development in Dairy Plant and Equipment'. *International Journal of Dairy Technology* 27(4): 198–210.

Estreicher, S.K. (2002). 'From Fermentation to Transportation'. *Historical Note*: 991–4. www.mrs.org/publications/bulletin (accessed 6 April 2023).

Evans, D., Campbell, H. & Murcott, A. (eds) (2013), *Waste Matters: New Perspectives of Food and Society*. Oxford: Wiley.

Evans, D.M. *et al* (2020). 'Understanding Plastic Packaging: The Co-evolution of Materials and Society'. *Global Environmental Change* 65: 102166.

Farrer, K.T.H (1980). *A Settlement Amply Supplied: Food Technology in Nineteenth Century Australia*. Melbourne: Melbourne University Press.

Fitzgerald, D. (2020). 'World War II and the Quest for Time-Insensitive Foods'. *Osiris* 35(1): 291–309.

Fontaine, L. (1996). *History of Pedlars in Europe*. Durham, NC: Duke University Press.

Ford, R. (2020). 'Controlling Contagion? Watercress, Regulation and the Hackney typhoid Outbreak of 1903'. *Rural History* 31(2): 181–94.

Fortes, M. & Fortes, S.L. (1936). 'Food in the Domestic Economy of the Tallensi' *Africa. Journal of the International African Institute* 9(2): 237–76.

Foster, D. & Kennedy, J. (2006). *H.J. Heinz Company*. San Francisco, CA: Arcadia Publishing.

Foster, W.F. (1944). *The Coopers' Company*. Cambridge: The University Press.

Freidberg, S. (2009). *Fresh*. Cambridge, MA: Harvard University Press.

Freire, M.D.A., Santana, I.A. & Reyes, F.G.R. (2006). 'Plasticizers in Brazilian Food-Packaging Materials Acquired on the Retail Market'. *Food Additives and Contaminants* 23(1): 93–9.

Frolich, X. (2011). 'Accounting for Taste: Regulating Food Labeling in the "Affluent Society" 1945–1995'. Doctoral dissertation: Massachusetts Institute of Technology.

FSA (2008). 'Criteria for the Use of the Terms Fresh, Pure, Natural Etc. in Food Labelling'. http://www.foodlaw.rdg.ac.uk/pdf/uk-08017-guidance-marketing-terms.pdf (accessed 6 April 2023).

Fuentes, C., Enarsson, P. & Kristoffersson, L. (2019). 'Unpacking Package Free Shopping'. *Journal of Retailing and Consumer Services* 50: 258–65.

Fukushima, D. (2004). 'Industrialization of Fermented Soy Sauce Production Centering around Japanese Shoyu'. In Steinkraus, Keith H. (ed), *Industrialization of Indigenous Fermented Foods*. New York: Dekker, 1–98.

Garcia, R. & Adrian, J. (2009). 'Nicolas Appert: Inventor and Manufacturer'. *Food Reviews International* 25(2): 115–25.

Geueke, B. (2016). 'Can Coatings'. *Food Packaging Forum*, 15 December. https://www.foodpackagingforum.org/food-packaging-health/can-coatings (accessed 6 April 2023).

Giddens, A. & Sutton, P.W. (2014). *Essential Concepts in Sociology*. Cambridge: Polity Press.

Gilmour, S.C. (1955). *Paper Its Making, Merchanting and Usage*. London: Longmans, Green & Co Ltd.

Goldenberg, N. (1989). *Thought for Food: A Study of the Development of the Food Division, Marks & Spencer: An Autobiography*. Orpington: Food Trade Press.

Goodman, D. (2001). 'Ontology Matters: The Relational Materiality of Nature and Agro-Food Studies'. *Sociologia Ruralis* 41(2): 182–200.

References

Goody, J. (1982). *Cooking, Cuisine and Class*. Cambridge: Cambridge University Press.

Gormley, R. (2008). '10 Developing Frozen Products for the Market and the Freezing of Ready-Prepared Meals'. In Evans, J.A. (ed), *Frozen Food Science and Technology*. Oxford: Blackwell.

Gray, M. (1939). 'The History and Development of Packaging'. *Journal of the Royal Society of Arts* 87(4511): 633–58.

Gray, M. (1955). *Package Design*. London: The Studio Publications.

Gregory, R.A. *et al* (2019). 'Exploring Bristol's Historic Glass Industry'. *Post-Medieval Archaeology* 52(2): 256–99.

Gronow, J. (2007). 'First-Class Restaurants and Luxury Food Stores'. In Atkins, P., Lummel, P.,& Oddy, D. (eds), *Food and the City in Europe since 1800*. Aldershot, Hants: Ashgate.

Guildhall Library, London (1978). *Cries of London*. Lympne Castle, Kent: Harry Margary.

Hagberg, J. & Holmberg, U. (2017). 'Travel Modes in Grocery Shopping'. *International Journal of Retail & Distribution Management* 45(9): 991–1010.

Hammersley, M. & Atkinson, P. (2007). *Ethnography*. London: Routledge, (3rd ed).

Harrison, V.G.W. (1961). 'Technical Advances in Packaging'. *Journal of the Royal Society of Arts* 195(5063): 821–39.

Hartley, D. (1999). *Food in England*. London: Little Brown.

Harvey, M., Quilley, S. & Beynon, H. (2002). *Exploring the Tomato*. Cheltenham, Glos: Edward Elgar Publishing Limited.

Hassall, A.H. (1855). *Food and Its Adulterations*. London: Longman, Brown, Green & Longmans.

Hawkins, G. (2013). 'The Performativity of Food Packaging'. In Evans, D., Campbell, H. & Murcott, A. (eds), *Waste Matters: New Perspectives of Food and Society*. Oxford: Wiley.

Heller, S. (1999). 'Appetite Appeal'. *Social Research* 66(1): 213–24.

Hendry, J. (1995). *Wrapping Culture: Politeness, Presentation, and Power in Japan and Other Societies*. Oxford: Oxford University Press.

Henry, M. & Morris, C. (2022). 'Fantasies of Logistics in Aotearoa New Zealand'. In Stead, V. & Hinkson, M. (eds), *Beyond Global Food Supply Chains: Crisis, Disruption, Regeneration*. Singapore: Springer Nature.

Herrmann, C., Rhein, S. & Sträter, K.F. (2022). 'Consumers' Sustainability-Related Perception of and Willingness-to-Pay for Food Packaging Alternatives'. *Resources, Conservation and Recycling* 181: 106219.

Hills, R.L. (1988). *Papermaking in Britain 1488–1988*. London: The Athlone Press.

Hine, T. (1995). *The Total Package*. Boston: Little Brown.

Hisano, A. (2017). 'Selling Food in Clear Packages: The Development of Cellophane and the Expansion of Self-Service Merchandising in the United States, 1920s–1950s'. *International Journal of Food Design* 2(2): 139–52.

Holleran, C. (2016). 'Representations of Food Hawkers in Ancient Rome'. In Calaresu, M. & van den Heuvel, D. (eds), *Food Hawkers: Selling in the Streets from Antiquity to the Present*. London: Routledge.

Horowitz, R. (2006). *Putting Meat on the American Table*. Baltimore: Johns Hopkins University Press.

Horrocks, S.M. (1995). 'Nutrition Science and the Food Industry in Britain, 1920–1990'. In den Hartog, A.P. (ed), *Food Technology. Science and Marketing: European Diet in the Twentieth Century*. East Linton, Scotland: Tuckwell Press.

Howard, A.J. (1949). *Canning Technology*. London: Churchill.

Hynes, S. *et al* (2021). 'The Impact of Nature Documentaries on Public Environmental Preferences and Willingness to Pay: Entropy Balancing and the Blue Planet II Effect'. *Journal of Environmental Planning and Management* 64(8): 1428–56.

Jackson, P. *et al* (2018). *Reframing Convenience Food*. Cham, Switzerland: Palgrave Macmillan.

Jasanoff, S. *et al* (2001). *Handbook of Science and Technology Studies*. London: Sage.

Jenkins, A. (1970). *Drinka Pinta*. London: William Heinemann Ltd.

Jenkins, W.A. & Harrington, J.P. (1991). *Packaging Foods with Plastics*. Lancaster, PA: Technomic.

Johnson, S. (2014). *How We Got to Now*. New York: Riverhead Books.

Johnston, J.P. (1977). *A Hundred Years Eating*. Dublin: Gill and Macmillan Ltd.

Johnston, J. & Baumann, S. (2015). *Foodies: Democracy and Distinction in the Gourmet Foodscape*. London: Routledge, (2nd ed).

Jones, J.P. *et al* (2019). 'Nature Documentaries and Saving Nature: Reflections on the New Netflix Series Our Planet'. *People and Nature* 1(4): 420–5.

Jones, L.A. & Park, S. (1993). 'From Feed Bags to Fashion'. *Textile History* 24(1): 91–103.

Jones, O. (1949). *Canning Practice and Control*. London: Chapman Hall, (3rd ed).

Jones, P. & Kipps, M. (ed) (1995). *Flight Catering*. Harlow, Essex: Addison Wesley Longman Limited.

Judge, A.I. (1914). *A History of the Canning Industry*. Baltimore: The Canning Trade.

Khetarpaul, N. & Punia, D. (2008). *Food Packaging*. New Delhi: Daya Publishing.

Kilby, K. (1989). *The Cooper and His Trade*. Fresno, CA: Linden Publishing.

Kiple, K.F. & Ornelas, K.C. (eds) (2000). *The Cambridge World History of Food*. Cambridge: Cambridge University Press.

Klein, J. (2022). 'Repositioning Potatoes in the PRC'. In Klein, J. *et al* (ed), *Cultural China 2021: The Contemporary China Centre Review*. London: University of Westminster Press.

Kuijt, I. & Finlayson, B. (2009). 'Evidence for Food Storage and Predomestication Granaries 11,000 Years Ago in the Jordan Valley'. *Proceedings of the National Academy of Sciences* 106(27): 10966–70.

Kurkjian, C.R. & Prindle, W.R. (1998). 'Perspectives on the History of Glass Composition'. *Journal of the American Ceramic Society* 81(4): 795–813.

Laistrooglai, A., Mosikarat, P. & Wigran, M. (2000). *Packaging Design with Natural Materials: A Study for Conservation*. Bangkok: Silpakorn Univeristy Research & Development.

Lane, Y.F. (2017). 'Good Business: Charity, Capitalism, and the Moral Economy of the Watercress and Flower Girls' Mission, London 1866–1914'. Doctoral dissertation: Rutgers, The State University of New Jersey-New Brunswick.

Larousse Gastronomique (1988). *English Text*. London: Hamlyn.

Latour, B. (1996). 'On Actor-Network Theory: A Few Clarifications'. *Soziale Welt* 47(4): 369–81.

Law, J. (2009). 'Actor-Network Theory and Material Semiotics'. In Turner, B. (ed), *The New Blackwell Companion to Social Theory*. Oxford: Blackwell.

Law, J. (ed) (1986). *Power, Action and Belief: A New Sociology of Knowledge*. London: Routledge.

Law, J. & Callon, M. (1988). 'Engineering and Sociology in a Military Aircraft Project: A Network Analysis of Technological Change'. *Social Problems* 35(3): 284–97.

Leander, L. (1995). *Tetra Pak: A Vision Becomes Reality*. Lund: Tetra Pak International.

Lebreton, L. *et al* (2018). 'Evidence That the Great Pacific Garbage Patch Is Rapidly Accumulating Plastic'. *Scientific Reports* 8(1): 1–15.

Leeds, E.T. (1941). '17th and 18th-century Wine-Bottles of Oxford Taverns'. *Oxoniensia* 6: 44–55.

Levenstein, H. (1993). *Paradox of Plenty*. Oxford: Oxford University Press.

Levenstein, P. (1988). *Messages from Home*. Columbus: Ohio State University Press.

Levinson, M. (2006). *The Box*. Princeton, NJ: Princeton University Press.

Levinson, M. (2008). 'Freight Pain—The Rise and Fall of Globalization'. *Foreign Affairs* 87: 133–40.

Licence, T. (nd). 'What the Victorians Threw Away: The Database'. Available online: http://www. whatthevictoriansthrewaway.com/the-database/ (accessed 6 April 2023).

Lindström, T. & Österberg, F. (2020). 'Evolution of Biobased and Nanotechnology Packaging–A Review'. *Nordic Pulp & Paper Research Journal* 35(4): 491–515.

Lorence, M. (2020). 'Package and Product Development Testing in a Microwave Oven'. In Erle, U., Pesheck, P. & Lorence, M. (eds), *Development of Packaging and Products for Use in Microwave Ovens*. Sawston, Cambridge: Woodhead Publishing.

References

Low, A.M. (1939). *Science in Industry*. London: Oxford University Press.

Lummel, P. (2007). 'Born-in-the-City: The Supermarket in Germany'. In Atkins, P., Lummel, P., Oddy, D. (eds), *Food and the City in Europe since 1800*. Aldershot, Hants: Ashgate.

Lyon, P. & Kinney, D. (2013). 'Convenience and Choice for Consumers: The Domestic Acceptability of Canned Food between the 1870s and 1930s'. *International Journal of Consumer Studies* 37(2): 130–5.

MacGregor, D.R. (1952). *The Tea Clippers*. London: Percival Marshall & Co. Ltd.

Mah, A. (2002). *Plastic Unlimited*. Cambridge: Polity.

Males, J. & Van Aelst, P. (2021). 'Did the Blue Planet Set the Agenda for Plastic Pollution? An Explorative Study on the Influence of a Documentary on the Public, Media and Political Agendas'. *Environmental Communication* 15(1): 40–54.

Man, D. (2015). *Shelf Life*. Chichester: Wiley.

Mansfield, B. (2003). 'Fish, Factory Trawlers, and Imitation Crab: The Nature of Quality in the Seafood Industry'. *Journal of Rural Studies* 19(1): 9–21.

Mansfield, B. (2008). 'Spatializing Globalization: A "Geography of Quality" in the Seafood Industry'. *Economic Geography* 79(1): 1–16.

Markowitz, G. & Rosner, D. (2000). 'Cater to the Children: The Role of the Lead Industry in a Public Health Tragedy, 1900–1955'. *American Journal of Public Health* 90(1): 36–46.

Marlier, S. & Sibella, P. (2002). 'La Giraglia, a Dolia Wreck of the 1st Century BC from Corsica, France: Study of Its Hull Remains'. *The International Journal of Nautical Archaeology* 31(2): 161–71.

Mayhew, H. (2012). *London Labour and London Poor*. Oxford: Oxford University Press.

McCafferty, E.D. (1923). *Henry J. Heinz*. New York: Bartlett Orr Press.

McCully, E.A. (2006). *Marvelous Mattie: How Margaret E. Knight Became an Inventor*. New York: Farrar, Straus and Giroux.

McGinn, K.L. (2007). 'History, Structure, and Practices: San Pedro Longshoremen in the Face of Change'. In Dutton, J.E. & Ragins, B.R. (eds), *Exploring Positive Relationships at Work: Building a Theoretical and Research Foundation*. New York: Psychology Press.

McMillin, K.W. (2008). 'Where Is MAP Going?' *Meat Science* 80(1): 43–65.

Mehren, G.L. (1948). 'Consumer Packaging of Fruits and Vegetables in California'. *Journal of Marketing* 12(3): 327–36.

Meigh, E. (1960). 'The Development of the Automatic Glass Bottle Machine. A Story of Some Pioneers'. *Glass Technology* 1(2): 25–50.

Meigh, E. (1972). *The Story of the Glass Bottle*. Stoke-on-Trent: C.E. Ramsden & Co. Ltd.

Meneley, A. (2008). 'Time in a Bottle: The Uneasy Circulation of Palestinian Olive Oil'. *Middle East Report* 248: 18–23.

Metzger, G. (2009). 'Pōhā with tītī (muttonbird) Placed inside Blades of Kelp'. *ourheritage.ac.nz | OUR Heritage*. https://otago.ourheritage.ac.nz/items/show/8728 (accessed 11 April 2021).

Meussdoerffer, F.G. (2009). 'A Comprehensive History of Beer Brewing'. In Eßlinger, H.M. (ed), *A Comprehensive History of Beer Brewing*. Weinheim: WILEY-VCH Verlag GmbH & Co.

Milne, L. (2020). *Take One Tin: 80 Delicious Meals from the Storecupboard*. London: Kyle.

Ministry of Food (1945). *The ABC of Cookery*. London: Imperial War Museum, (Facsimile ed 2008).

Mintz, S.W. (1985). *Sweetness and Power: The Place of Sugar in Modern History*. London: Penguin.

Moller, H., Kitson, J.C. & Downs, T.M. (2009). 'Knowing by Doing: Learning for Sustainable Muttonbird Harvesting'. *New Zealand Journal of Zoology* 36(3): 243–58.

Moody, B.E. (1985). 'A Century of Mechanical Bottle Making'. *Glass Technology* 26(2): 108–17.

Moorshead, T.C. (1925). 'The Glass Bottle Industry and Future Developments'. *Journal of the Society for Glass Technology* 9: 282–315.

Morgan, B. (1964). *Express Journey*. London: Newman Neame Ltd.

Morris, C. (2006). 'On the Absence of Māori Restaurants: The Politics of Food and Indigeneity in Aotearoa/New Zealand'. *Appetite* 47(3): 395.

Morris, C. (2013). 'Kai or Kiwi? Māori and 'Kiwi' Cookbooks, and the Struggle for the Field of New Zealand Cuisine'. *Journal of Sociology* 49(2–3): 210–23.

Moseley, K.L. (2020). 'Food, Body Weight, and Everyday Life in England, c. 1954–1990' Unpublished PhD, University of Cambridge.

Murcott, A. (1982). 'On the Social Significance of the "Cooked Dinner" in South Wales'. *Social Science Information* 21(4/5): 677–95.

Murcott, A. (1983). 'Women's Place: Cookbooks' Images of Technique and Technology in the British Kitchen'. *Women's Studies International Forum* 6(2): 33–9.

Murcott, A. (2019). *Introducing the Sociology of Food and Eating*. London: Bloomsbury.

Murcott, A. (2023). 'Sociologies of Food and Eating'. In Petersen, A. (ed), *Handbook on the Sociology of Health and Medicine*. Cheltenham: Elgar.

Murcott, A., Belasco, W. & Jackson, P. (eds) (2013). *The Handbook of Food Research*. London: Bloomsbury.

Murray, S. (2007). *Moveable Feasts: The Incredible Journeys of the Things We Eat*. London: Aurum.

Napleton, L. (2001). *Look! It Cooks*. Totnes, Devon: Prospect Books.

National Canners Association (NCA) (1963). *The Canning Industry: Its History, Importance, Organizaion, Methods, and the Public Service Values of Its Products*. Washington DC: Information Division, National Canners Association.

Nelson, S.C., Ploetz, R.C. & Kepler, A.K. (2006). 'Musa Species (banana and plantain)'. *Species Profiles for Pacific Island Agroforestry* 15(2): 251–9.

Newman, G. (1943). 'Foreword'. In Enock, A.G., *This Milk Business: A Study from 1895 to 1943*. London: Lewis & Co.

Nixon, G. (2010). *Feedsack Secrets: Fashion from Hard Times*. Kansas City: Star Books.

Oddy, D.J. (2003). *From Plain Fare to Fusion Food*. Woodbridge, Suffolk: The Boydell Press.

Oddy, D.J. (2007). 'The Growth of Britain's Refrigerated Meat Trade, 1880–1939'. *The Mariner's Mirror* 93(3): 269–80.

Opie, R. (1989). *Packaging*. London: Macdonald & Co.

Osepchuk, J.M. (2009). 'The History of the Microwave Oven: A Critical Review'. *2009 IEEE MTT-S International Microwave Symposium Digest*: 397–1400.

Page, B., Edwards, M. & May, N. (2011). 'Metal Packaging'. In Coles, R. & Kirwan, M. (eds), *Food and Beverage Packaging Technology*. Oxford: Blackwell, (2nd ed).

Paine, F.A. & Paine, H.Y. (1992). *A Handbook of Food Packaging*. New York: Springer.

Parkinson, C. (1944). 'Packaging for Protection'. *The Science News-Letter* 46(17): 266–7.

Parry, R.T. (ed) (1993). *Principles and Applications of Modified Atmosphere Packaging of Foods*. Gaithersburg, Maryland: Springer Science & Business.

Pearson, G.S. (2016). 'The Democratization of Food: Tin Cans and the Growth of the American Food Processing Industry, 1810–1940'. Doctoral dissertation: Lehigh University.

Pecci, A. *et al* (2017). 'Use and Reuse of Amphorae. Wine Residues in Dressel 2–4 Amphorae from Oplontis Villa B (Torre Annunziata, Italy)'. *Journal of Archaeological Science: Reports* 12: 515–21.

Penn, K. (c.1948). *S.D.I.* London: Soft Drinks Industry (War Time) Association.

Pennell, S. (1998). '"Pots and Pans History": The Material Culture of the Kitchen in Early Modern England'. *Journal of Design History* 11(3): 201–16.

Petrick, G.M. (2009). 'Feeding the Masses: H.J. Heinz and the Creation of Industrial Food'. *Endeavour* 33(1): 29–34.

Petrick, G.M. (2010). 'An Ambivalent Diet: The Industrialization of Canning'. *OAH Magazine of History* (July) 24(3): 35–8.

References

Petrick, G.M. (2011). '"Purity as Life": H.J. Heinz, Religious Sentiment, and the Beginning of the Industrial Diet'. *History and Technology* 27(1): 37–64.

Petrick, G. (2012). 'Industrial Food'. In Pilcher, J.M., *The Oxford Handbook of Food History*. Oxford: Oxford University Press.

Petroski, H. (1992). *To Engineer Is Human: The Role of Failure in Successful Design*. New York: Vintage.

Petroski, H. (2003). 'The Evolution of the Grocery Bag'. *The American Scholar* 72(4): 99–111.

Petty, C. (1987a). 'Food, Poverty and Growth: The Application of Nutrition Science, 1918–1939'. *The Society for the Social History of Medicine Bulletin* 40: 37–40.

Petty, C. (1987). 'The Impact of the Newer Knowledge of Nutrition: Nutrition Science and Nutrition Policy, 1900–1939'. Doctoral dissertation: London School of Hygiene & Tropical Medicine.

Pfaender, H.G. (1966). *Schott Guide to Glass*. London: Chapman & Hall.

Pilditch, J. (1961). *The Silent Salesman*. London: Batsford.

Pollan, M. (2009). *In Defense of Food*. New York: Penguin.

Pollard, S. (1959). 'Review of The British Tinplate Industry: A History by W.E. Minchinton'. *The Journal of Economic History* 19(1): 140–2.

Potter, S. (1959). *The Magic Number*. London: Max Reinhardt Ltd.

Poulain, J.P. (2002). 'The Contemporary Diet in France: "De-structuration" or from Commensalism to "Vagabond Feeding"'. *Appetite* 39(1): 43–55.

Powell, H.J. (1880). '21st Ordinary Meeting: The Manufacture of Glass for Decorative Purposes'. *Journal of the Society of Arts* 29(19): 546–50.

Powell, H.J. (1896). 'Technical Education in Relation to Glass Manufacture'. *Journal of the Society of Arts* 45: 849–51.

Powell, H.J. (1919). 'Glass-Making before and during the War'. *Journal of the Royal Society of Arts* 67(3473): 485–95.

Powell, M. (2012). 'From Feed Sack to Clothes Rack'. *Textile Society of America Symposium Proceedings* 732.

Purcell, N. (1985). 'Wine and Wealth in Ancient Italy'. *The Journal of Roman Studies* 75: 1–19.

Purkiss, D. *et al* (2022). 'The Big Compost Experiment: Using Citizen Science to Assess the Impact and Effectiveness of Biodegradable and Compostable Plastics in UK Home Composting'. *Front. Sustain* 3: 942724.

Pursell, C.W. (1962). 'Tariff and Technology: The Foundation and Development of the American Tin-Plate Industry, 1872–1900'. *Technology and Culture* 3(3): 267–84.

Raffald, E. (1997). *The Experienced English Housekeeper*. Lewes, East Sussex: Southover Press.

Reader, W.J. (1976). *Metal Box: A History*. London: Heinemann.

Rees, G. (1969). *St Michael: A history of Marks and Spencer*. London: Weidenfeld & Nicolson.

Rees, J. (2013). *Refrigeration Nation*. Baltimore: The Johns Hopkins University Press.

Renne, E.P. (2007). 'Mass Producing Food Traditions for West Africans Abroad'. *American Anthropologist* 109(4): 616–25.

Riley, A. (2012). 'Plastics Manufacturing Processes for Packaging Materials'. In Emblem, A. & Emblem, H. (eds), *Packaging Technology*. Oxford: Woodhead Publishing.

Risch, S.J. (2009). 'Food Packaging History and Innovations'. *Journal of Agricultural and Food Chemistry* 57(18): 8089–92.

Roberts, R. (1990). *The Classic Slum*. London: Penguin.

Robertson, G.L. (2002). 'The Paper Beverage Carton: Past and Future'. *Food Technology* 56(7): 46–52.

Robertson, G.L. (2013). *Food Packaging: Principles and Practice*. New York: CRC Press.

Robertson, G.L. (2014). 'Food Packaging'. In van Alfen, N.K. (ed), *Encyclopedia of Agriculture and Food Systems*. Amsterdam: Elsevier, (2nd ed).

Root, W. & de Rochemont, R. (1976). *Eating in America: A History*. New York: Morrow.

Ross, J.R. (1997). *The Cryovac Story*. CT: Cryovac Division, W.R. Grace & CO.

Sacharow, S. & Griffin, R.C. (1980). *Principles of Food Packaging*. Westport, Conn.: AVI Publishing Co, (2nd ed).

Schmiechen, J. & Carls, K. (1999). *The British Market Hall*. New Haven: Yale University Press.

Scholliers, P. (2014). 'Constructing New Expertise: Private and Public Initiatives for Safe Food'. *Medical History* 58(4): 546–63.

Scholliers, P. (2015). 'Convenience Foods: What, Why, and When'. *Appetite* 94: 2–6.

Seltenrich, N. (2015). 'A Hard Nut to Crack: Reducing Chemical Migration in Food-Contact Materials'. *Environmental Health Perspectives* 123(7): A174–A179.

Shapiro, L. (1986). *Perfection Salad*. New York: Henry Holt.

Shapiro, L. (2004). *Something from the Oven*. New York: Penguin Books.

Shaw, G., Curth, L. & Alexander, A. (2004). 'Selling Self-Service and the Supermarket'. *Business History* 46(4): 568–82.

Shaw, J.F. (1936). 'The Development of Mass Production in the Glass Bottle Industry'. *Journal of the Institution of Production Engineers* 15(6): 295–308.

Sheller, M. & Urry, J. (2006). 'The New Mobilities Paradigm'. *Environment and Planning A* 38(2): 207–26.

Shepherd, S. (2000). *Pickled, Potted and Canned: The Story of Food Preserving*. London: Headline.

Shove, E. (2003). *Comfort, Cleanliness and Convenience: The Social Organisation of Normality*. Oxford: Berg.

Silliker, J.H. *et al* (1977). 'Preservation of Refrigerated Meats with Controlled Atmosphere'. *Meat Science* 1(3): 195–204.

Silverman, D. (2019). *Interpreting Qualitative Data*. London: Sage.

Skrabec, Q. (2007). '*Michael Owens and the Glass Industry* (Kindle Locations 3064–3066)'. Kindle Edition.

Smith, A.F. (1996). *Pure Ketchup*. Columbia, SC: University of South Carolina Press.

Smith, D.F. *et al* (2005). *Food Poisoning, Policy and Politics*. Woodbridge, Suffolk: The Boydell Press.

Smith-Howard, K. (2014). *Pure and Modern Milk*, Oxford: Oxford University Press.

Souza, P.M.S. *et al* (2013). 'PLA and Montmorilonite Nanocomposites: Properties, Biodegradation and Potential Toxicity'. *Journal of Polymers and the Environment* 21(3): 738–59.

Spence, R.M.M. (1980). 'A Study of Post-Harvest Changes in Watercress: Rorippa Nasturtium-Aquaticum (L.) Hayek'. Doctoral dissertation: University of Bath.

Star, S.L. (1988). 'Introduction: The Sociology of Science and Technology'. *Social Problems* 35(3): 197–205.

Stevens, M.J. (2006). 'Kāi Tahu me te Hopu Tītī ki Rakiura: An Exception to the "Colonial Rule"?' *The Journal of Pacific History* 41(3): 273–91.

Stobart, J. (2013). *Sugar & Spice*. Oxford: Oxford University Press.

Strasser, S. (1980). *Satisfaction Guaranteed*. New York: Pantheon Books.

Stroud, D. & Walker, K. (2013). *Marketing to the Ageing Consumer*. London: Palgrave Macmillan.

Suddendorf, T. *et al* (2020). 'It's in the Bag: Mobile Containers in Human Evolution and Child Development'. *Evolutionary Human Sciences* 2: e 48.

Summers, M. (2015). *A Biography of Nicholas Appert 1749–1841*. Reading: Downs Way Publishing.

Talbot, O. (1974). 'The Evolution of Glass Bottles for Carbonated Drinks'. *Post-Medieval Archaeology* 8(1): 29–62.

Taverner, C. (2003). *Street Food*. Oxford: Oxford University Press.

Téchoueyres, I. (2007). 'Food Markets in the City of Bordeaux'. In Atkins, P., Lummel, P. & Oddy, D. (eds), *Food and the City in Europe since 1800*. Aldershot, Hants: Ashgate.

Thirsk, J. (2007). *Food in Early Modern England*. London: Hambledon.

References

Thompson, E.P. (1967). 'Time, Work-Discipline, and Industrial Capitalism'. *Past & Present* 38: 56–97.

Thorne, S. (1986). *The History of Food Preservation*. Kirkby Lonsdale, Cumbria: Parthenon Publishing.

Todorova, D.A., Lasheva, V.G. & Sokolova, L.B. (2015), 'Paperboard Packaging for Liquid Foods'. *Food and Packaging* 6: 29–34.

Trentmann, F. (2017). *The Empire of Things*. London: Allen Lane.

Turner, W.E.S. (1926). 'The Composition of Glass Suitable for Use with Automatic Machines'. *Journal of the Society of Glass Technology* 10: 80–94.

Twede, D. (2002). 'Commercial Amphoras: The Earliest Consumer Packages?' *Journal of Macromarketing* 22(1): 98–108.

Twede, D. (2005). 'The Origins of Paper Based Packaging'. *Proceedings of the Conference on Historical Analysis and Research in Marketing* 12: 288–300.

Twede, D. (2016). 'History of Packaging'. In Brian Jones, D.G. & Tadajewski, M. (eds), *The Routledge Companion to Marketing History*. Abingdon, Oxon: Routledge.

Twede, D. & Goddard, R. (1998), *Packaging Materials*. Leatherhead, Surrey: Pira International.

University of Southampton (2014). *Roman Amphorae: A Digital Resource* [data-set]. York: Archaeology Data Service. Available at: https://archaeologydataservice.ac.uk/archives/view/amphora_ahrb_2005/cat_amph.cfm (accessed 6 April 2023).

Usherwood, B. (2000). '"Mrs Housewife and Her Grocer": The Advent of Self-Service Food Shopping in Britain'. In Andrews, M. & Talbot, M.M., *All the World and Her Husband*. London: Cassell.

Vacher, F. (1892). *The Food Inspector's Handbook*. London: The Sanitary Publishing Co Ltd.

Walker, T. R *et al* (2021). 'Single-Use Plastic Packaging in the Canadian Food Industry: Consumer Behavior and Perceptions'. *Humanities and Social Sciences Communications* 8(1): 1–11.

Weber Macena, M. *et al* (2021). 'Plastic Food Packaging: Perceptions and Attitudes of Portuguese Consumers about Environmental Impact and Recycling' *Sustainability* 13(17): 9953.

Weedon, C.E. (1976). 'The Glass Container Industry 1916–1976'. *Glass Technology* 17: 165–81.

Weinreb, A. (2017). *Modern Hungers: Food and Power in Twentieth-Century Germany*. Oxford: Oxford University Press.

Whyte, R. *et al* (2001). 'Traditional Māori Food Preparation Methods and Food Safety'. *International Journal of Food Microbiology* 69(3): 183–90.

Wilbur, R.L. & Ophüls, W. (1914). 'Botulism: A Report of Food-Poisoning Apparently due to Eating of Canned String Beans, with Pathological Report of a Fatal Case'. *Archives of International Medicine* 14(4): 589–604.

Wilk, R. (2006). *Home Cooking in the Global Village*. Oxford: Berg.

Wilk, R. (2009). 'Anchovy Sauce and Pickled Tripe: Exporting Civilized Food in the Colonial Atlantic World'. In Belasco, W. & Horowitz, R. (eds), *Food Chains: From Farmyard to Shopping Cart*. Philadelphia: University of Pennsylvania Press.

Williams, E.W. (1963). *Frozen Foods*. Boston, MA: Cahners.

Wilson, B. (2012). *Consider the Fork: A History of How We Cook and Eat*. London: Penguin.

Wilson, C. A. (1976). *Food and Drink in Britain*. Harmondsworth: Penguin.

Work, H.H. (2014). *Wood, Whiskey and Wine*. London: Reaktion.

Xanthos, D. & Walker, T.R. (2017). 'International Policies to Reduce Plastic Marine Pollution from Single-Use Plastics: A Review'. *Marine Pollution Bulletin* 118(1–2): 17–26.

Zeide, A. (2018). *Canned: The Rise and Fall of Consumer Confidence in the American Food Industry*. Oakland, CA: University of California Press.

INDEX

Index

Index

Index